1724446
3/02

741.64 POW
Powers, Alan.
Front cover : great book jacket
and cover design /
RICE

BELLEVUE PUBLIC LIBRARY
BELLEVUE, NE 68005

Please Do Not Remove Card
From Pocket

GAYLORD S

FRONT COVER

Sarah Champion
Fortune Hotel
Martyn Bedford
Geoff Dyer
Howard Marks
Emer Martin
Jean McNeil
Grant Morrison
Helena Mulkerns
Emily Perkins
Will Self
William Sutcliffe
Fortune Hotel
From the editor of
Disco Biscuits

FRONT COVER

GREAT BOOK JACKETS AND COVER DESIGN

ALAN POWERS

MITCHELL BEAZLEY

FRONT COVER

GREAT BOOK JACKETS AND COVER DESIGN

ALAN POWERS

Copyright © Octopus Publishing Group Ltd 2001

First published in Great Britain in 2001 by Mitchell Beazley,
an imprint of Octopus Publishing Group Ltd,
2-4 Heron Quays, Docklands, London E14 4JP

Commissioning Editor *Mark Fletcher*
Art Directors *Vivienne Brar and Geoff Borin*
Project Editor *John Jervis*
Designed by *blu inc. graphics ltd.*
Editor *Penny Warren*
Production *Catherine Lay and Alex Wiltshire*
Picture Researcher *Jo Walton*
Proofreader *Alison Wormleighton*
Indexer *Ann Parry*

A CIP catalogue record for this book is available from the British Library.

ISBN 1 84000 421 5

All rights reserved. No part of this work may be reproduced or utilized in any form or by any means, electronic or mechanical, including photocopying, recording or in any information storage and retrieval system, without the prior permission of the publisher.

Set in Gill Sans
Produced by Toppan Printing Co., (HK) Ltd
Printed and bound in China

Contents

Top: James Hanley, *Aria and Finale*, London, Boriswood Ltd, 1932. Jacket design by James Boswell (see page 16).

The Evolution of the Book Jacket

Top: L. Couperus, *God en Goden* (God and gods), Amsterdam, Veen, 1903. Cover design by Jan Toorop. Toorop was a painter and illustrator in Holland, influenced by batik designs from the Dutch colonies in Indonesia. This is a fine example of a book blocking in Art Nouveau style, for an author of symbolist tales. By 1912, however, this style had gone out of fashion, and Couperus requested his publisher to commission a book cover in 'anything but a modern style.'

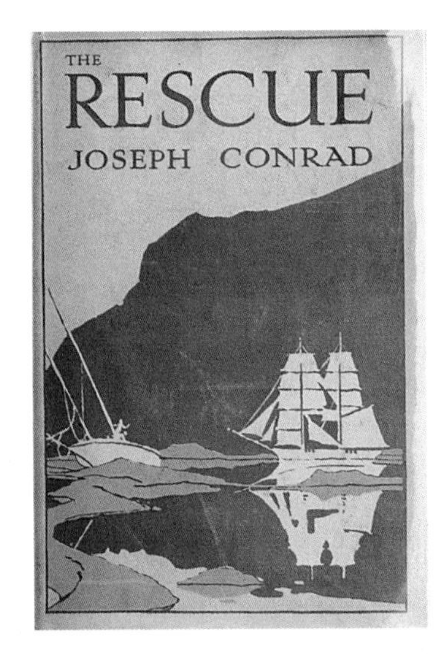

Middle: Joseph Conrad, *The Rescue*, London, J. M. Dent & Sons Ltd., 1920. Designer unknown. The use of flat colours to make a poster-like image was popular in the 1920s, but this is a neatly composed jacket with a balance of text and evocative illustration.

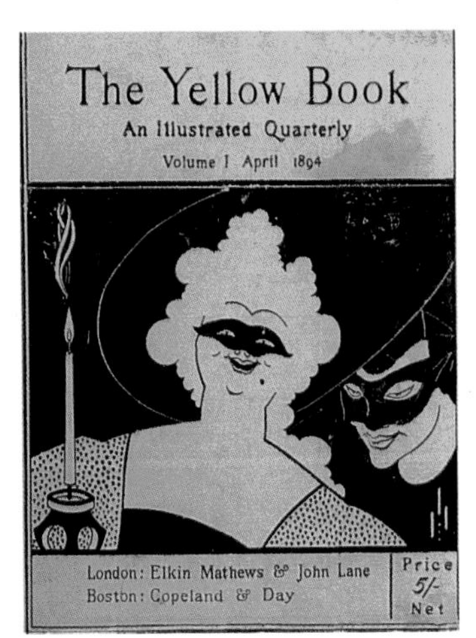

Bottom: Henry Harland, literary editor, *The Yellow Book*, An Illustrated Quarterly, Volume One, April 1894, London, Elkin Matthews and John Lane. Cover design by Aubrey Beardsley. The quintessence of the 1890s, *The Yellow Book* was conceived on New Year's Day 1894 and launched four months later, with Aubrey Beardsley as Art Editor. When Oscar Wilde was arrested a year later in London, the newspaper headlines proclaimed, '*Yellow Book* under his arm' as proof of decadence, and the publisher John Lane recalled, 'It killed *The Yellow Book* and it nearly killed me.' In fact Wilde, who was excluded from the contributors, said 'It is horrid and not yellow at all' – the second claim in defiance of the evidence.

A book jacket or cover is a selling device, close to advertising in its form and purpose, but also specific to a product that plays a teasing game of hide and seek with commerce. The reason for this ambiguity is that books have never been purely consumer goods. Many books have a built-in resistance to obsolescence, as a combined result of their physical form and content. People become attached to them and, perhaps, even after nearly two centuries of mass-production, some distant memory of their preciousness and scarcity in the pre-industrial age still clings to them.

The printed book, which is usually associated with scholarship and wisdom rather than with worldly transactions, has an aura that is perhaps one reason why books have been so slow to acquire any other form of decorative cover apart from the traditional binding. It may also account for a surprising lack of available information about book jackets. Even today, collecting book jackets is relegated to a class of trivia unworthy of the true collector. There are many detailed studies of book binding, but no standard work on the history of the book jacket. This contrasts oddly with the reality of book-collecting, in which twentieth-century classics achieve high prices – even higher if they include a jacket that is in good condition.

The scarcity of surviving jackets has its origins in the historical practice of removing and throwing away the cover after purchasing the book, a practice which itself reflected the low esteem in which jackets were held for many years. Keeping the jacket on a book would be like storing clothes in the carrier bag from the shop where they had been bought and, indeed, the aim of many jackets was no more than to keep the binding cloth underneath in good condition while the book was in the shop and then during transit to the purchaser's home.

Book jackets first appeared in England in the nineteenth century, in a culture that was still discovering the rules of consumerism. Their early evolution came about in fits and starts, constrained by cultural inhibitions that are now difficult to understand. When decoration was present on the outside of the book, it took the form of either blocking onto binding cloth, or pasting printed paper sheets onto the front and back boards. In both cases, the design content may have been very similar to a book jacket, and the blockings of books from the 1890s, in particular, are often charming and original. These books were evidently meant to be displayed face upward as items of interior decoration, since the whole attention is given to the front board. *The Yellow Book*, an illustrated quarterly famous for its associations with Aubrey Beardsley and Oscar Wilde, was one such example, and owning a copy was a badge of belonging to the avant-garde culture.

Only after 1900 did book jackets begin to become commonplace, and even then, the great majority consisted simply of a repetition of the blocking from the binding on a sheet of paper. There was possibly some additional information on the back, but little in the form of a promotional "blurb" or a summary of the content. When pictures were used on covers, it was often for more specialized types of book, particularly for stories for children. Increased competition within the book trade before the First World War, however, created the first wave of designed jackets, and a writer in 1911 commented that "the exigencies of trade have caused publishers to tax their ingenuity to the utmost, and they vie with each other in presenting their wares in as attractive a form as possible. They are apparently convinced that a book, like a woman, is none the worse, but rather the better, for having a good dressmaker. To this end, they have enlisted artists of distinction to design book covers and end papers, and now it is quite a commonplace remark that, so far as certain classes of literature are concerned, 'the cover sells the book'."

This first wave of jackets was so relatively fragile that the 1914–18 war was able to set back their further development until the 1920s. During this decade, advertising and the study of salesmanship both became more widespread, largely inspired by the economic buoyancy of the United States. Branded and packaged goods, as opposed to generic products sold by measure, were a growing feature among foods, medicines, and a range of household products from the 1880s onward. Books could learn from this practice, for not only could a publisher establish a brand image, but he could make different genres of book more easily identifiable for the convenience of the customer. Consumers, who were growing up in a culture richer in visual images than any before, and were experiencing motion-picture films for the first time, were beginning to take in visual images subliminally as well as to read text for information. In addition, colour was more readily available for printing.

Top: John Masefield, *Martin Hyde*, London, Wells Gardner, Darton & co., 1910. Jacket design by T. C. Dugdale.
This historical romance by the future poet laureate is typical of children's books which pioneered the use of specially drawn illustrations for book jackets.

Middle: M. P. Shiel, *The Purple Cloud*, London, Chatto & Windus, 1901. Designer "W.J.R".
The author of this pioneering science-fiction was described in a review of an earlier book as "the Apostle of Breathlessness". Shiel (1865–1947) describes how a purple gas destroys all but two members of humanity. The front board and spine carry a blocked design suitable to the sensational quality of the tale. The novel was filmed in the 1950s as "The World, the Devil and the Flesh".

Bottom: Charles Dickens, *A Christmas Carol*, London, William Heinemann, 1915. Jacket design by Arthur Rackham.
Rackham made his reputation as an illustrator of reprinted children's classics with *Rip Van Winkle*, 1905. This jacket only hints at the content of one of the best-known tales, and its use of the door knocker cleverly represents an invitation to enter the book.

Before the First World War, artists often produced a painted artwork for colour printing, which involved an expensive making of "colour process blocks" whose reproductive quality was inferior to more skillful methods that involved "colour separation" by the artist. Whether by letterpress or lithography, covers drawn in this way could be printed more effectively to achieve a stronger visual impact, as can be seen in the work of designers such as Edward McKnight Kauffer, whose understanding of technical processes helped to boost his early career.

Such experience soon fed back into the art schools, where the distinction between "fine" and "commercial" art was breaking down anyway, partly as a result of the necessity for artists to earn a living in a sluggish market for pictures. In the 1920s and '30s, publishers, if they so wished, could buy the services of some of the finest artists of the time for their covers, from academicians such as Sir William Orpen and Sir William Nicholson (designer of William Heinemann's windmill logo), to brilliant youngsters such as Eric Ravilious, Edward Bawden, Barnett Freedman, and Rex Whistler.

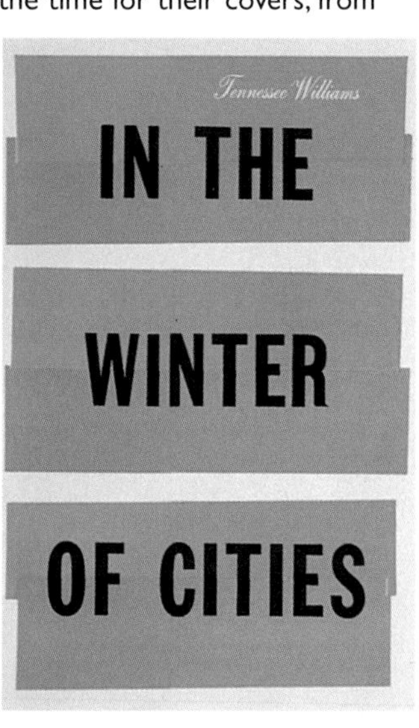

In an age of publishing individualism, the look of the jacket much depended on the taste of the firm's directors. Richard De La Mare at Faber and Faber was one of the great patrons of the time, while Victor Gollancz employed Stanley Morison to create his long-lasting series of yellow typographic jackets.

In the United States, the typographic designer W. A. Dwiggins (1880–1956), closely attached from 1920 onward to the publishing firm of Alfred Knopf, brought a new gaiety to book covers causing, as a contemporary wrote, "those slim vertical strips [of book spines] to crackle and vibrate and sing." Dwiggins's jackets stood out in the American market, which was mostly considered by writers of the time to be of a low standard, although it is possible that today we might value more highly the typical designs that contemporaries considered vulgar. Good American book jacket design rapidly asserted itself, so that by 1949, Charles Rosner could say that US jackets, especially those designed by Alvin Lustig for New Directions, showed, "an unlimited use of imagination", bringing the latest findings in visual communication derived from abstract art directly into the marketplace and into the home.

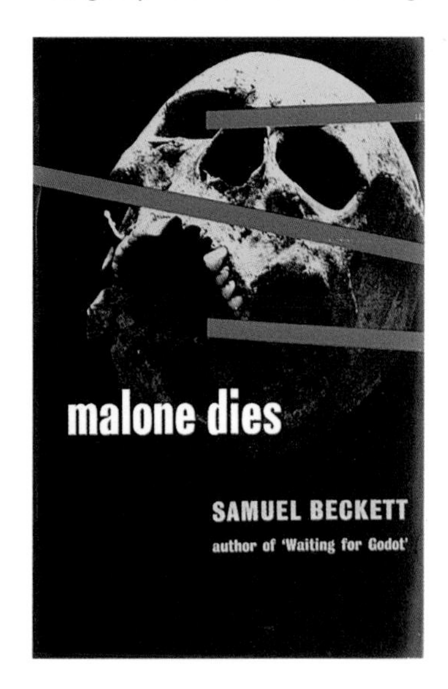

Top: Richard Strachey, *Many Happy Returns*, London, Constable, 1933. Jacket design by Ray Strachey.
A successful design by the author's wife, using a collage effect with bus tickets and loose script lettering to match.

Middle: Tennessee Williams, *In the Winter of Cities*, Norfolk, Conn., New Directions, 1957. Jacket design by Elaine Lustig-Cohen.
Indirect suggestion through abstract formal design, seamlessly linked to the presentation of the book title.

Bottom: Samuel Beckett, *Malone Dies*, London, John Calder Ltd., 1958. Designer unknown.
A striking use of photography with an abstract overlay to convey the shocking quality of Beckett's work which had recently burst on a surprised reading and theatre-going public, following the London production of *Waiting for Godot* in 1955.

Top: John Fowles, *The Magus*, London, Jonathan Cape, 1966. Jacket design by Tom Adams.
Tom Adams made his reputation with the jacket for Fowles's psychological thriller, *The Collector*, 1963. The jacket for its successor gives primacy to images from the novel, and the lettering is reduced in scale, although well placed against a blank field in the design.

Bottom: Edgar Rice Burroughs, *Tarzan and the Foreign Legion*, New York, Edgar Rice Burroughts, Inc., 1947. Jacket design by John Coleman Burroughs.
Composed as a magazine story in 1944, this was one of many sequels to Burrough's most famous work, the original *Tarzan of the Apes*, 1914. No publisher wanted this tale of the Pacific War, so Burroughs published it himself, with a cover designed by his son.

The book trade in continental Europe remained strangely detached from these Anglo-Saxon activities. The typical French, Italian, or German book was issued in plain paper, as a half-finished if still readable product awaiting completion in the form of a bespoke binding, with a plain if stylish typographic wrapper. This throwaway elegance still affects book design in these countries, and it may be symptomatic of the Europeanization of English culture that a non-glossy, non-pictorial cover has become the latest phase in the cycle between restraint and excess, as seen in the latest house style of the publishers Faber and Faber.

The launch of Penguin Books by Allen Lane in 1935 was the beginning of one of the largest changes in publishing since the invention of the printing press. Only the conservatism of the book trade, which amounted almost to a set of restrictive practices, had hitherto prevented books from being made and sold so cheaply, but the conditions of the Depression led publishers to take desperate measures. Lane's risk-taking intuition meant that all publishers, sooner or later, had to respond to the vastly increased market for book-buying that Lane had started to tap. The Penguin design, which involved devising a new brand and series identity within a tight cost constraint, was based largely on the Albatross Library, a European series of English language reprints. The books went a long way toward repudiating the sensationalism of cover design associated with American "dime novels". Even among paperback publishers, however, a certain snobbery continued to prevail, with Penguin taking a decidedly upmarket position in Britain, while acknowledging that across the Atlantic conditions required adapting to a less sophisticated market both in terms of selection of titles and visual presentation. Throughout its many transformations, Penguin is one company that still has an immediately recognizable quality, and among the smaller paperback publishers, Black Sparrow produces books that are collectible for their covers if for nothing else.

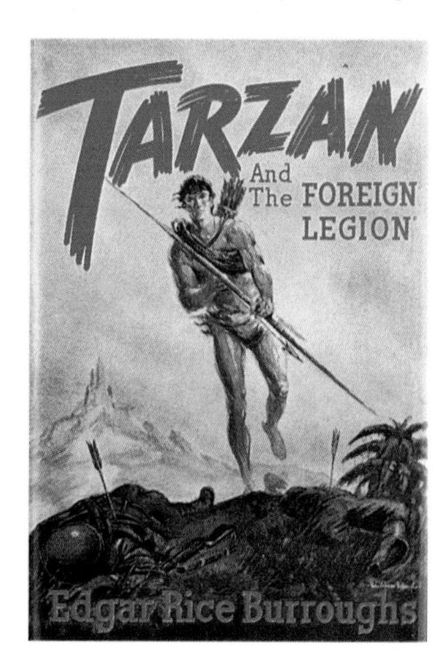

In the publishing world of today, the distinction between hardback and paperback still exists, but more as a function of marketing than of production. Books may be launched first in hardback, in the traditional way, but most publishers issue their own paperbacks rather than selling rights to a specialist paperback publisher. A book with an established visual identity as a hardback will probably keep the same cover in paperback, although publishers who deal in reprints and imports are more likely to create an overall identity for their imprint.

The position of the designer in the book trade has changed too. The cover is usually still treated as a special stand-alone item, independent of the typographic design inside the book. The in-house designer will probably be involved in a strategy for the look of all the company's

Above: Douglas Adams, *The Douglas Adams Series*, London, Pan, 1987. Cover art direction and design by Gary Day-Ellison.
Proclaimed on the back as 'a trilogy of four', Douglas Adams's quirky tales of space travel are well matched by Gary Day-Ellison's interchangeable covers. Each split image can be assembled as a centrepiece by shuffling the pack, and the spines carry the number '42' in Lucher colour-test style dots, a number well known to contain the secret of the universe.

products, and there may be a freelance art director employed to commission individual artists within a consistent style. In most publishing houses, the dummy-prototype of the jacket (nowadays easily mocked up with a computer and laser-printer) has to be approved by the sales team, who have regular contact with retail buyers and claim to have a sixth sense for what will be commercially successful. If the book is a new one, the author may be asked for approval, but he or she is unlikely to be able to contradict the professionals. Producing successful book jackets is an inexact science at best, for the field is always changing. Some jackets achieve classic status almost instantly, however. It is hard now to separate Louis de Bernières's *Captain Corelli's Mandolin* from the squiggly lettering and silhouettes of Jeff Fisher.

Jacket styles tend to go in waves. Like any product in a crowded marketplace, they need to stand out, and this can be achieved by speaking quietly amidst a lot of noise as readily as by shouting in a void. After the raucous clamour of the 1960s, high on the discovery of cheap colour printing, airbrushing, Letraset, and other excitements, the style of the 1970s was often deliberately reticent and supposedly nostalgic. There was undoubtedly a loss of creativity, however, and Mike Dempsey, a former art director for Fontana books, wrote of the way that designers had become "marionettes whose movements and wishes are tightly controlled." He summed it up as, "The bland leading the bland."

The illustrator and designer have an unprecedented range of tools at their disposal today for creating and manipulating images. Computers allow for an infinite number of overlays and colour transformations, giving images the visual equivalent of an echo effect on a synthesizer. Profusion seems to be giving way to a renewed simplicity, with a preference for one strong image on a cover, possibly distorted or combined with text anchored in a flat coloured field which is often as bright as possible.

Perhaps a deep-seated love of books among those whose lives revolve around them has saved the book from succumbing to all the deleterious effects of marketing and promotion that might be thought to threaten it. Book buyers are willing to be charmed, but are not the kind of consumers who take kindly to being treated as fools, so some space is maintained, despite everything, for real imagination and creativity, and this pays off again and again. The threat of the digital book, which might at least offer the opportunity for designing a CD cover, seems at present unlikely to bring the age of Gutenberg to an abrupt end, and the information revolution, against expectation, actually seems to have assisted circulation both of new and of second-hand books.

Top: Keith Ovenden, *The Greatest Sorrow*, London, Hamish Hamilton, 1998. Photographs and design by Richard Ivey.
Richard Ivey is a freelance photographer who has designed a number of book and magazine covers using manipulated and collaged images to interpret the subject matter. The novel concerns Philip Leroux, an Oxford philosophy don, and his relationship with a dead colleague, hence the Oxford setting and the melancholy absorbed figure.

Middle: Sarah Champion, editor, *Fortune Hotel*, London, Hamish Hamilton, 1999. Design by Ashworth/Sissons. Images by John Holden.
A collection of short stories with a confident handling of text and image on the cover.

Bottom: Keith Ovenden, *Eine Art Vermächtnis*, Munich, C. H. Beck Verlag, 1999. Photograph by Richard Ivey; Art Director, Leander Eisenmann.
Since the Oxford context would not be so recognisable to a German readership, the figure from the cover of the English edition is isolated with a shadowy presence, telling the story more symbolically.

Book designers, however, now have a new challenge: jacket legibility in a thumbnail icon on a website is almost as much a requirement as legibility across a crowded shop.

Alvin Lustig wrote in 1947 of the way that, in addition to the primary objective of helping to sell a book, his work for New Directions allowed him to achieve another, secondary aim of "projecting a series of 'public' symbols of higher than usual standards." Despite their lowly status, book covers act as a communicative bridge between the richness of a text, which works its way into public consciousness, and the physical world. The twentieth century, while full of images, has been relatively weak in its production of genuine visual symbols that have a depth of meaning. The best book jackets have a quality that goes beyond words, although even the worst, of which a few examples are included here, nearly always have some entertaining features.

Book jacket design is accessible enough for an amateur to study, and examining a wide range of examples is an excellent training in what visual communication really means. The book cover is different to food packaging in its scope for conveying some depth and even contradiction. It is a kinetic art, which involves different viewing distances, and different sequences of handling as the front or the spine may be seen first and each needs to move the spectator into a physical engagement with the book. Tony Goodwin, who was manager of a bookshop before becoming fiction editor for Penguin, wrote that "the whole mass of whispered mental associations which a cover will invoke are too complex, transitory, and varied to be conjured by the direct brutal frontal assault that tries to bully you into buying with an anecdotal realism." The design of book covers helps to make a book something more than mere "information", something that, even though it may have many thousands of identical siblings, still demands a relationship, something that when given, defines the values of the giver and recipient. The best book covers possess a form of hidden eroticism, connecting with some undefended part of the personality in order to say "take me, I am yours".

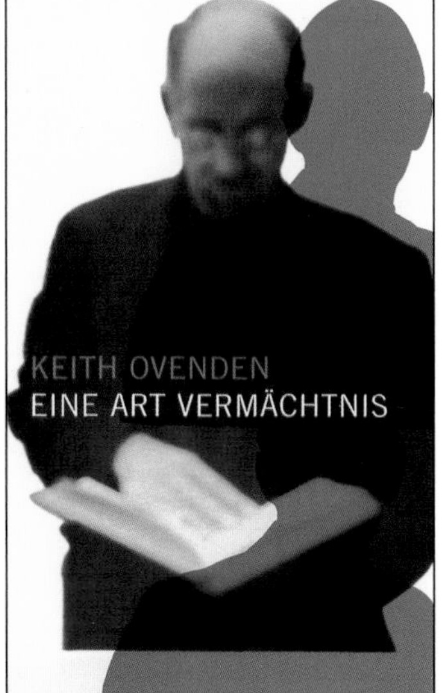

LEE-ELLIOTT
F.
GRIESE

The Impact of Modernism:

The 1920s and 1930s

All the right conditions for the book jacket existed for years before it arrived. While modernism in design is often attributed to technical developments, the book jacket is largely a social phenomenon, a symptom of great changes in the structure of the world at the cusp of the nineteenth and twentieth centuries – changes that are normally grouped under the umbrella term "modernism". The word conjures images of Parisians hissing the first night of the "Rite of Spring" in 1913, Americans outraged by artworks at the Armory Show in New York in the same year, and Dadaists performing antics in Zurich cafés while old Europe tore itself apart on the Western Front during the First World War.

Book jackets of a kind that aimed to be more than the linear paper bags of the previous era sprang into life in this period. They were part of an awakening by the sleepy business of publishing to the new opportunities for communication offered by motor cars, cinema, cheap newspapers, and, within a few years, broadcasting. Although we talk of an information revolution happening in the last ten years of the twentieth century, there was also one of equivalent scale at the beginning of the century. Thus modernism in book jackets is a broader matter than avant-garde visual style – it is a genuine symptom of modernity as an unstoppable force, taking any number of forms.

◄ F. Griese, *Winter*, London, Longman, Green & Co., 1929. Jacket design by Thayer Lee-Elliott (see page 18).

The Modernist Jacket

Because modern art is nowadays most frequently found in art museums, which are committed to representing the purity of art – separated from any implication of a business transaction – we are not accustomed to seeing the relationship between the formal character of modernism and the commercial world from which, historically, it so often drew its inspiration. In the early years of the twentieth century, business and advertising were testing grounds for completely new ideas. New means of communication developed almost spontaneously, in typography and styles of drawing, film, and photography. A new visual language emerged when Charlie Chaplin's silhouette and eccentric walk were recognized all over the world by people who would never hear about Cubist painting during their whole lives.

Since book jackets only had a marginal existence before 1930, their role in forming a new style was limited at first, but soon they acted both as an advertisement for modernism as a style, and as a means by which modern artists could earn much-needed money during a time of scarcity. Often they also expressed some of the political yearnings of these artists for a better society. Nearly always, the jacket was the most modern part of the book in visual terms, since within the book the standard page layouts remained conservative, as they have, indeed, to the present day.

▲ **Mary Butts, *Death of Felicity Taverner*, London, Wishart, 1932. Jacket design by James Boswell.**
A complex multiple image by a leading English graphic artist, illustrating a strange novel by Mary Butts (1891–1937) about a predatory alien incomer to the settled English countryside of Dorset, where Butts lived, who plans to convert it to a sanitized tourist attraction. The red and blue hint at the novel's conflicting sets of values.

► **Roger Vercel, *Captain Conan*, London, Constable, 1935. Jacket design by Victor Reinganum.**
Victor Reinganum (1907–95) trained in Paris in the school of Fernand Léger, whose simple poster-like style is apparent in this jacket. The airbrush technique also recalls the popular 1930s posters of A. M. Cassandre. As well as being a prolific illustrator, Reinganum produced his own paintings, which were influenced by surrealism.

◄ Henry Green, *Party Going*, London, Hogarth Press, 1939. Jacket design by John Banting.
The cover by John Banting (1902–72) is close to the naive, in accord with the tendency of the Hogarth Press, run by Leonard and Virginia Woolf.

▼ Henry Green, *Living*, London, J. M. Dent, 1929. Jacket design by K. Romney Towndrow.
Green (1905–73) made his reputation with this novel based on his experiences of working in a factory in Birmingham. The effective jacket owes something to the Soviet style of portraying the heroic worker, but also accurately depicts the reflected light from molten iron being poured into moulds.

▲ Booth Tarkington, *Claire Ambler*, New York, Doubleday Doran & Co., 1928. Artist unknown.
With its imagery, colours, and "Broadway" typeface, this jacket represents all the aspects of the 1920s that were recycled in the 1970s. Surprisingly few designs of the 1920s actually fit this model so closely. The drawing cleverly adopts the manner of tile designs, popular in the period.

► H. E. Bates, *The Woman Who Had Imagination*, New York, Macmillan, 1934. Artist unknown.
It is hard to tell whether this jacket is modern deliberately or by accident. Its typography and arrangement of rules would not have looked out of place on an avant-garde text of the 1960s. Clearly influenced by the design exercises of the German Bauhaus school, it might have been the experiment of a young in-house designer.

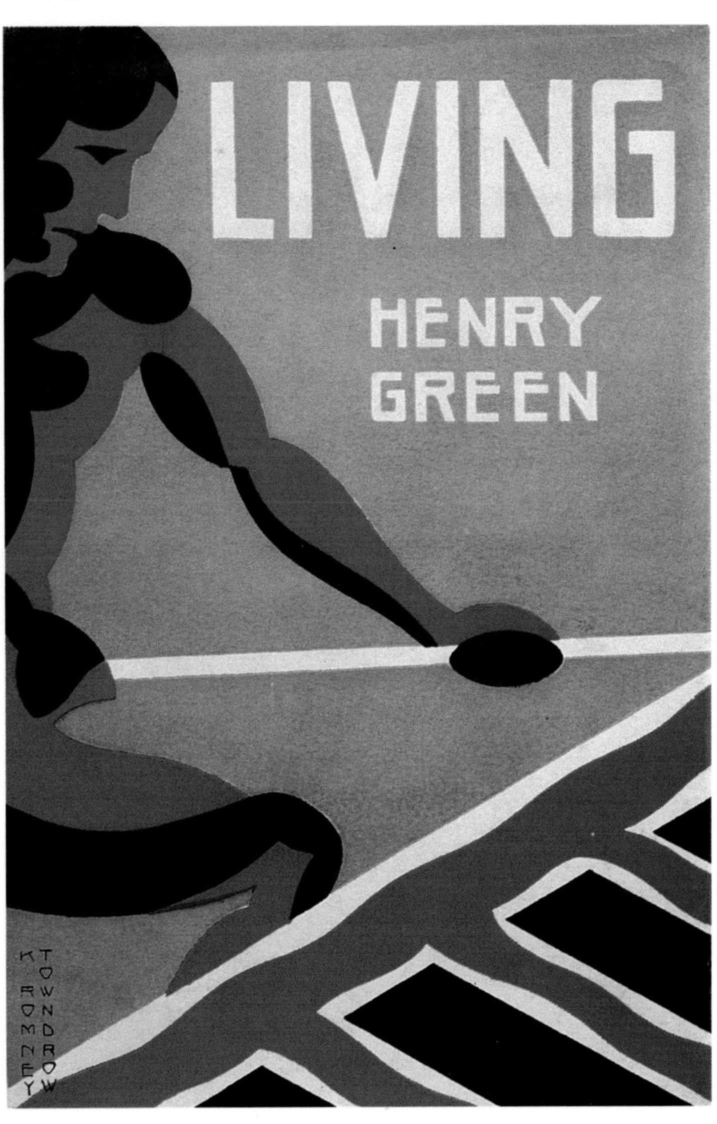

Designing in Monochrome

Until recently, full-colour printing was an extravagance. The cost of producing a book jacket would hardly be increased with a coloured ink on a coloured paper, however, and, with these means, a degree of individuality for the jacket could be achieved. The actual printing medium was the line block, created photographically from an original drawing. It worked best when the drawing was composed in simple shapes without shading. It is difficult to produce perspective effects in one colour, but a flat design can work very well. Paper and ink colour needed to be matched to the subject, and the design could play with solid printed areas against those where the background colour came through. Lettering was usually included by the artist as part of the design. In the 1880s, Japanese prints were influential in creating a monochrome graphic style, since they were usually composed with blocks of colour, simplifying the complexity of observed phenomena. Cubism, in its broadest popular sense, also favoured flatness, and provided further inspiration in the 1920s. The jackets of this era have much in common with posters, which were governed by the same technical constraints. The covers were commonly printed on matt paper, which is pleasurable to the touch, but their coloured papers often fade on the spine, so each jacket's true glory is only revealed when the title is pulled from the shelf.

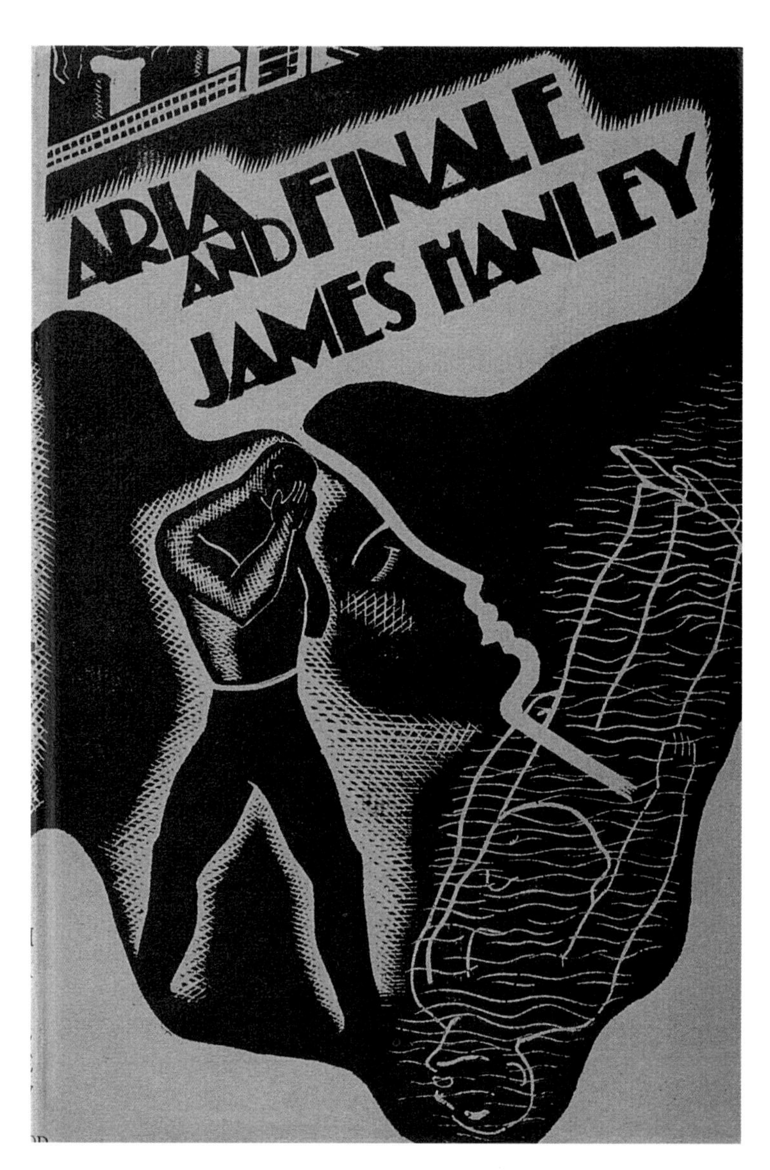

◄ Knut Hamsun, *August*, London, Cassell, 1932. Artist unknown.
Bold pen lettering combines with a suggestive silhouette image. The use of the triple rules and the off-centre placing of the picture give the composition a dynamic quality.

▲ James Hanley, *Aria and Finale*, London, Boriswood Ltd, 1932. Jacket design by James Boswell.
The New Zealand artist James Boswell (1906–71) joined the Communist party in 1932 and gave up painting to concentrate on graphic work, often in the manner of the German expressionist painter George Grosz. The jacket for *Aria and Finale* is suggestive, if rather confused, creating a counter-change of light and dark areas, with a version of the typeface Broadway for the title, a style of lettering favoured for revivals of art deco.

► **A. H. Adair, *Dinners Long and Short*, London, Victor Gollancz, 1928. Jacket design by Edward McKnight Kauffer.**
An object lesson in achieving pictorial depth with simple means. The single colour is used with a paler tint, so that the title lettering can appear behind the glass, while the coffee cup clips it at the bottom edge and therefore appears to stand forward in its deliberately naive perspective. The lettering is appropriately whimsical with its use of dots in all the "counters" of "a" and "o".

▼ **Ray Strachey, *Shaken by the Wind: A Story of Fanaticism*, London, Faber and Gwyer, 1927. Jacket design by Edward McKnight Kauffer.**
An example of Kauffer's Cubist phase (see pp. 44–5), using two single colour printings on a buff paper. The design is abstract, but there is a suggestion of machinery and of a human figure. Ray Strachey was the second wife of Oliver Strachey, elder brother of the biographer and essayist Lytton Strachey, for whose books Kauffer also designed jackets.

◄ **Storm Jameson, *The Single Heart*, London, Ernest Benn Ltd. Series design by Stanley Morison.**
The decorative arabesque frame was probably redrawn from a seventeenth-century example to give identity to a fiction reprint series, Benn's Sixpenny Library, which was founded by Victor Gollancz (see pp. 22–3) when he was managing director of Benn Brothers in 1920–8.

Graphic Innovation

▲ Sally Carson, *Crooked Cross*, London, Hodder & Stoughton, 1934. Jacket design by Thayer Lee-Elliott.
The composition of the head resembles vorticist drawings of Ezra Pound by Henri Gaudier-Brzeska drawn before the First World War, which had recently been rediscovered. The use of interlocking volumes and glimpses of the white background is skilfully managed. The "Crooked Cross" – the Nazi swastika, which was still a matter of neutral curiosity at this time – appears on the spine.

The limitations of printing technology in the inter-war period acted as a stimulus to designers and helped to create an unmistakable look, which has often been imitated. Designers often used the diagonal as a compositional device to achieve a dynamic effect, whether in the lettering, the layout, or the image itself. Two or three colour workings gave an unexpected richness of vocabulary. The early cinema, with its use of back-lit silhouettes, close-ups, and unexpected camera angles, was surely influential in creating this style.

It was difficult to sell pictures in this period, and as a result many talented artists turned to "commercial art", at a time when most advertising images were drawn by hand. Thayer Lee-Elliott remains a largely unknown figure although he could have been a recognized artist of the period. His book jacket designs indicate his skill and versatility in a modern style, equal to the much better-known Kauffer. He understood the value of bold simplicity particularly well. At the other end of the scale, Vanessa Bell (1879–1961) is well known as a painter and as sister of the novelist Virginia Woolf. But she also designed jackets for a number of books issued by Leonard and Virginia Woolf from the Hogarth Press in the same relaxed decorative style that visitors can see applied to wall surfaces and textiles in her home, Charleston Farmhouse in Sussex.

► F. Griese, *Winter*, London, Longman, Green & Co., 1929. Jacket design by Thayer Lee-Elliott.
The blocky lettering used by Lee-Elliott is similar in style to that of Edward McKnight Kauffer. Here it is skilfully used to suggest a snowy landscape with black and two tones of grey. The open spaces of paper and the small size of the author's name enhance the effect.

▼ William Faulkner, *Light in August*, New York, Harrison Smith & Robert Haas, 1932. Jacket design by Arthur Hawkins.
The designer has made a brilliant use of diagonal blocks of tone to create the effect of sunrays from behind a thundercloud. The yellow border is a surprising touch, but it helps to tie in the otherwise weak lettering as well as adding to the sultry effect.

► Anonymous, *Smoked Spectacles: A Moral Adventure*, London, Faber and Gwyer, 1929. Jacket design by Alan Rogers.
The diagonal takes the form of an isometric projection in this design. It uses colours that are reminiscent of 1930s tiled bathrooms. Faber and Gwyer was the early name of publishers Faber and Faber. There was only one Faber, but the second was invented to improve the sound of the name when Gwyer was dropped.

◄ Virginia Woolf, *The Years*, London, Hogarth Press, 1937. Jacket design by Vanessa Bell.
In contrast to the tight, flat design and drawing of the other examples shown on these pages, Vanessa Bell brought a painter's concern for movement and texture to the design of jackets, making even the limited medium of the line block reproduction sensitive to the touch of the pen. Two colours are cleverly used here, and the downward-pointing black rose hints at symbolism beyond conventional decoration. The lettering is deliberately casual, but the distinctive visual representation would be instantly recognizable to Virginia Woolf's fans.

Edward Bawden and Eric Ravilious

Among the artist-designers whose careers were launched in England in the 1930s, Edward Bawden (1903–89) and Eric Ravilious (1904–42) both had distinctive and versatile styles. Forming a strong friendship as students, they adopted an approach to decorative art which was neither modernist, arts and crafts, nor neo-classical. Medieval influences can sometimes be traced in their work (for instance in the avoidance of pictorial depth), sometimes a neo-Victorian exuberance, and at other times a tender seventeenth-century feeling for the hidden language of symbolism. Both were essentially graphic artists, familiar with engraving techniques, lithography, pen drawing, and the use of coloured washes derived from a serious pursuit of watercolour. The sum was something typically English but entirely fresh, and their skill in designing lettering made them ideal as book-jacket artists. Never pompous, their work rewards prolonged study, as in the abstraction of the heads on the cover for *Elephants & Castles*. Ravilious's career was cut short by his loss on active service as a war artist – he remains most famous for his wood engraving of an eighteenth-century batsman for *Wisden's Cricketers' Almanac*. Bawden designed jackets throughout his life, and as a lover of nineteenth-century novels, nothing pleased him more than illustrating moments of grotesque comedy in everyday life.

◄ Compton Mackenzie, *Buttercups & Daisies*, London, Cassell, 1931. Jacket design by Edward Bawden.
It is impossible not to want to open the book and find out why a cow with a tweed cap has invaded a sedate tea party in a doll's house-like room. Bawden uses the simplest technical means – a single-colour line block – to create a jacket full of character, in which the decorative lettering and the diagonal, so typical of the 1930s, add to the sense of impending disaster.

▲ Alfred Duggan, *Elephants & Castles*, London, Faber and Faber, 1963. Jacket design by Edward Bawden.
This novel of the classical world has a jacket that is both informative and decorative. The heroic classical triumph is subtly undermined by the sense of caricature in the main figures, and also, perhaps, by the manner in which the horse is cropped out of the frame, making it more suggestive of movement than of a whole horse. Bawden was working with colour separations here to create a bold effect. The main image is a linocut, a humble printing medium which is used with brilliant results.

▼ **J. M. Richards, *High Street*, London, Country Life, 1939. Decorative paper boards by Eric Ravilious.**
This book originated in Ravilious's drawings of London shops, mostly old-fashioned and eccentric ones. The cover reveals his ability to grasp the design potential of a whole object: it is designed like a shop front, with fascia lettering for the title, and a stall-board below for the author's and artist's names. The spill of light from the window provides a decorative texture running in horizontal bands in a manner close to that of Barnett Freedman, who was a friend and contemporary.

► **Sacheverell Sitwell, *Southern Baroque Art*, London, Gerald Duckworth, 1930. Series jacket for Duckworth's Georgian Library by Eric Ravilious.**
This jacket was designed for a range of cheap reprints of recently published books, which included the first major work by the youngest of the three Sitwells, first published in 1923. The lettering is set in type, and the design allows space for the details of each book within its elaborate wood-engraved pattern of shooting stars in the night sky.

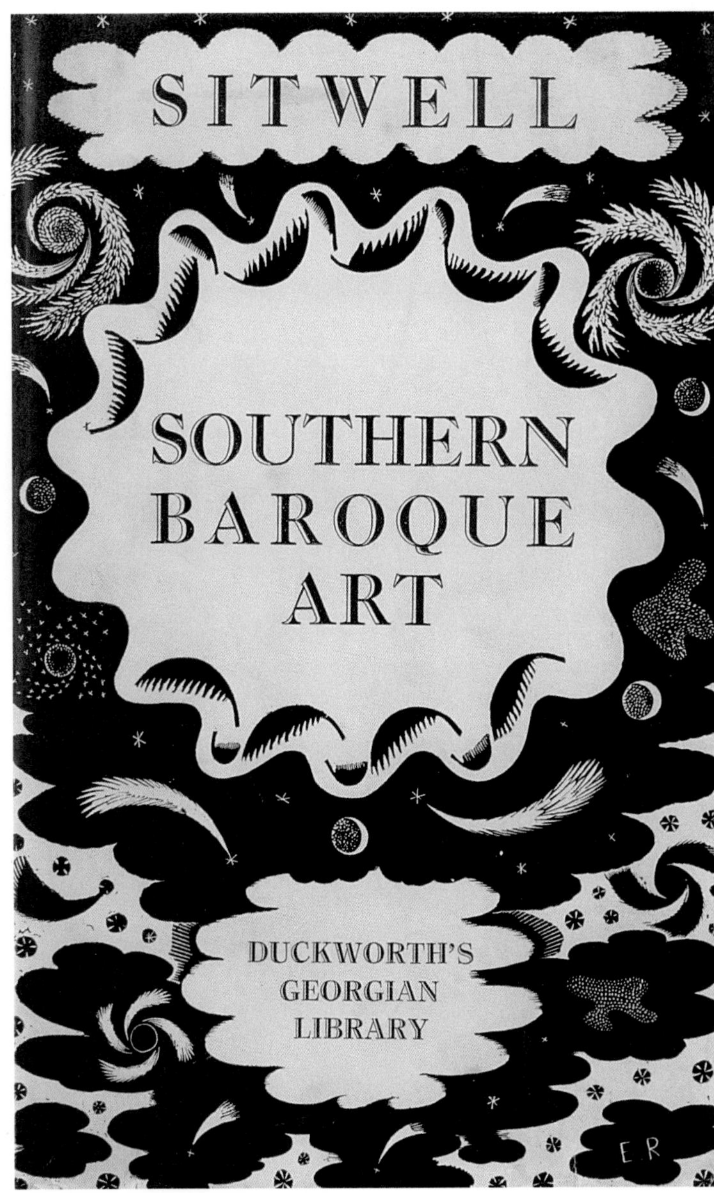

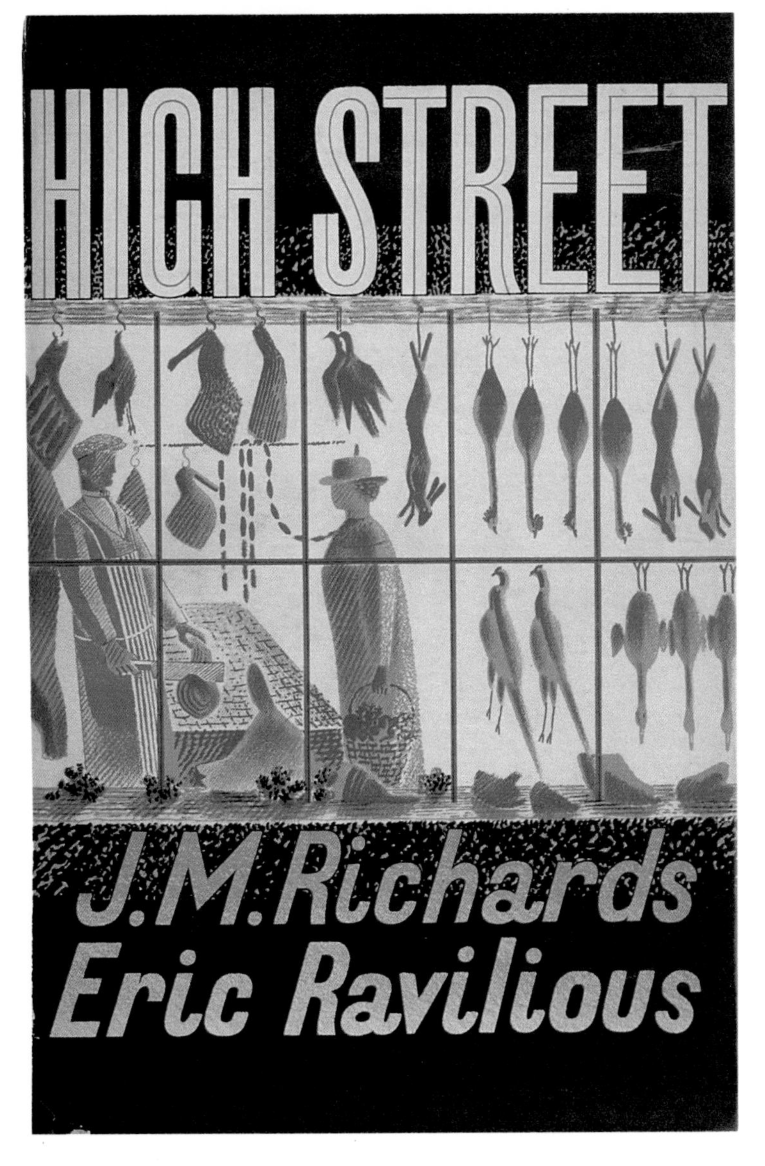

◄ **John Pope-Hennessy, *London Fabric*, London, B.T. Batsford, 1941. Jacket design by Eric Ravilious.**
A lithographic jacket in three colours for this wartime book, treated by Ravilious almost in the manner of a seventeenth-century emblem book. Its mysterious symbolic use of architecture relates to the essays on various London buildings which form the contents of the book.

Victor Gollancz

Victor Gollancz (1893–1967) started his own publishing firm in 1928. He had an early success with the play *Journey's End* by R. C. Sherriff, a serious treatment of the First World War. In 1930, with economic depression deepening, he launched a cheap paperback imprint, Mundanus Ltd. For this, he employed Stanley Morison (1889–1967), designer of the world-famous Times Roman font. Morison's most famous achievement for Gollancz was the series of yellow jackets. Gollancz, who loathed "picture jackets", decided on yellow after spending an afternoon touring the main railway stations of London to discover the most effective background colour. In France and Italy, yellow was already a recognized colour for novels (*une jaune* or *un giallo* being synonyms for cheap fiction). Black and magenta type contrasted with this background, providing immediate recognition of a Gollancz book. The covers were printed on a paper specially made so that they would not fade. Morison's contribution was a combination of copywriting and design in which the words play tricks on the reader. Covers have an excess of information or a tantalizing sparseness, nearly always with a compelling pointing hand in the bottom right-hand corner of the front board, encouraging the reader to turn over. Despite the playfulness of the designs, the title and author are always clearly stated.

THE
THEORY & PRACTICE
OF
SOCIALISM
BY JOHN STRACHEY
Author of The Coming Struggle for Power,
The Nature of Capitalist Crisis, etc., etc.

MR. STRACHEY'S INTRODUCTION BEGINS AS FOLLOWS: "This Book attempts to say plainly what the Working Class Movement of the world is striving for. Such general re-statements of socialism and communism become necessary from time to time. For socialism and communism are living, growing concepts. Moreover, there are today special reasons for attempting to say exactly what

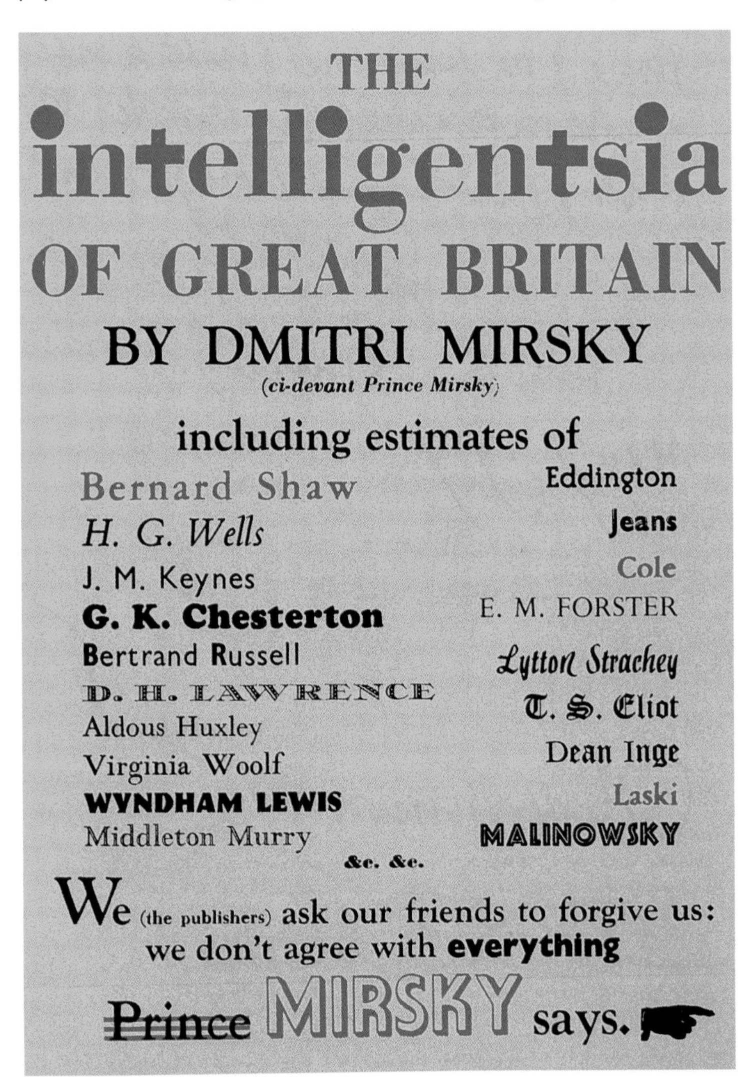

◄ John Strachey, *The Theory & Practice of Socialism*, London, Victor Gollancz, 1936. Jacket design by Stanley Morison. The mixture of typefaces, sizes, and colours deliberately breaks all the rules of good taste in typography, but is similar to much advertising design in the 1930s. Sometimes the Gollancz jacket copy extended over both covers and inside flaps, sometimes, by contrast, there was hardly any "blurb" at all.

▲ Dmitri Mirsky, *The Intelligentsia of Great Britain*, London, Victor Gollancz, 1935. Jacket design by Stanley Morison. A criticism of British intellectuals by a Russian aristocrat who in 1934 chose unwisely to return from exile to Stalin's Russia, where he was shortly arrested and later died in a labour camp. The typography of the jacket, almost certainly from the hand of the conservative Catholic Stanley Morison, plays with as many typefaces as possible, emphasizing the ambiguity of the author's position.

▼ John Faulkner, *My Brother Bill*, London, Victor Gollancz, 1964. Designer unknown.
Victor Gollancz's distinctive yellow style was continued into the post-war period, but here the presentation is more staid and classical than in some of the pre-war examples.

► Bob Biderman, *Paper Cuts*, London, Victor Gollancz, 1990. Designer unknown.
The Gollancz yellow jacket tradition is brought up to date in this story of environmentalists clashing with the logging industry in Oregon. The signature of the pointing hand returns, together with the extract from the text and the strong colour contrasts.

MY BROTHER BILL

an affectionate reminiscence by

JOHN FAULKNER

"When William Faulkner died in July of 1962 his reputation was at its height. He had won a Nobel Prize. He was read and admired and imitated by younger writers in many countries. His works were criticised, analysed and interpreted by students and professors with a solemn industry usually reserved for the masterpieces of authors at least 100 years dead . . . Today the first of what was known about Faulkner the man, in contrast to Faulkner the writer, is published . . . John, airplane pilot, W.P.A.

◄ Richard Jessup, *Cincinnati Kid: A Poker Novel*, London, Victor Gollancz, 1964. Designer unknown.
The Gollancz list included many writers of thrillers and detective stories. The "Playbill" lettering of the title of this novel was a well-recognized code for the Wild West.

One of the pleasures of book-collecting is to come across a famous book in its original jacket, and to understand the relationship between the contents and the image. An original jacket still says something about the world into which the book was launched, and the publisher's expectation of the kind of reader he was hoping to attract.

Few authors have ever demanded or been allowed much choice about the images used or the design of their book jackets, and instances of deep and meaningful collaboration between artist and author are not necessarily to be expected. Exceptions to this, however, are two books featured on these pages: *To The Lighthouse* and *The Hobbit*. In the former case, the artist was the author's sister, Vanessa Bell, while the publisher was Virginia Woolf herself, in partnership with her husband Leonard, at the Hogarth Press. For *The Hobbit*, his first work of fiction, the Oxford don J. R. R. Tolkien drew his own jacket, with a stylized art nouveau landscape and runic lettering round the border. It may have been a schoolboyish effort, but it was one that remained standard for future hardback editions. Staff from the production department at George Allen & Unwin helped him with technical advice, including a tactful hint to manage without a red printing, which added a red flush on the central mountain, making it look rather like an iced cake.

▲ Aldous Huxley, *Brave New World*, London, Chatto & Windus, 1932. Artist unknown.
Although Aldous Huxley was himself a "Sunday" painter, Chatto & Windus, a firm with a high standard of visual presentation, commissioned a smooth professional design for his most famous novel, which indicates little about the disturbing contents of the book. *Brave New World* sold 23,000 copies in the first two years in the UK.

► F. Scott Fitzgerald, *The Great Gatsby*, New York, Scribner's, 1925. Jacket design by F. Cugat.
Original book jackets seldom create such strong and appropriate images for their texts as this full-colour design for Scott Fitzgerald's most famous work. As the blurb on the back states, Gatsby, despite his invisibility in the story, "will live as a character, we surmise, as long as the memory of any reader lasts."

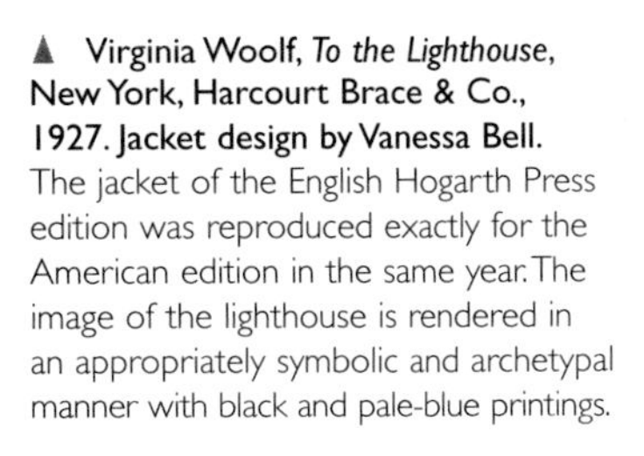

▲ **Virginia Woolf, *To the Lighthouse*, New York, Harcourt Brace & Co., 1927. Jacket design by Vanessa Bell.**
The jacket of the English Hogarth Press edition was reproduced exactly for the American edition in the same year. The image of the lighthouse is rendered in an appropriately symbolic and archetypal manner with black and pale-blue printings.

▲ **Christopher Isherwood, *Goodbye to Berlin*, London, Hogarth Press, 1939. Artist unknown.**
The jacket matches the title's famous opening line, "I am a camera", but is far removed from the imagery of the film *Cabaret* (1968) which was derived from the book's tales of Sally Bowles set against the rise of Nazism. The date of publication on the eve of the Second World War adds poignancy.

▲ **Ernest Hemingway, *In Our Time*, Paris, Three Mountains Press, 1924. Artist unknown.**
Hemingway's early book of short stories was published in a limited edition of 170 copies and offered for sale by Sylvia Beech at Shakespeare & Co., the famous expatriate bookshop in Paris which had published James Joyce's *Ulysses* two years before. The jacket is a collage of newspapers.

▲ **J. R. R. Tolkien, *The Hobbit, or there and back again*, London, George Allen & Unwin, 1937. Designer J. R. R. Tolkien.**
Written initially to entertain his family, *The Hobbit* was partly a throwback to Edwardian fairytale romances, and soon became an established classic.

▲ **John Steinbeck, *Of Mice and Men*, New York, Covici Friede, 1937. Artist unknown.**
Steinbeck's third novel concerns two itinerant farm labourers, one of whom is strong but dim-witted and becomes exploited by his weak but cunning companion. The cover alludes to the content in the illustration both of the figures and the paired trees – a rather literal interpretation.

▲ **John Steinbeck, *The Grapes of Wrath*, New York, Viking Press, 1939. Jacket design by Elmer Hader.**
A realistic portrayal, somewhat in the manner of US government-sponsored "New Deal" art, of this famous novel's content. A poor farming family leaves the "badlands" of Oaklahoma in the hope of finding a better life in the "promised land" of California, only to meet disillusion and problems of a different kind.

Strange and Surreal

▲ Isak Dinesen, *Seven Gothic Tales*, London, Putnam, 1934. Jacket design by Rex Whistler.
Under her pseudonym of Isak Dinesen, Baroness Karen Blixen, author of *Out of Africa*, gave in her title an opportunity for one of Rex Whistler's evocations of a romantic mood. He had a thorough understanding of architecture which enabled him to use it decoratively to frame a delicate watercolour scene.

► Hugh Walpole, *Four Fantastic Tales*, London, Macmillan, 1932. Jacket design by Rex Whistler.
Exaggeration of the macabre adds an element of humour to Whistler's romanticism, and the whole composition is brought to life with swirling smoke and draperies. Colour reproduction was just adequate for Whistler's artwork to be photographed and printed from half-tone colour blocks.

Founded in Paris in the 1920s, the surrealist movement claimed to be descended from all artists who had relied on the imagination to see beyond material appearances. It was as much a literary as an artistic movement, and made a counter-claim for subject matter in art against the tendency to abstraction. Salvador Dali, although only briefly a member of the official movement, has remained for most people the typical surrealist artist, with his distorted, melting objects usually seen under the sun of a desert landscape.

It was not necessary to actually be a surrealist in the 1920s and '30s in order to be part of a wider romantic movement. Rex Whistler (1905–44) was an English artist with an instinctive feeling for past styles, and with great skill, he added something distinctive from the twentieth century to his imagined world of baroque and gothic. His sense of period style, combined with an amazing facility for drawing, made him much in demand for book jackets, the best of which have a haunting quality that stays in the mind's eye. Surrealism is in many respects an extreme form of symbolism, and shares in the power of the visual arts to awaken deeper responses in viewers if the appropriate signals are transmitted. This is one of the purposes of a good book jacket, and certain artists have an instinct for finding imagery that achieves a life of its own apart from the text it introduces.

▲ Salvador Dali, *Hidden Faces*, London, Nicholson & Watson, 1947. Jacket design by Salvador Dali.
Dali was a productive writer and well-known for his surrealist antics in London and New York by the time this book came out. The playful lettering of his name contrasts with the provocative swastika.

► John Hawk, *The House of Sudden Sleep*, New York, The Mystery League Inc., 1930. Jacket design by "Gene".
A stylish design that uses three colours and black line cross-hatching to create an atmosphere that is comic as well as threatening.

◄ H. G. Wells, *Star Begotten*, London, Chatto & Windus, 1937. Jacket design by Harold Jones.
A late text by one of the early twentieth century's great writers of fantasy as well as fact. The cover is an early work by Harold Jones (1904–92) who later specialized in children's books, in which his symbolic imagination added to the significance of the content.

▼ James Hanley, *The Secret Journey*, London, Chatto & Windus, 1936. Jacket design by Harold Jones.
The title of this novel is enough to set the imagination going, but the image of Jones's jacket, with its rows of industrial housing, like a frame from a 1930s documentary, already begins to alter and shape one's expectations.

Barnett Freedman

Many artists in inter-war Britain designed books jackets as a way of earning some income. Many did it well, but Barnett Freedman (1901–57) was in a class of his own, both technically in terms of his understanding of printing method, and artistically in his delicacy of drawing and ability to provide a memorable image. He was equally skilled at designing appropriate styles of lettering, which were legible but always individual and alive. Freedman grew up in a poor Jewish immigrant family in the East End of London and won scholarships to art school. He was a "character", and a memorable teacher who used to say, "What do you mean by commercial art? There is only good art and bad art." Freedman's favourite medium was lithography. Until the 1920s, the actual drawing of the image on the stone would have been the work of a professional artist in the printing works, who would "translate" the design brought in by a freelance. The Curwen Press, however, made agreements with the trade unions to allow their favoured artists to draw directly at the press and the idea spread. This direct work was necessary for Freedman's style because he often scraped away solid areas of his chalked drawing directly on the lithographic stone.

◄ **John Howard Griffin, *The Devil Rides Outside*, London, Collins, 1953. Jacket design by Barnett Freedman.**
The jacket shows a calm pastoral vision of the Kentish countryside, with a contrasted black inset hinting at human drama, all achieved with three colour workings, the yellow tint being overlaid on white paper.

▲ **Amos Tutuola, *The Palm Wine Drinkard*, London, Faber and Faber, 1952. Jacket design by Barnett Freedman.**
The title of this West African classic provides an occasion for a medley of images with lettering lurching about the lower half of the page in sympathy with the theme. At the Royal College of Art, Freedman, in common with all other students, attended the lettering classes given by Edward Johnston, the world authority on the subject.

► Sacheverell Sitwell, *Dance of the Quick & the Dead*, London, Faber and Faber, 1936. Jacket design by Barnett Freedman.
Freedman's favourite colour scheme of yellow, red, and black is used to illustrate the suggestive title. Freedman achieved the flecks in the solid red panel with a tool he invented and called a "jumper". It cut through the chalked drawing directly on the lithographic stone.

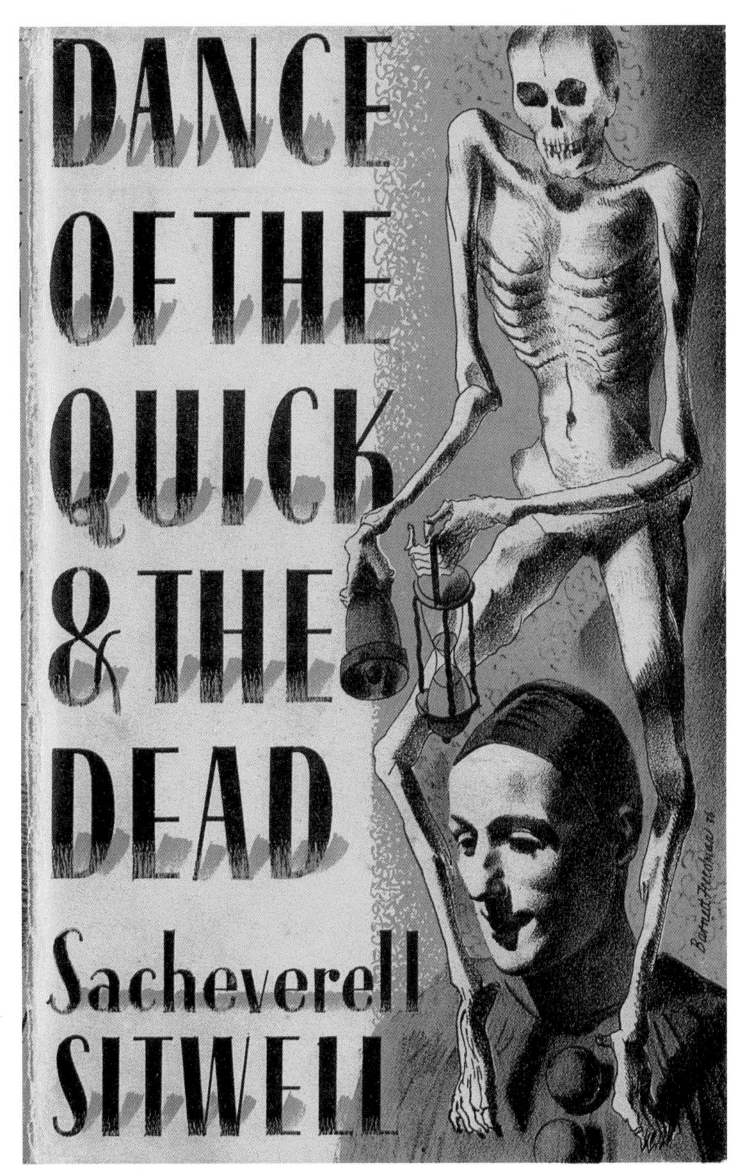

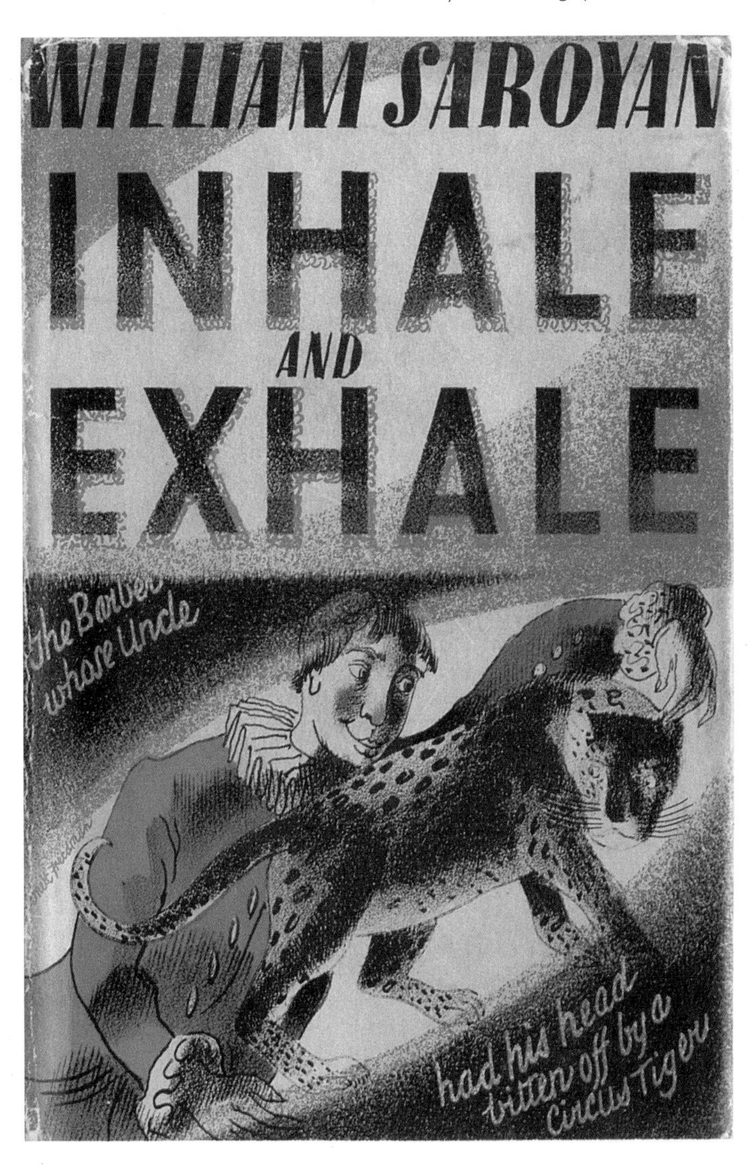

◄ William Saroyan, *Inhale and Exhale*, London, Faber and Faber, 1936. Jacket design by Barnett Freedman.
For a book by the author of *The Daring Young Man on the Flying Trapeze*, Freedman used a technique often found in his illustrations of framing a vignette image with hand-written snatches of text, like an unconventional version of a picture and caption.

Penguin: The Creation of a Brand

The launch of Penguin Books in 1935 was a key moment in publishing history. It was an enterprise which mixed innovative boldness with professionalism and attention to detail, not least in the visual appearance of the books. At seventeen Allen Lane (1902–70), whose original surname was Williams, went to work at the famous London publishers The Bodley Head, founded and directed by John Lane, a relation of his mother's. At Lane's request, the whole Williams family changed their name to Lane. By the early 1930s, after John Lane's death, The Bodley Head was struggling financially, and Allen Lane proposed cheap paperback reprints as a remedy. His fellow directors dismissed the idea, so Lane, with his two brothers, set up an independent company and launched the first ten titles at sixpence in July 1935. This price contrasted with a normal price for a cheap hardback fiction reprint of five times as much. The books were drawn from the backlists of The Bodley Head (whose name appears on the earliest Penguins) and other publishers, such as Jonathan Cape, who gave some good authors in return for cash in hand, convinced that the scheme would fail.

Inspired by the name Albatross Library, launched in 1932, the directors had a shortlist of ten animals and birds, but were locked in indecision until a typist, Jean Clark, working in earshot of the meeting, proposed "Penguin" from behind a partition. As the original designer Edward Young recalled, "It was the obvious answer, a stroke of genius. The meeting broke up immediately. I went straight off to the Zoo to spend the rest of the day drawing penguins in every pose from the dignified to the ridiculous, and the following morning produced, at first shot, the absurdly simple cover design which was soon to become such a familiar sight on the bookstalls."

Penguin adopted similar design specifications to Albatross and, like them, chose different colours to indicate different kinds of book: orange for fiction, dark-blue for biography, green for crime and mystery, and so on. The earliest Penguins had a thin dust wrapper repeating the information on the printed jacket, including a blurb on the front flap and author details on the back.

Booksellers objected to the low prices, so the Lanes tried Woolworths, and convinced the firm's buyer, who was persuaded when his wife happened to drop in to his office during the discussion and gave her endorsement as a standard consumer. Woolworths, where sixpence was the standard price, gave Penguin its initial boost, which was followed up by a rapid expansion of titles, and the launching of other imprints within the company, notably Pelican for non-fiction. In addition, the publication of topical books exposing Nazi Germany and arguing against appeasement in the years before the Second World War was rewarded by large sales, assuring for Penguin a generous quota when paper rationing began, since allowances were based on immediate pre-war consumption.

The hostility towards Penguin from the established book trade persisted for years, but Allen Lane's combination of high cultural standards with good business sense remained unbeatable. When the American paperback revolution began in 1939, Lane refused to copy its pictorial covers, although before 1939 the short-lived Penguin Illustrated Classics series used wood engravings of a high-minded kind.

▲ André Maurois, *Ariel*, London, Penguin Books, 1935. Cover design Penguin Books.
This life of the poet Percy Bysshe Shelley was the first in the numbered series of Penguins. It is soberly presented with the main information set in the leading English modern typeface, Gills Sans, with the words "Penguin Books" in Ultra Bodoni. This typeface was based on styles of the 1830s which a hundred years later had become popular again.

▲ Ernest Hemingway, *A Farewell to Arms*, London, Penguin Books, 1936. Cover design Penguin Books.
Hemingway's novel, first published by Jonathan Cape in 1929, told of a love affair between a lieutenant and a nurse. In 1936, The Bodley Head went into receivership and its name ceased to appear on Penguin covers thereafter, although it was relaunched and became a successful publisher in post-war Britain.

▲ Izaak Walton, *The Compleat Angler*, Harmondsworth, Penguin Books, 1939. Illustration by Gertrude Hermes.
In keeping with the "Penguin Illustrated Classics", but not part of the series, this was one of the rare Penguins to use a lemon yellow on the cover – a good match for Gertrude Hermes's engravings. Walton's famous last line, "Study to be quiet" was a difficult instruction on the eve of the Second World War.

▲ Henry Thoreau, *Walden, or life in the woods*, Harmondsworth, Penguin Books, 1938. Illustration by Ethelbert White.
One of the ten titles launched in the "Penguin Illustrated Classics" series in 1938, with Robert Gibbings as Art Editor. The medium of wood engraving was adaptable to mass production on cheap paper, bringing a sense of quality previously reserved for the rich into Penguin's sixpenny range.

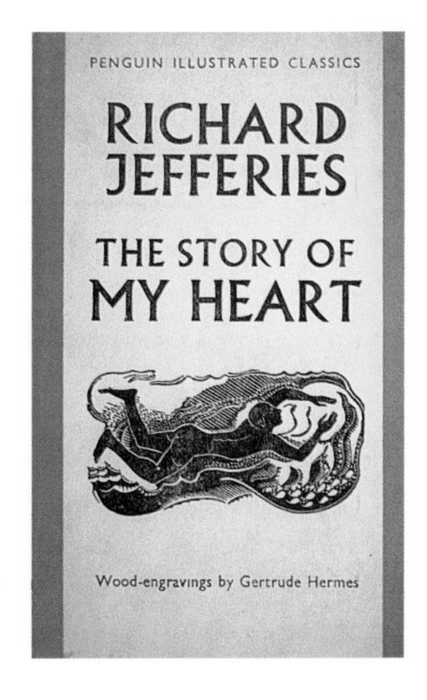

▲ Richard Jefferies, *The Story of My Heart*, Harmondsworth, Penguin Books, 1938. Illustration by Gertrude Hermes.
G. B. Harrison wrote in an introduction to Jefferies's autobiographical work, which was first published in 1883 and reprinted in the Penguin Illustrated Classics series, "Jefferies at heart was not a gentle naturalist, but a lusty pagan, delighting in all physical emotion." The engraving on the cover conveys this affirmation of life.

▲ Roger Fry, *Vision & Design*, Harmondsworth, Pelican Books, 1938. Cover design Pelican Books.
This collection of essays by Britain's leading art critic, which was reprinted four years after his death, was the twentieth in the Pelican series which aimed to cover "Science, Economics, History, Sociology, and Art".

▲ Thomas Sharp, *Town Planning*, Harmondsworth, Pelican Books, 1940. Cover design Penguin Books.
Pelican was chosen as a title for the series after Allen Lane heard a woman ask with a slip of the tongue, "Have you got any Pelican books?" at St Pancras Station bookstall. He realized that if he did not make this similar-sounding bird his own, one of his upstart competitors might exploit the name.

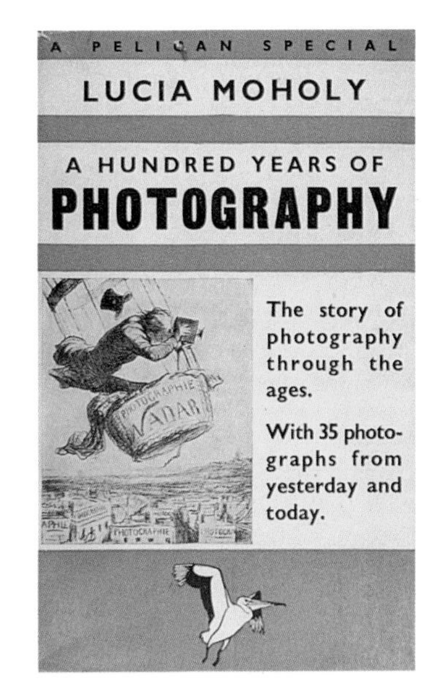

▲ Lucia Moholy, *A Hundred Years of Photography*, Harmondsworth, Penguin Books, 1939. Front cover. Cover design Penguin Books.
An original title ("Pelican Special") by the first wife of László Moholy-Nagy. Cover illustrations were unusual for early Penguins, although this cartoon of Nadar by Daumier is not acknowledged. There was a section of plates inside the book, all still for the price of sixpence.

▲ Lucia Moholy, *A Hundred Years of Photography*, Harmondsworth, Penguin Books, 1939. Back cover. Cover design Penguin Books.
Penguins used their back covers either to advertise their own books (which was also done with any leftover pages at the back of the book itself), or, after the outbreak of war, to carry advertising for any number of products from shaving soap to Mars Bars.

Early Paperback Series

Traditionally, publishers issue a hardback edition, particularly of fiction, at a premium price to cover the main costs of publication, followed by a cheaper paperback edition. The first paperbacks came about as a result of the growth of rail travel in the nineteenth century, which brought a demand for cheap editions of novels. In 1842 in Germany, Bernard Tauchnitz of Leipzig began his series of English-language reprints which were sold, normally at railway bookstalls, outside the copyright jurisdiction of the original publishers, but always with their agreement and a voluntary payment of royalties. Their style was European, with uncut pages and white covers. The Tauchnitz house style was reworked in 1935, following its takeover by John Holroyd-Reece, who in 1932 founded the Albatross Library as a competitor. It had a more modern image, but followed the same pattern of selling in a different copyright zone to the original edition. Albatross covers were the work of Giovanni (Hans) Mardersteig, of Verona. After the success of Albatross, the names of birds became a pattern, producing most famously Penguin Books (see pp. 30–1), but also the shorter-lived Toucan series. Albatross also originated the idea of colour-coding the covers to indicate different kinds of book, something adopted by Penguin and by the revised Tauchnitz Library in the form of coloured rules.

TAUCHNITZ EDITION
COLLECTION OF BRITISH AND AMERICAN AUTHORS
VOL. 4937

A PORTRAIT OF THE ARTIST AS A YOUNG MAN
BY
JAMES JOYCE

LEIPZIG: BERNHARD TAUCHNITZ
PARIS: LIBRAIRIE GAULON & FILS, 39, RUE MADAME

Not to be introduced into the British Empire and U.S.A.

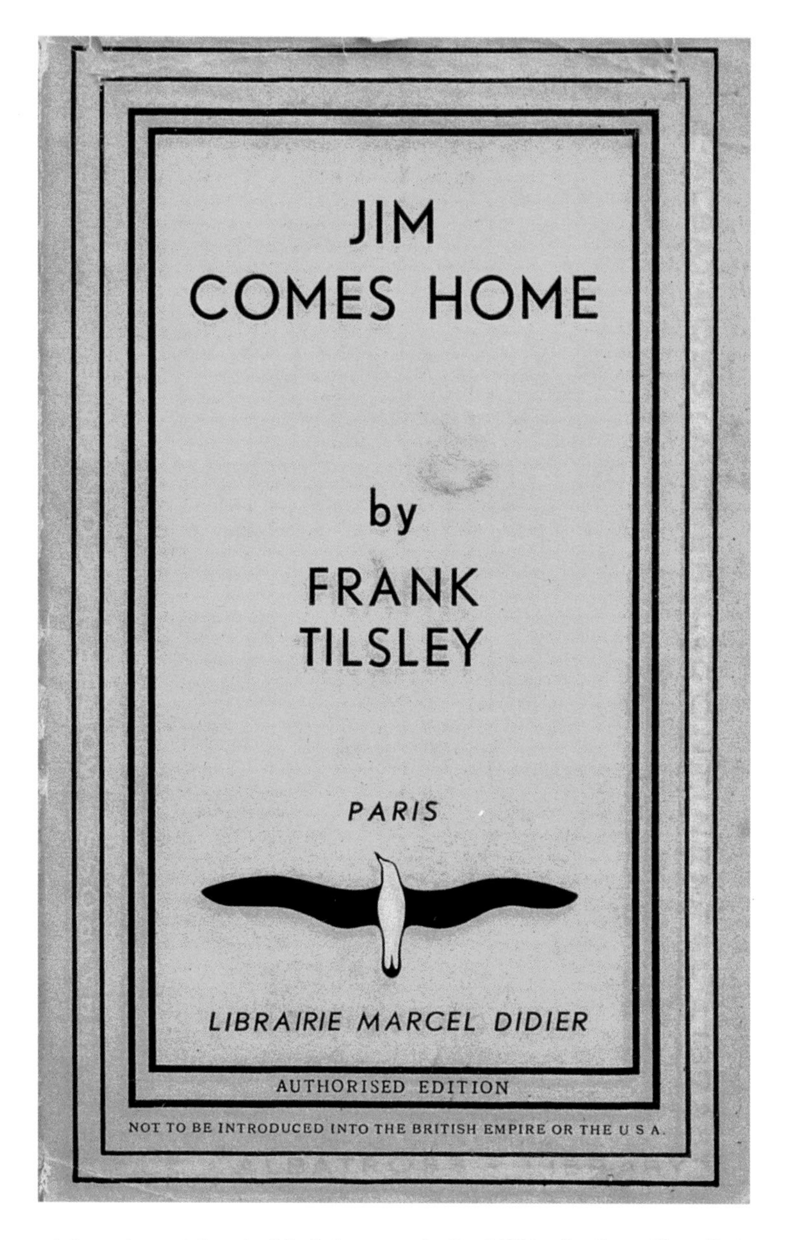

◄ James Joyce, *A Portrait of the Artist as a Young Man*, Leipzig, Hamburg, Paris, Bernard Tauchnitz, 1930. Artist unknown.
Joyce's classic fictionalized autobiography was first published as a serial in *The Egoist*, 1914–15. Tauchnitz had been selling English-language books in Europe for nearly 100 years when this edition was produced, which retained a squarish format that was difficult to put in a coat pocket.

▲ Frank Tilsley, *Jim Comes Home*, Paris, Albatross Books, 1947. Series design by Giovanni Mardersteig.
The pre-war look of Albatross books was continued into the post-war period, when Penguin, initially inspired by Albatross, was becoming a worldwide publishing company.

▶ **Takashi Ohta and Margaret Sperry, *The Golden Wind*, New York, Charles Boni Paper Books, 1929. Cover design by Rockwell Kent.**
The series was established by publisher Charles Boni after he lost his shares in a previous company. It began as a mail-order book club in 1929, with distinguished line-drawn covers by Rockwell Kent, but turned into a retail series in 1930 before falling victim to the Depression in 1932. Piet Schreuders writes, "The paper and the typography were of a quality which was, and still is, rare for paperbacks."

◀ **Angus MacVicar, *The Ten Green Brothers*, London, Toucan, 1936. Artist unknown.**
A year after the successful launch of Penguin Books, another exotic bird proclaims a paperback series. Some publishers relaunched titles from their existing lists in similar format, specially in the high-turnover field of crime and mystery.

▲ **John Buchan, *The Island of Sheep*, Leipzig, Hamburg, Paris, Bernard Tauchnitz, 1937. Artist unknown.**
An example of the redesigned Tauchnitz format, following the takeover by John Holroyd-Reece. John Buchan (1875–1940) was a politician who is chiefly famous for *The Thirty-Nine Steps* (1915). Alfred Hitchcock's 1935 film of this book, starring Robert Donat as the hero, Richard Hannay, would have stimulated demand for more Buchan titles.

Colour and Printing

Using strong colours to sell books was common in the nineteenth century, when cheap reprints of novels for railway travellers were commonly issued in paper-covered boards with gaudy images printed from wood engravings. The "quality" trade prided itself on discretion until the 1920s, when strong colour became a trend in fashion and interior decoration. Colour was less used during the First World War, partly because the chemicals used for coloured inks and dyes were the same as those needed for making explosives. There were still a number of problems in colour printing: the best paper for the job was heavily coated with china clay to prevent absorption of the ink, but it gave an unpleasant touch and did not grip well around a book. It worked best when artists could compose an image in "colour separations", which would be made into separate printing blocks or plates with specially mixed pure colours, rather than having colours produced by overlaid half-tone dots. The famous series of covers for Batsford in the 1920s and '30s was designed by Brian Cook, a relation of the founding family of this distinguished imprint. The early examples employed the Jean Berté process of colour printing which achieved greater vibrancy of colour with water-based inks that were printed from rubber rollers engraved by hand.

▲ John Dos Passos, *1919*, New York, Harcourt, Brace & Co., 1932. Designer unknown.
The map showing the political divisions of Europe at the Treaty of Versailles maximizes the strength of colour on a high white paper. Having the sea black (a favourite colour in the 1920s) helps to project the strong reds.

► Francis and Vera Meynell, editors, *The Week-End Book: A Sociable Anthology*, London, The Nonesuch Press, 1924. Jacket design by Edward McKnight Kauffer.
The first edition of a popular anthology. Kauffer was skilled at designing in simple colour shapes: his image here of a steam locomotive illustrates the opening poem, "Week-End" by Harold Munro, beginning, "The train, the twelve o' clock for paradise."

▲ **Leon Feuchtwanger, *Success*, London, Martin Secker, 1930. Designer unknown.**
Papers with repeat patterns, used historically for bookbinding, especially in Italy, were popular in the 1920s and could be designed in a modern style. The heavy Germanic lettering in red is given maximum prominence on its black panels in this simple but effective three-colour printing job.

◄ **Seán O'Faoláin, *Midsummer Night Madness*, London, Jonathan Cape, 1932. Jacket design by "Ripos'am".**
Two-colour printings were applied to a coloured paper to create an abstract cover design.

▼ **Ralph Dutton, *The English Country House*, London, B. T. Batsford, 1935. Jacket design by Brian Cook.**
As the inks used in the Jean Berté printing process were transparent, they could be overlaid to get more tones from fewer printings. It was necessary, however, to use the brightest possible pigments to achieve this. Brian Cook eventually tired of the garish effects that resulted, as seen here, and reverted to more conventional methods.

▲ **Humphrey Pakington, *English Villages and Hamlets*, London, B. T. Batsford, 1934. Jacket design by Brian Cook.**
Part of the "Face of Britain" series, which was distinguished by Brian Cook's poster-like covers. The sans serif type went with the modern look of the colours, and gave the idea of English tradition an unexpected modernist kick.

◄ ▼ Evelyn Waugh, *Love among the Ruins*, London, Chapman & Hall, 1962. Osbert Lancaster, *Progress at Pelvis Bay*, London, John Murray, 1941. Jackets by the respective authors. Based on Antonio Canova's famous sculpture of Cupid and Psyche, Waugh's elegant drawing shows his continuing interest in design. Lancaster's characteristic clean lines illustrate this deadpan guide to a dreadful English seaside resort.

Authors often like to scribble, doodle, or paint. Noël Coward, for example, enjoyed painting, especially in Jamaica where he went to escape the English climate (moral and fiscal, as well as weather). Osbert Lancaster, a man as witty in his way as Coward, made architecture the subject of several illustrated books, writing terse, subversive commentaries to accompany his drawings. Some authors are self-evidently amateur artists and, like T. S. Eliot's drawing for his *Old Possum's Book of Practical Cats*, their work's charm may lie in its naivety. Others produced more sophisticated work: Evelyn Waugh, for example thought of becoming an artist and illustrated his first novel, *Decline and Fall*, with sparse sardonic cartoons. Jean Cocteau, now best remembered for films such as *Orphée*, produced drawings which provided a distinctive trademark for his books. Michael Ayrton, who, like Cocteau, was fascinated by the reworking of classical myths, was artist, sculptor, and writer, and his excess of talent may have confused a public that prefers creative artists to be neatly labelled.

► T. S. Eliot, *Old Possum's Book of Practical Cats*, London, Faber and Faber, 1939. Jacket drawing by T. S. Eliot. Old Possum, was a nickname for T. S. Eliot used by Ezra Pound.

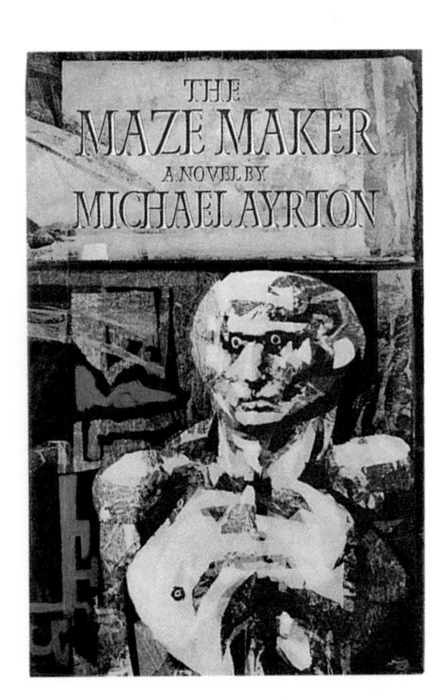

► **Michael Ayrton, *The Maze Maker*, Harlow, Longman, 1967. Jacket illustration by Michael Ayrton.**
Michael Ayrton illustrates his fictional treatment of the story of Daedalus, the subject of many of his late sculptures. As a result of the book, he was commissioned to design a maze for an American banker in the Catskill mountains. George Steiner wrote, "There seemed to be nothing Ayrton could not do in a style defiantly his own…."

◄ **Jean Cocteau, *Les Enfants Terribles*, Le Livre de Poche, Paris, 1971. Jacket design by Jean Cocteau.**
First published in 1929, Cocteau's short novel of a bizarre and mutually destructive brother-sister relationship has remained one of his best-known works. The cover drawing is typical of many Cocteau graphics that borrowed from the ambiguities and simplifications of Cubism to restate primal themes.

▲ **Noël Coward, *Pomp and Circumstance*, London, Heinemann, 1960. Jacket design by Noël Coward.**
In his song "Mad Dogs and Englishmen", Coward mocked the pretensions of the British empire. In similar mocking spirit, this novel borrows its title from Sir Edward Elgar's marches and the cover portrays in flat Matisse-like colours a scene in Jamaica, where Coward spent much of the year in his later life.

Dutch Graphic Design

The culture of printing in Holland has developed vigorously alongside other movements in architecture and design. A number of designers worked in several fields, like H. T. Wijdeveld, who was an architect and theatre-designer, as well as being the editor and designer for the magazine *Wendingen*. This vitality was supported by adventurous commissioning from business and state enterprises in the inter-war period. Innovations included letter-forms, layouts, and the use of photomontage in association with the new typography of the 1920s. As Jan Tschichold, who later worked for Penguin Books in England, explained in his important and influential book *The New Typography* (1928), "In photomontage, with the help of given or selected photographs, a new pictorial unity is created which, being deliberate and no longer accidental, has an axiomatic claim to the title of Art." The Dutch painter Cesar Domela, associated with the De Stijl movement, moved to Berlin in 1927 and, until the rise of Nazism in 1933, worked as a graphic designer as well as pursuing his research in pure art. He made frequent use of photomontage, not in the satirical manner of the German artist John Heartfield, but in a more poetic relationship with the books whose jackets he designed.

◄ Michail Sjolochow, *De Stille Don (Quiet Flows the Don)*, The Hague, De Baanbreker, 1931. Jacket design by Cesar Domela.
For the Dutch edition of this book, Domela created a photomontage of mounted Cossacks facing a crowd of peasants. The two colours are cleverly deployed and despite the amount of information, the result is still clearly legible.

▲ Horst Biernath, *Arne Björn, Fährt ins Glück (Arne Björn, Journey in Happiness)*, Berlin, Zetschriftenverlag, 1933. Jacket design by Cesar Domela.
A yearning image of freedom made by Domela at a time of turmoil in Berlin, his adopted home. The use of the map, with a line of direction on it, is a concise way of communicating the contents of the book.

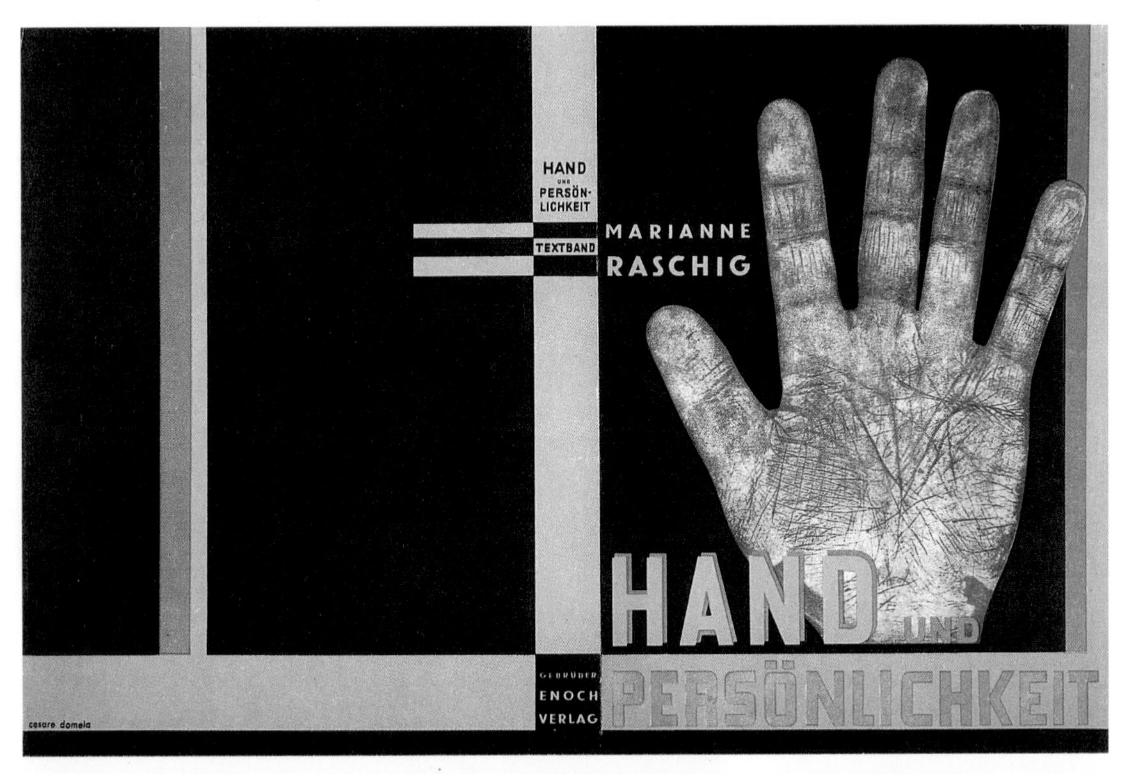

◄ **Marianne Raschig, *Hand und Persönlichkeit* (*Hand and Personality*), Hamburg, Gebruder Enoch Verlag, 1931. Jacket by Cesar Domela.**
The positioning of the image of the hand, behind the title lettering but coming forward from the framing rules, helps to give three-dimensionality to the flat image. In *The New Typography*, Jan Tschichold condemned the use of decorative rules with blank spaces at the intersections, but Domela uses the spaces for conveying information on the book's spine.

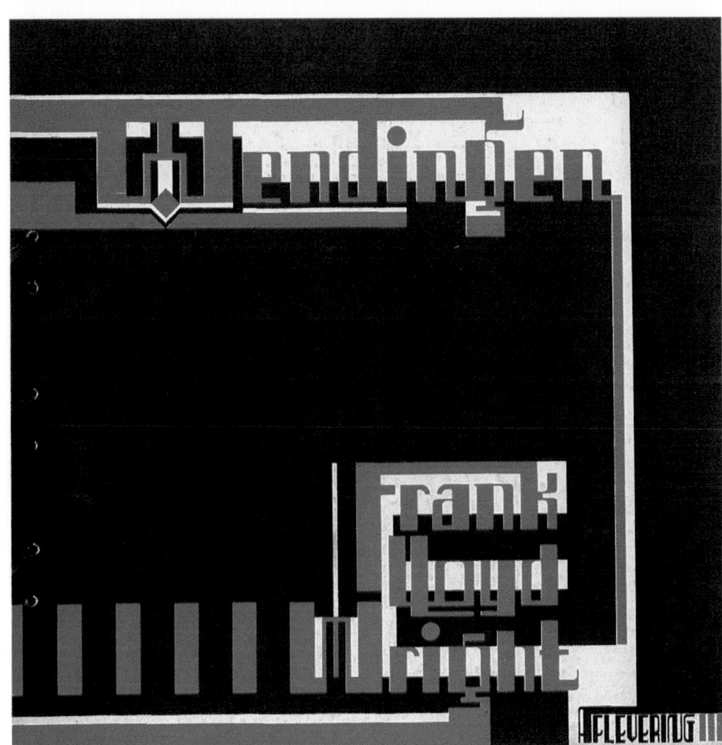

▲ ***Wendingen*, "Frank Lloyd Wright special issue", Amsterdam, C.A. Mees, 1925. Cover design by H.T. Wijdeveld.**
Wendingen was an inclusive and eclectic magazine, covering art, architecture, and theatre. It had a square format, and was bound, Japanese style, with raffia, indicating the strong oriental influence on Dutch culture. This important publication on the work of the American architect has been reprinted as a classic of its time.

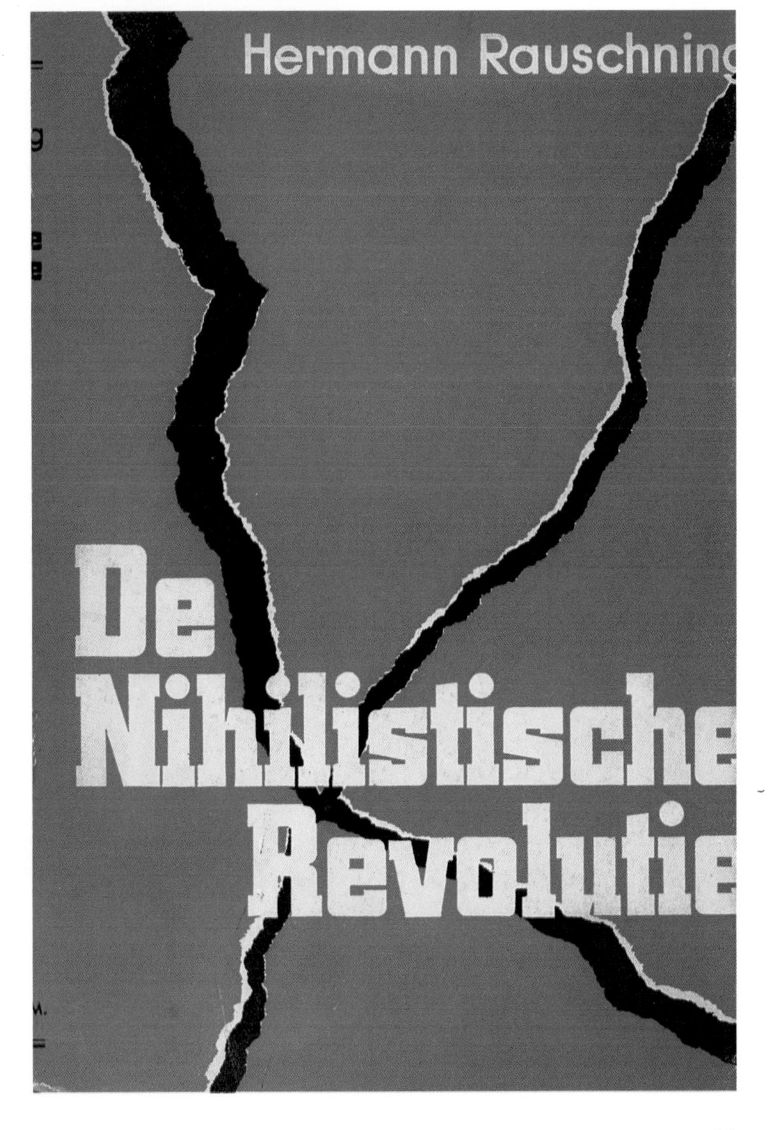

► **Hermann Rauschning, *De Nihilistische Revolutie* (*The Nihilistic Revolution*), The Hague, Leopold, 1939. Jacket design by Helmut Salden.**
Simple means create a striking cover, which is similar to many 1950s jacket designs. The translator of this German text noted that the cover "claims to strike a balance between the demands made by marketing … and the cover as a symbol of the book's content," an eternal issue for the book-jacket designer.

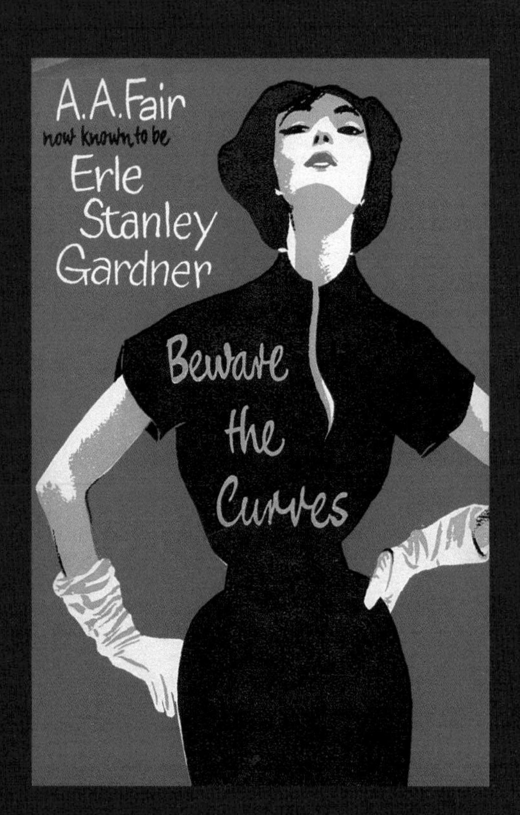
A.A.Fair
now known to be
Erle
Stanley
Gardner
Beware
the
Curves

The Creation of Style:

The 1940s to the 1960s

Book-jacket designers of the inter-war period were odd-job men, whether descending from the heights of fine art, or getting their feet on the ladder from the corner of the publisher's office or the printer's factory. In the period during and after the Second World War, "commercial artists" and "industrial artists" turned into "graphic designers" and took a fresh view of the value of their activity. Most of the best ones, like Paul Rand or Alvin Lustig, learned on the job through experience, and benefitted from European modernist culture which was becoming widely available through magazines and the diaspora of emigration. Book-cover design encompassed an extraordinarily wide range of styles and techniques, and in a culture that was still dominated by the printed image and word, there was a steep increase both in quantity and quality of book-cover design.

Despite the enormous potential for a new integrated approach to the design of books, jackets and covers remained a Cinderella area. Their design was often left to the last minute and subject to competing opinions from different individuals in the publishing house. Despite the enormous amount of design talent available, the book trade, in English-speaking countries, at least, was more often content to achieve decent dullness than to sparkle, and books whose insides and outsides were stylistically matched were rare indeed.

◄ A. A. Fair (Erle Stanley Gardner), *Beware the Curves*, London, William Heinemann, 1957. Jacket design by "Stein" (see page 68).

Lettering

Pictures and lettering may be considered as separate aspects of a jacket design, but they can be combined together so that it is hard to tell where one finishes and the other begins. The lettered jacket may initially present an archaic or impoverished appearance, recalling the times when jackets were meant to be discarded as soon as the book was bought, but skilled designers have discovered that letterforms can communicate much subliminal information about the cultural milieu of a book.

Lettering was taught to nearly all art students in the 1930s and '40s, while other artists, like David Jones, discovered it for themselves through the example of the famous lettercutter, Eric Gill (1882–1940). David Jones's jacket for his long poem, *Anathémata*, is an example in which the early Christian letterforms with their irregularities not only locate the poem in the distant past but also introduce its religious content.

The letters themselves can suggest the book's content, as with Michael Harvey's jacket for Hammond Innes's *Atlantic Fury*, torn by a gale into spindrift. Harvey, who trained with Reynolds Stone, another pupil of Gill, was probably the most prolific producer of lettered jackets in Britain, providing a house style for several publishers, and notably for the hardback novels of Graham Greene published by The Bodley Head in the 1960s and '70s.

▲ Arthur Koestler, *The Age of Longing*, London, Collins, 1951. Jacket design by Peter Curl.
Koestler was one of the leading post-war intellectuals. The perspective and falling withered leaves of this jacket give a feeling of post-war anxiety.

◄► David Jones, *Anathémata*, London, Faber and Faber, 1952, jacket by David Jones and Graham Greene, *The Human Factor*, London, The Bodley Head, 1978, jacket by Michael Harvey.
The painter David Jones began to write after a nervous breakdown in 1932 and, at the same time, began to make lettered inscriptions. Several of these are illustrated to accompany the text of *Anathémata*, a work that evokes both the layers of history in Britain, hence the Latin form of London, and the centrality of Christianity to civilization, hence the monograms below the title.

▲ **Iris Murdoch, *A Severed Head*, London, Chatto & Windus, 1961. Jacket design by John Woodcock.**
Novels by Iris Murdoch (1919–99), all originally published by Chatto & Windus, show a wide variety of jacket styles. Some of them were designed by artists she knew personally, such as Reynolds Stone and Tom Phillips. *A Severed Head* is concerned with adultery, incest, castration, and suicide – none of which could be inferred from the jacket. The book was filmed in 1971 by Dick Clement with Lee Remick and Claire Bloom.

◄ **Hammond Innes, *Atlantic Fury*, London, Collins, 1962. Jacket design by Michael Harvey.**
Despite the graphic response to the title, the cover is classic in its disciplined lettering. The thrillers of Hammond Innes, set in extremes of climate with groups of tough men, were popular both as books and as films.

► **Graham Greene, *A Burnt-Out Case*, London, William Heinemann, 1961. Jacket design by Lacey Everett.**
The novel is set in a leper colony in the Congo, so the flower adds an element of irony. The spiky character of the lettering follows the fashion of the 1950s, although the strong colour is more typical of the 1960s.

Edward McKnight Kauffer

▲ Martin Armstrong, *St Christopher's Day*, London, Gollancz, 1928. Jacket design by Edward McKnight Kauffer.
This and the jacket for H. G. Wells, opposite, are examples of Kauffer's work for the newly founded firm of Victor Gollancz (see pp. 22–3), in both cases using an economical two-colour design and thus avoiding the realistic full-colour effect which Gollancz specially disliked. The figures are schematic but expressive in a crowded composition.

► R. M. Fox, *Smoky Crusade*, London, Hogarth Press, 1938. Jacket design by Edward McKnight Kauffer.
Although the style of the hand-drawn lettering is similar to Kauffer's work of the 1920s, the use of photomontage and the sharp colouring are more typical of the 1930s. Kauffer learned from Bauhaus designers, notably Herbert Bayer and Moholy-Nagy, the art of simple layout using diagonals and tense relationships between visual masses.

Edward McKnight Kauffer was born in 1890 in Montana. He made his career designing posters for the London Underground, which was the greatest nursery for graphics and design in the 1920s. Before the end of that decade, his work spanned from the illustration of limited editions for the Nonesuch Press to the production of brochures and cards for commerical firms. This versatility was approved and emulated by many other artists who enjoyed the challenge of an interesting design brief as well as the income that such work could produce in unsettled times. Kauffer's work on books reflects not only his ability as an artist in making memorable simplified images, but also his sensitivity to literature. Indeed, the austere poet T. S. Eliot became one of his friends and supporters. During the 1930s, Kauffer's style began to reflect not only the pre-1914 decorative Cubism which won him early fame, but the montages and novel typography of the Bauhaus and the bizarre juxtapositions of the surrealists. In July 1940, Kauffer and his companion, the designer Marion Dorn, left England for the US, and the last fourteen years of Kauffer's life were spent productive, but unhappy, in New York.

► H. G. Wells, *The Open Conspiracy*, London, Victor Gollancz, 1928. Jacket design by Edward McKnight Kauffer.
The use of colour takes up the title's invitation. Kauffer was never bashful about putting his name or initials in a prominent position on his work.

▼ Paul Bowles, *Let It Come Down*, New York, Random House, 1952. Jacket design by Edward McKnight Kauffer.
There is a palpable shift of style in this late Kauffer jacket, which is almost conservative in its realism, although still masterly in simplification and colour matching.

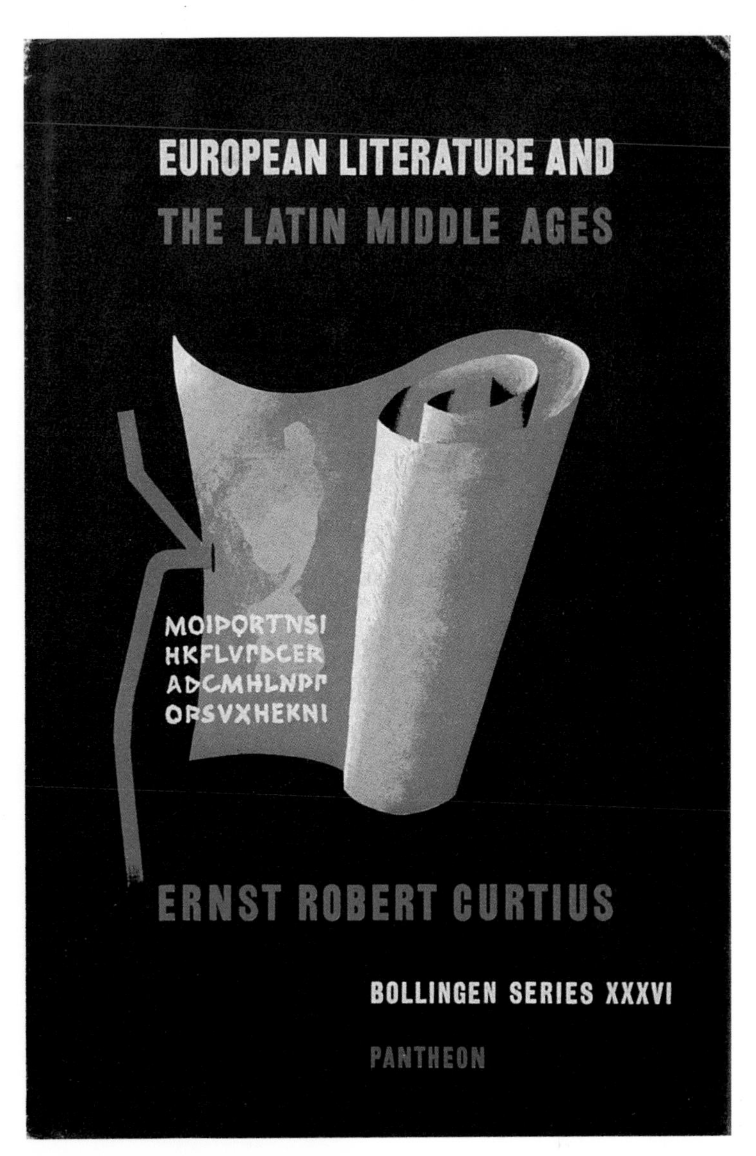

◄▲ Ernst Robert Curtius, *European Literature and the Latin Middle Ages*, 1952–3, and *Selected Prose of Hugo von Hofmannsthal*, 1952. New York, Pantheon Books. Jacket designs by Edward McKnight Kauffer.
Both titles are part of the Bollingen series, published on behalf of Princeton University. The series was named after the home of the psychologist C. G. Jung in Switzerland and reflects his interest in the spiritual role of culture. These are academic books which might not normally have received the attentions of a jacket designer, but even in their simplicity, the Kauffer jackets lend them a certain distinction.

European Writers

The post-war years saw an unprecedented interest in European fiction in the English-speaking world. The names of Jean-Paul Sartre (1905–80) and his companion Simone de Beauvoir (1908–86) were symbolic of the glamour of the Parisian intellectual café life, combined with a sense of toughness and anguish. De Beauvoir now seems in some ways the more significant of the two, with her understanding that the subjected role of women in the post-war world was not only a matter of gender but representative of the repressions of class and colonialism. European writing was not all about despair, however. The "magic realism" fantasies of Italo Calvino (1923–87) were one example of a fiction whose political message was not so overt, consisting rather of a kind of intellectual escapism. In his books, mythology and folklore played their part in a way that greatly influenced writers operating under the influence of postmodernism in the 1980s.

In continental Europe, such books would have appeared in plain typographic covers, but the jackets produced for early hardback translations of these "highbrow" novels offered scope for the illustrative talents of post-war British artists, working in a range of styles.

▲ **Italo Calvino, *Baron In The Trees*, London, Collins, 1959. Artist unknown.**
Two years after its original publication, Calvino's fantasy of an eighteenth-century baron who insists on living in trees made a distinguished appearance in this English edition.

◄ **Friedrich Deich, *The Sanity Inspectors*, London, Putnam, 1956. Jacket design by Gerard Hoffnung.**
A feeling of existential anxiety typical of the 1950s pervades this drawing by one of England's leading humorous illustrators.

◄ **Milan Kundera, *The Joke*, London, Macdonald, 1967. Jacket by Alan Spain.**
The title's irony is not lost in this design which conveys information on a variety of subliminal levels. The date of this publication by one of Czechoslovakia's leading dissidents coincided with the "Prague Spring" of 1968.

▲ **Simone de Beauvoir, The *Blood of Others*, Secker & Warburg, 1948. Jacket design by Victor Reinganum.**
A striking design for the second of de Beauvoir's major works, it is perhaps overcomplicated by overlaying abstract colour areas on black-and-white drawing.

▲ **Françoise Sagan, *Bonjour Tristesse*, London, John Murray, 1955. Jacket design by F. Quilter.**
A striking design for the most famous title by a leading proponent of feminism in post-war fiction.

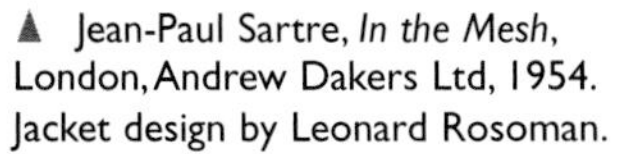

▲ **Jean-Paul Sartre, *In the Mesh*, London, Andrew Dakers Ltd, 1954. Jacket design by Leonard Rosoman.**
One of Britain's leading artist-illustrators provided a finely observed drawing for the first British publication of a Sartre novel. The drawn lettering helps the unity of design in the jacket.

► **Jean-Paul Sartre, *Intimacy*, London, Peter Nevill Ltd, 1949. Jacket design by Guy Nicholls.**
A realistic presentation, rendered in a typical 1950s scratchy ink line, but belonging more, perhaps, to the realm of pulp fiction than to highbrow publishing.

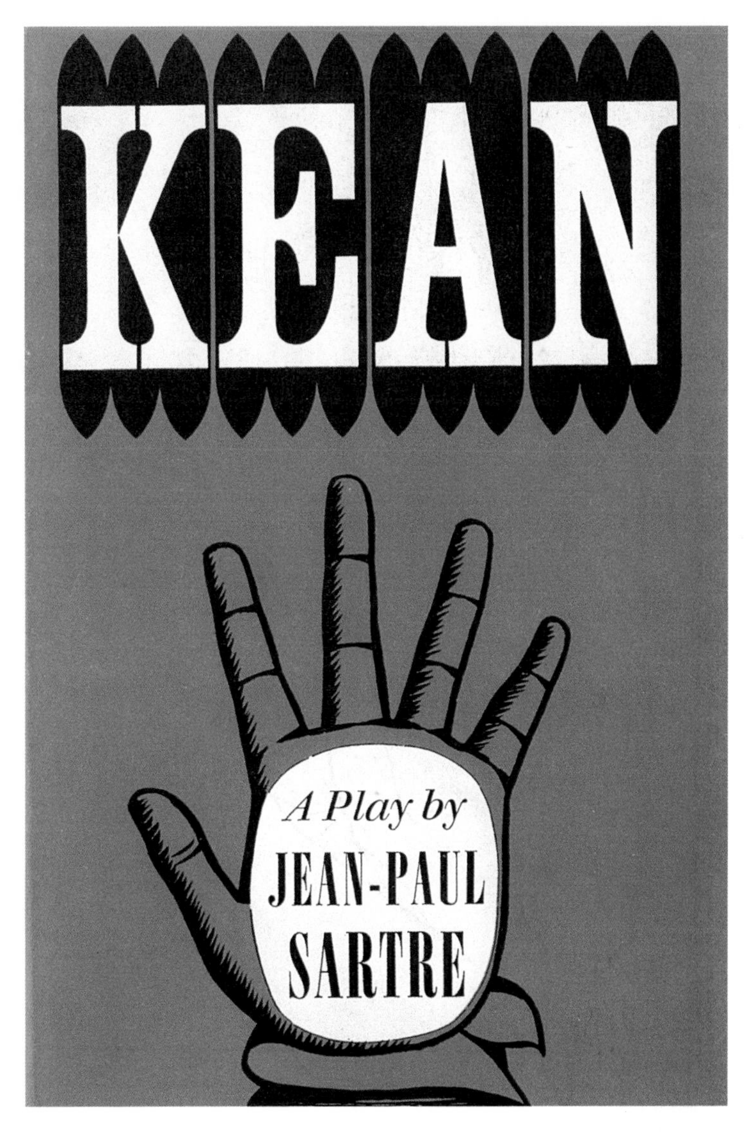

► **Jean-Paul Sartre, *Kean*, London, Hamish Hamilton, 1954. Artist unknown.**
Sartre's play is based on the life of the English actor, Edmund Kean (1787–1833), a romantic, self-destructive figure. The jacket picks up some of the theatrical character and the early nineteenth-century style.

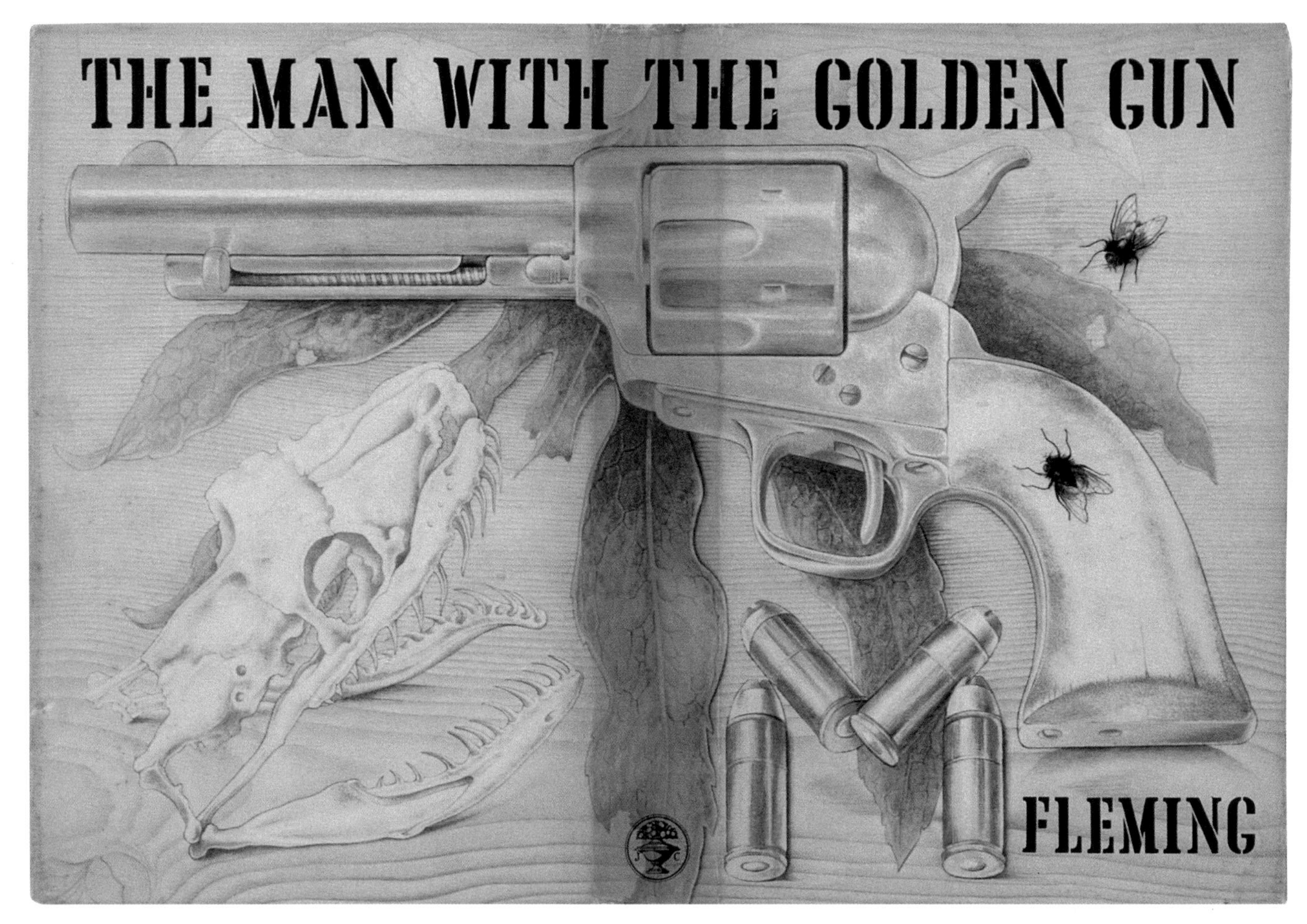

In 1953, Jonathan Cape published *Casino Royale*, the first novel by Ian Fleming (1908–64). Bond novels, published annually thereafter, acquired a following, and the filming of *Dr No* (published in 1958), with Sean Connery and Ursula Andress, gave them immortality. The components of the books, as Kingsley Amis wrote, were "evident familiarity with secret-service style activities (not least those of his country's enemies) . . . a formidable and physically repulsive villain, a strong sexual component, a glamorous and complaisant heroine, and – of course – James Bond himself." Ian Fleming took a lot of trouble with the jackets for his books, providing ideas for draughtsmen and buying their original artwork. He commissioned Richard Chopping, whom he considered "the only English master of *trompe l'oeuil"*, to design the jacket of *From Russia with Love* and subsequent Bond books. Fleming provided Chopping with a detailed brief and a supplement to Cape's normal fee of twenty-five guineas. The jacket designs, carried round the spine and back of the book, are restrained but effective in their focus on still-life objects which convey the macabre sense of doom in the stories, omitting, however, the gadgetry and sex for which they have become better-known.

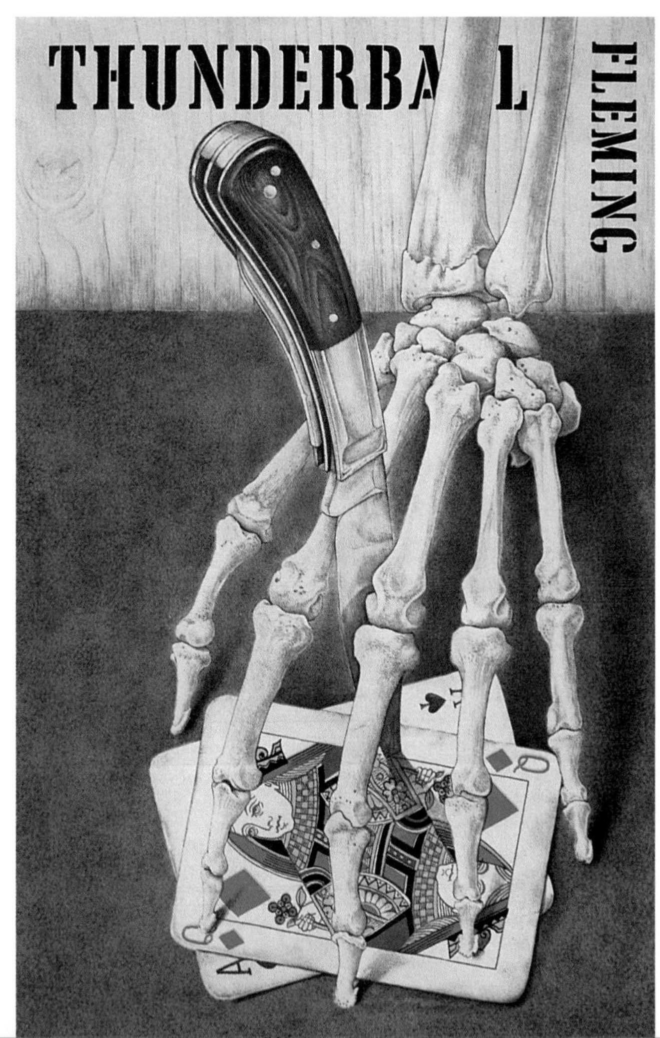

▲ ► Ian Fleming, *The Man with the Golden Gun*, 1965, and *Thunderball*, 1961, London, Jonathan Cape. Jacket designs both by Richard Chopping.
Fleming was delighted by the covers produced by Richard Chopping which form a distinctive series.

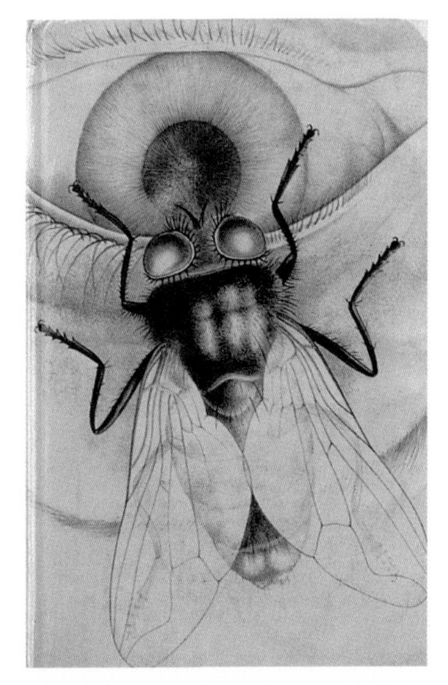

◄ Richard Chopping, *The Fly*, London, Secker & Warburg, 1965. Jacket by Richard Chopping.
Richard Chopping's illustration for his own novel shows his sinister detailed eye and imagination.

▼ Ian Fleming, *For Your Eyes Only*, London, Pan Books, 1962. Cover design by J. Oval.
With its Marilyn Monroe lookalike, the cover for this book of Bond stories comes close to the sultry sexuality of American paperback covers about which English publishers complained in the1940s and '50s.

▲ Ian Fleming, *Diamonds are Forever*, London, Jonathan Cape, 1956. Cover design by Pat Marriott.
The well-observed lines, creating an almost abstract composition, distinguish Pat Marriott's jacket for the third Bond novel, and contrast with the style of the Pan Bond paperback covers. The limited range of colours, emphasizing the smiling lips, is particularly effective.

► Ian Fleming, *Casino Royale*, London, Pan Books, 1955. Artist unknown.
The cover of *Casino Royale* in paperback contrasts with the highbrow graphics of Cape's hardback editions. It presents an image of James Bond prior to his association with the actor Sean Connery in the early series of Bond films produced by Alberto Broccoli.

Science Fiction

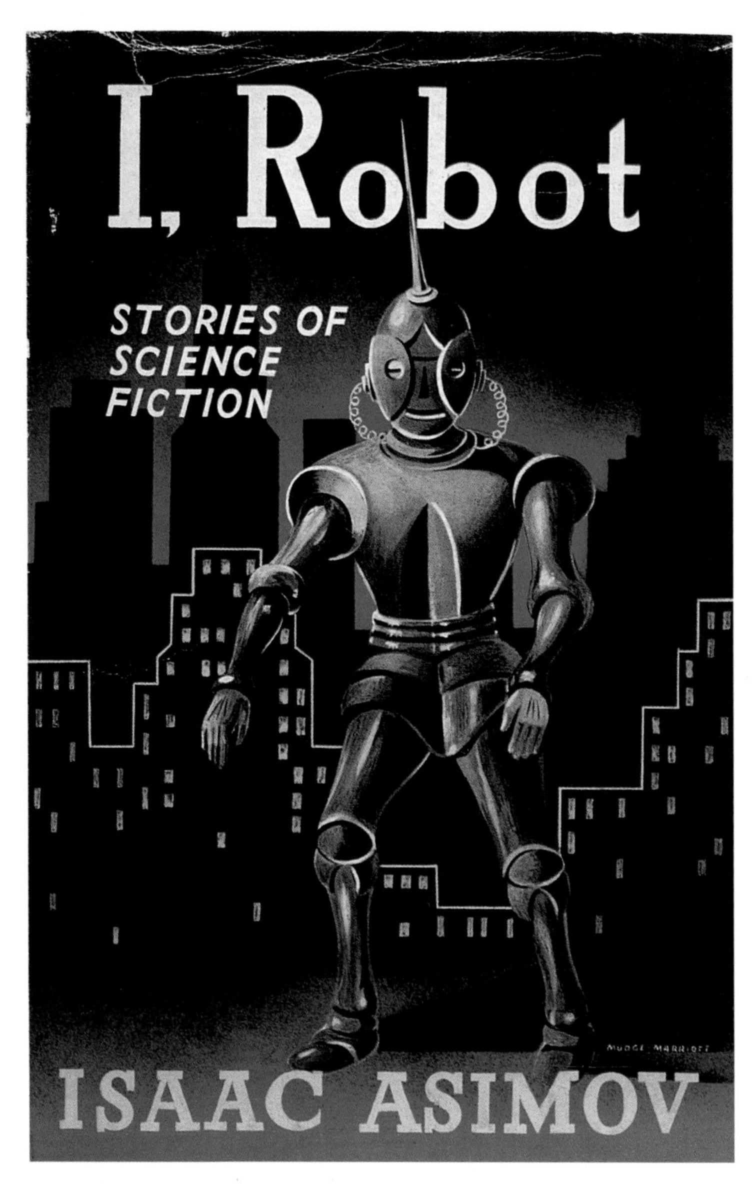

Projections of the future, involving aliens from outer space, journeys into the past, and intriguing technology, have much in common with ancient myths and parables, as well as with the imperialist spirit of the early twentieth century. The aliens surprisingly often display in fictionalized form the characteristics of a feared national enemy. A few early writers in this genre, notably Jules Verne and H. G. Wells, have remained classics. It has been claimed of both Isaac Asimov (1920–92) and Robert Heinlein (1907–88) that they retrieved the genre from the world of pulp paperbacks and gave it intellectual and moral credibility through good writing in the 1940s. In Asimov's case, he discovered sci-fi magazines on his family's candy stall, and because they included the word "science" persuaded his high-minded father that he should be allowed to have them. Asimov became famous, among other things, for formulating the "Three Laws of Robotics", in which robots in stories should obey their human masters and put their needs before their own. With these principles, Asimov claimed, "No writer could write a stupid robot story."

Heinlein was invalided out of the US Navy, and returned to an earlier task of writing. As Frank Robertson has written, "It was Heinlein who decided that science fiction would be more believable if believable people did all those unbelievable things."

◄▲ Isaac Asimov, *I, Robot*, London, Grayson & Grayson, 1952, jacket by Mudge Marriot, and John Wyndham, *Trouble with Lichen*, London, Michael Joseph, 1960, jacket by Hugh Marshall.
The cover of Asimov's early story collection betrays the pulp paperback ancestry of American science fiction, which was soon to become an important form of literature in its own right.

► L. Ron Hubbard, *Final Blackout*, Providence, Hadley Publishers, 1948. Artist unknown.
Hubbard (1911–86) was an explorer and prolific writer of pulp fiction, until the launch of his psychological theory of dianetics in 1950, and its transition into The Church of Scientology in 1955. He has been described as "the greatest humanitarian in history".

◄ **Robert A. Heinlein, *The Man Who Sold the Moon*, Chicago, Shasta Publishing, 1950. Jacket design by Hubert Rogers.**
A collection of stories by Heinlein, described by Frank Robertson as "the one author who has raised science fiction from the gutter of pulp space opera to the attitude of original and breathtaking concepts." The cover design, with its elegant lettering, makes the genre explicit while exhibiting a certain restraint.

▼ **Kurt Vonnegut, Jr., *Slaughterhouse-Five or The Children's Crusade*, New York, Seymour Lawrence, 1969. Jacket design by Paul Bacon.**
A distinguished design, but one which betrays none of the content of this account of the fire-bombing of Dresden in 1944, an event which Vonnegut witnessed as a prisoner-of-war. The science-fiction element comes with the main character, Bobby Pilgrim, a visitor from space who provides corrective lenses for earthlings.

► **Isaac Asimov, *The Gods Themselves*, London, Victor Gollancz, 1972. Cover design by Victor Gollancz.**
The combination of an established author and an English publisher with a strong house style for jackets (see pp. 22–3) has resulted in a jacket that is notable chiefly for its use of a letterform inspired by early computers, which were then considered futuristic.

Alvin Lustig

Alvin Lustig died of diabetes in 1955 before the age of forty, but in only fifteen years he did much to establish a new look for American jacket design. Some of his designs have remained in use ever since. After a few months studying with the architect Frank Lloyd Wright, Lustig worked for the progressive publisher New Directions, under its director James Laughlin. From 1945 to 1952, he designed the covers for the New Directions "New Classics" series, of which Steven Heller writes, "they appear as fresh and inventive today as when they were introduced almost 50 years ago."

European modernism was the chief influence on Lustig's work, from designers such as Domela and Kauffer to the wiry graphics of Paul Klee or the work of Catalan surrealist Joan Miró. Modernism was often witty, and Lustig succeeded in catching its insouciant, almost throwaway elegance. He proved that a jacket designer needs to have read a text intelligently in order to summarize its mood and content without trivializing it. This attention to the author's meaning enabled him to switch rapidly from one graphic style to another, while retaining a distinctive series identity through sheer quality rather than heavyweight branding.

◄ Paul Bowles, *The Sheltering Sky*, Norfolk, Conn., New Directions, 1949. Jacket design by Alvin Lustig.
At one point in his varied career, Lustig worked in film animation, creating the title sequence for the cartoon series *Mr Magoo*. This jacket resembles an animated abstract film of the kind made in Canada by Norman MacLaren in which abstract shapes move to music.

▲ Arthur Rimbaud, *Illuminations*, Norfolk, Conn., New Directions, 1947. Jacket design by Alvin Lustig.
Reading the late-nineteenth-century poet Rimbaud for the first time has changed many lives. Lustig matched the writer's volatile genius with a burst of flame hanging in space like a firework.

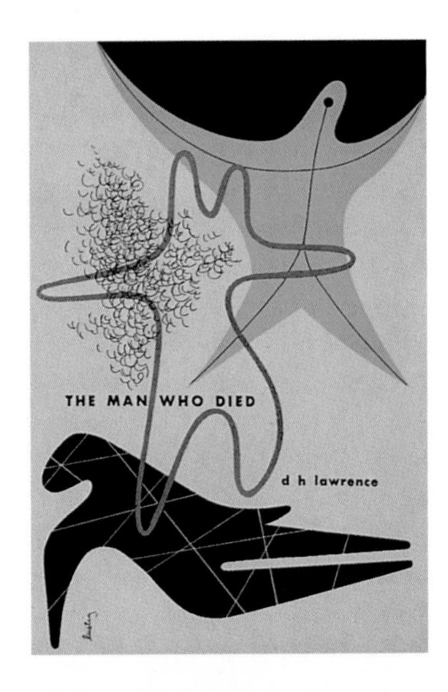

► **D. H. Lawrence, *The Man Who Died*, Norfolk, Conn., New Directions, 1946. Jacket design by Alvin Lustig.**
A simple but graphic portrayal of the idea of an out-of-body experience, which owes something to the style of Joan Miró.

▼ **Franz Kafka, *Amerika*, Norfolk, Conn., New Directions, 1948. Jacket design by Alvin Lustig.**
Kafka's fantasy about a continent he never visited has been described as "the excitement of adventure in the great American spaces Kafka knew only from books." He believed that "designs and miracles" were still alive in America.

▲ **Alain Fournier, *The Wanderer* (*Le Grand Meaulnes*), Norfolk, Conn., New Directions, 1946. Jacket design by Alvin Lustig.**
This tender cover avoids an explicit narrative rendering of the tale of young love lost, the only work of the brilliant young writer killed in the First World War, but through a combination of curly lettering, the leaf, and the background pattern like geological strata, it evokes a feeling of curiosity and anticipation.

◄ **Charles Baudelaire, *The Flowers of Evil*, Norfolk, Conn., New Directions, 1947. Jacket design by Alvin Lustig.**
Images of tendrils of hair are specially powerful. Lustig's cover design for Baudelaire's famous collection of poems plays on the ambiguity of the title and evokes a physical presence even in the most schematic form of abstraction.

Through the Keyhole

Piet Schreuders, the authority on the design history of paperbacks, explains that the publishing firm of Dell Books was significantly different to most of its competitors, partly because it was situated not in New York but in the small industrial city of Racine, Wisconsin. George Delacorte, its founder had begun with comics and magazines, so, unlike most publishers, he was moving upmarket rather than downmarket when he decided to start publishing paperbacks. One distinctive feature of several Dell titles was the "mapback" cover, frequently used for detective thrillers, which showed the location of the murder or mystery, thus enabling the reader to visualize the plan of a house or apartment, the surrounding terrain, or sometimes a considerable section of a real city. In some cases, the authors themselves provided the details for the drawings.

All Dell books used a keyhole logo, with different motifs inside it according to the type of book. The eye motif, appropriately, was used for mysteries of all kinds. The simple unshaded colours and black outlines by the artist Ruth Belew have a particular period charm, but the salesmen objected to the "mapbacks" and claimed that promotional blurbs would be more effective. The practice therefore faded out after 1951.

▲ ► *The Crooking Finger* (above), 1946; *Speak No Evil* (right), 1943; and *Strawstack* (far right), 1944. Racine, Wisconsin, Dell Books. All illustrations by Ruth Belew.

Like a three-dimensional Cleudo board, the covers of the Dell "mapbacks" often illustrate the kind of locations on which so many mid-century murder stories depended for their puzzles of detection.

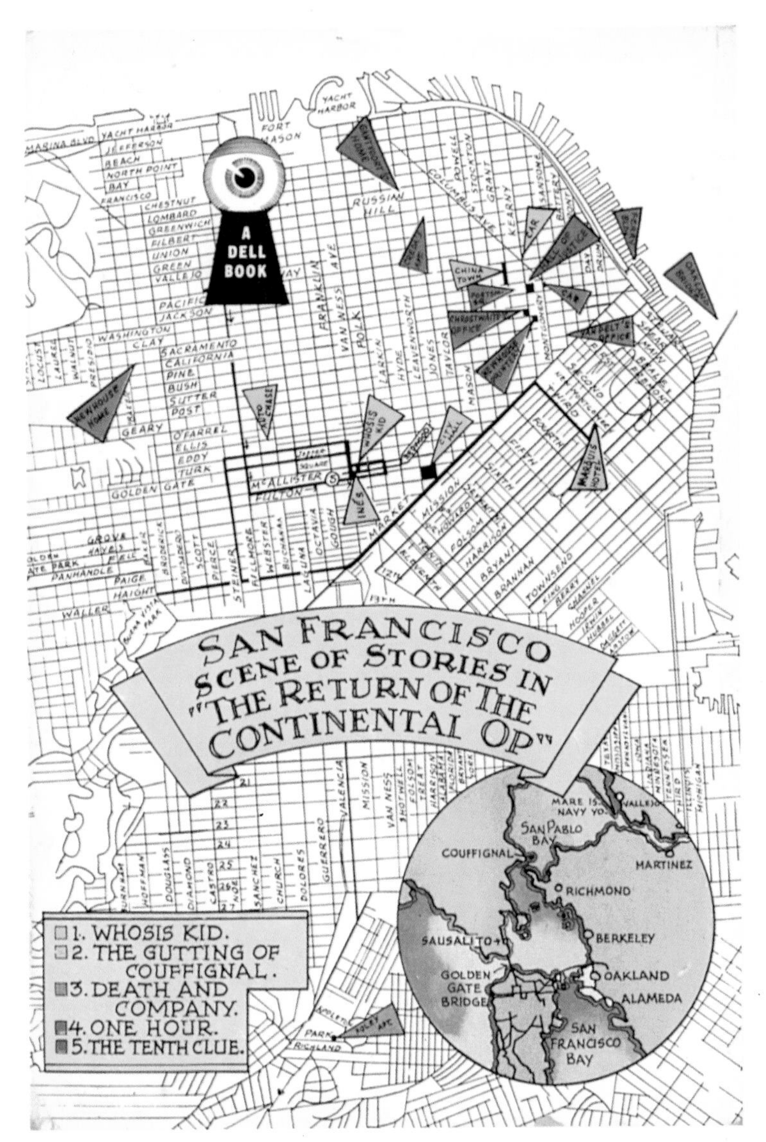

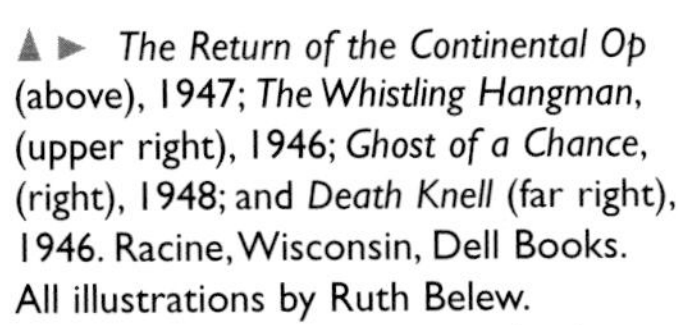
▲ ► *The Return of the Continental Op* (above), 1947; *The Whistling Hangman*, (upper right), 1946; *Ghost of a Chance*, (right), 1948; and *Death Knell* (far right), 1946. Racine, Wisconsin, Dell Books. All illustrations by Ruth Belew.

City maps presented on paperbacks might claim a practical or educational value. Tall apartment buildings provide a typically American setting for drama, evidently involving some athletic work on the exterior of the building.

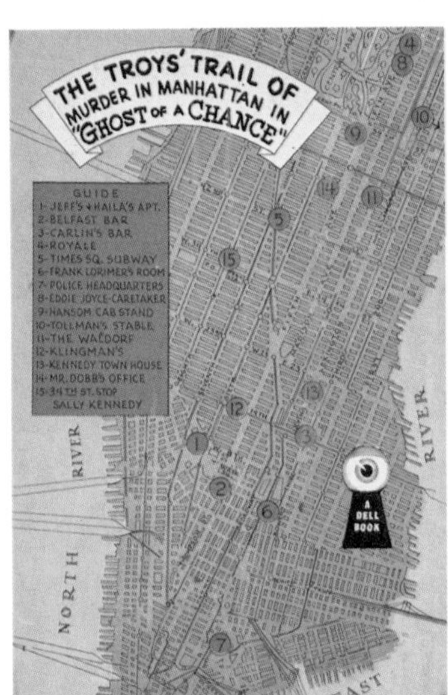

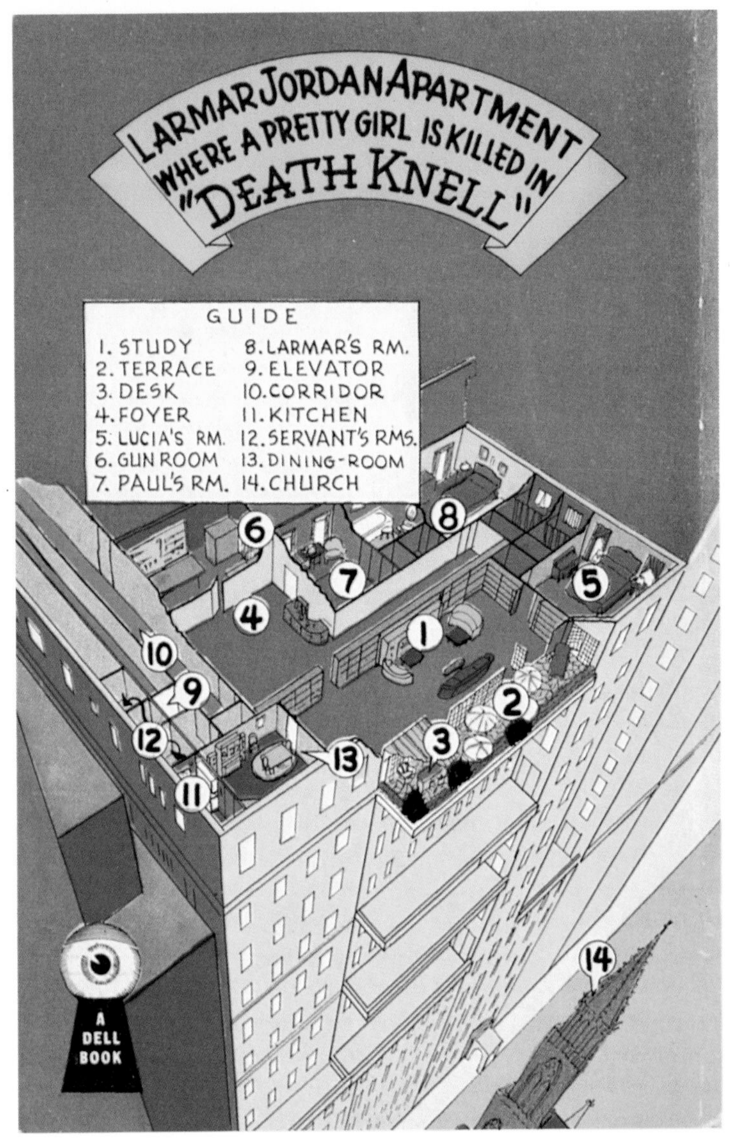

◄ Leon Uris, *Exodus*, Frankfurt, Büchergilde Gutenberg, 1961. Jacket design by Gerhard M. Hotop.
A simple but expressive collage-type design, with free-style hand-drawn lettering, which first developed in Germany in the 1920s. The continuity between the spine and the front board is a notable feature of this design.

▼ Ralph Ellison, *Invisible Man*, New York, Random House, 1952. Jacket design by Edward McKnight Kauffer.
A late jacket by Kauffer, using the device of intersecting lines that was used also in this period by Alvin Lustig. Kauffer's work was often ahead of its time, but by the 1950s the rest of the design world had caught up with him and the simplicity of this design, selecting a single eye for detailed treatment, is similar to other designs of the 1950s.

The 1950s now seems in many ways as remote in its beliefs as the years before the Second World War, even though many of the writers and artists who made their reputation during that era are still influential living figures. The memories of the war were still present in much contemporary fiction, while social problems of the time called attention to the continuing dissolution of "accepted standards", and exposed how much human misery had for years been concealed beneath them.

In the 1950s and '60s hand-drawn work of illustrators, however skilful, began to seem old fashioned by comparison with the new techniques that often used photography and played with lettering. In terms of graphic styles, the most successful jackets work with an economy of visual means, whether representational or abstract. They often play with various forms of collage as a way of producing an immediate impact, which serves to deepen their effect with a sense of dislocation between the title and the imagery.

It is interesting, fifty years on, to see how the work of Elaine Lustig Cohen has remained fresh and modern looking, while other examples, such as Hans Tisdall's Hemingway cover, have a distant 'period' quality. The distinction seems to depend on some scarcely definable quality of 'cool'.

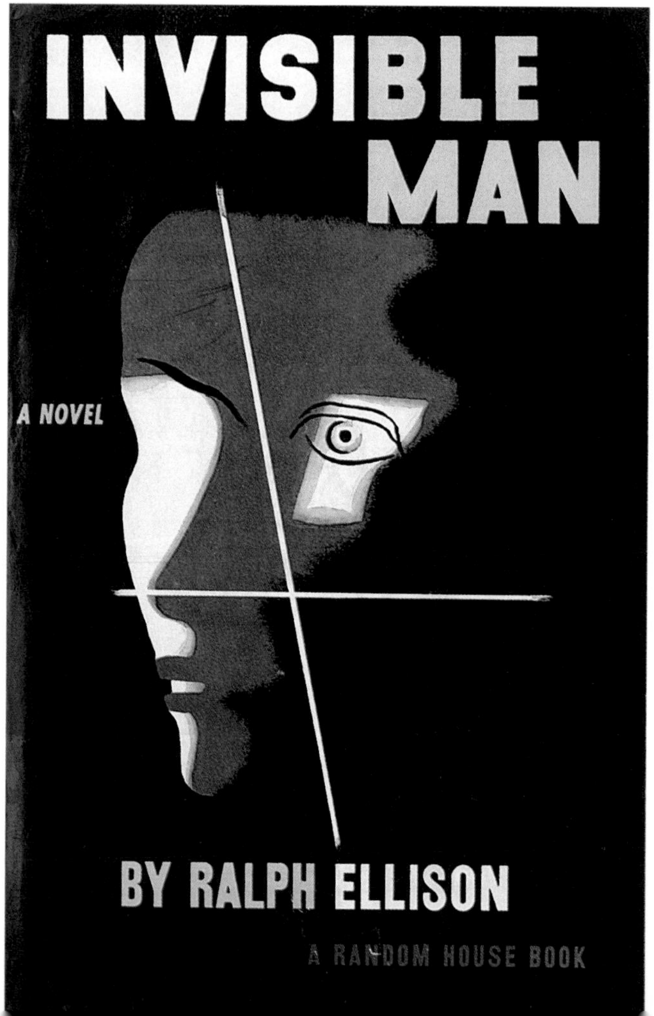

◄ **Tennessee Williams, *Baby Doll*, Norfolk, Conn., New Directions, 1959. Jacket design by Elaine Lustig Cohen.**
Designed for a collection of film scripts by the author of *A Streetcar Named Desire* (1947), this jacket evokes the grandeur of the ante-bellum South, an image that readers may expect to have shattered by what they find within. The orange label and bright lights lettering play on the menace of the title, but avoid falling into cliché.

▼ **Tennessee Williams, *Hard Candy*, Norfolk, Conn., New Directions, 1957. Jacket design by Elaine Lustig Cohen.**
A jacket by the widow of Alvin Lustig, herself a notable designer in a different style. Here the imagery of wrapped candy becomes as threatening as Alfred Hitchcock's birds.

▲ **Norman Mailer, *The Naked and the Dead*, London, Henderson & Spalding, 1959. Jacket design by James Holland.**
The English edition of Mailer's novel of the war in the Pacific, published in the US in 1948. The successful film of 1958 probably stimulated this English edition, but instead of a film image, there is a drawing by a well-known designer-illustrator with the ambiguous figure of a swimmer overlaid on the outline of an island.

▲ **Norman Mailer, *An American Dream*, New York, Dial Press, 1965. Jacket design by Paul Bacon.**
This story of a prominent professor of psychology who murders his wealthy wife was filmed the following year as *See You in Hell, Darling*. The graphic style shows the impact of pop art, echoing the interest of Jasper Johns in targets and in the American flag as subjects for art.

▲ **Anaïs Nin, *Under a Glass Bell and Other Stories*, New York, E. P. Dutton, 1948. Jacket design by Lester Kohs.**
An early collection by an author whose reputation has grown since her death in 1977 through her erotic journals. Born in Paris in 1903, her first book was a commentary on D. H. Lawrence. The design of the jacket is discreetly abstract in an age when visual information was beginning to flood the world.

▲ **Ernest Hemingway, *Across the Rain and Into the Trees*, London, Jonathan Cape, 1950. Jacket design by Hans Tisdall.**
Hemingway used to insist that the German-born artist Hans Tisdall (1910–97) should design all the covers for his English editions. Tisdall, who designed many other jackets for Cape – often consisting only of his elegant brush lettering – also worked as a textile designer, mural painter, and art teacher.

Penguin and the Paperback

At the end of the Second World War, the effects of which were entirely beneficial for paperback publishing, the Penguin imprint was ten years old. In 1946 Allen Lane hired the famous designer Jan Tschichold (1902–74), the first of many designers and art directors who ensured Penguin titles were not only cheap and well-edited, but designed to the highest standards. As Hans Schmoller, Tschichold's successor, explained, the cost of correcting the spacing of capital letters might be excessive for an edition of 3000 but would not matter for a print-run of 50,000 or 100,000. The covers moved in step with the refinements within. The King Penguin series, which began in 1941, consisted of hardbacks with illustrated paper-covered boards. Illustrated with colour plates, they were intended as gift books and were much enjoyed for their range of subjects and pre-war elegance. Poetry books were distinguished by patterned paper covers into the 1970s, while other series, such as the Penguin Shakespeare, revised an earlier format with a glossy but discreet cover. After the mid-1950s, novels began to have drawings on their covers, often by artists such as Quentin Blake, Paul Hogarth, and David Gentleman, who were just beginning their careers. However, before the 1960s, only American Penguins had fully pictorial covers, needed to compete in a very different bookselling market.

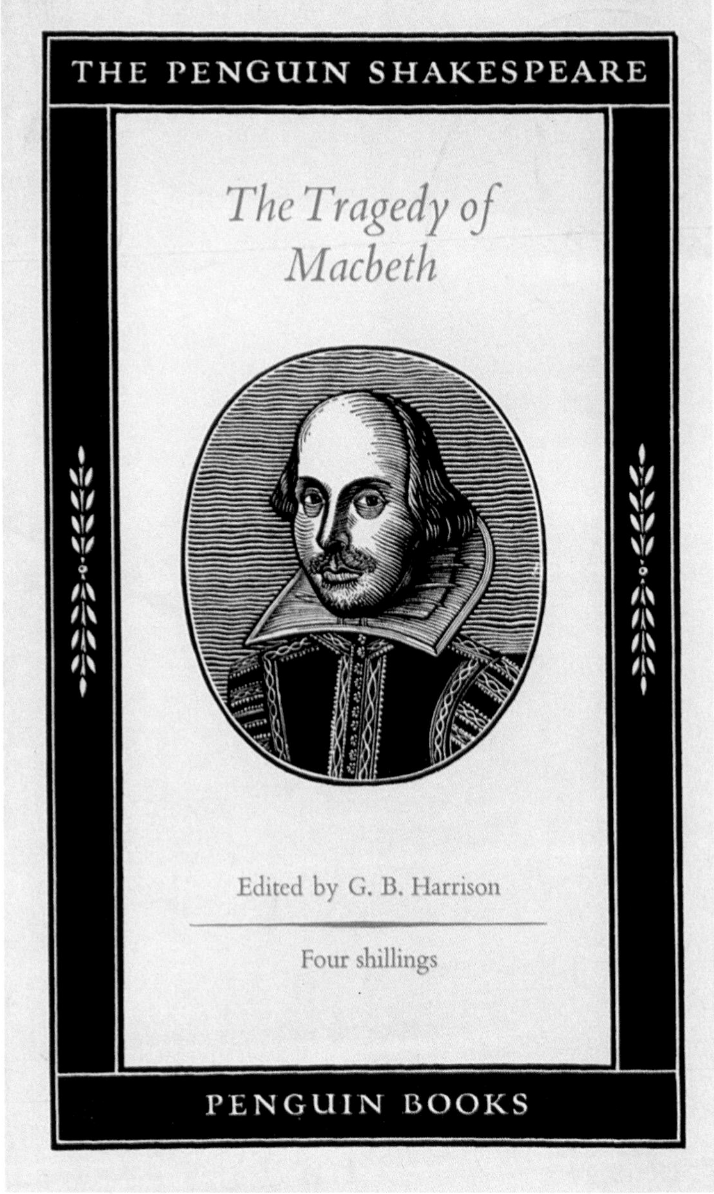

◄ **Kenneth Rowntree and Gwyn Jones, *A Prospect of Wales*, Harmondsworth, King Penguin, 1948. Jacket design by Kenneth Rowntree.**
After 1942, the King Penguin series was edited by the art historian Sir Nikolaus Pevsner, who would have known Rowntree through contacts at the *Architectural Review*. The book has sixteen watercolours by Rowntree in colour and a short introductory text, forming a "portfolio" in the Regency landscape tradition, of the kind evoked by the vignette on the cover.

▲ **William Shakespeare, *The Tragedy of Macbeth*, Harmondsworth, Penguin Books, 1949. Series jacket design by Jan Tschichold.**
Penguin first published individual Shakespeare plays in 1938, redesigning and extending the series in the 1950s. The covers included a vignette by the wood engraver Reynolds Stone, repeated in a rectangular form on the title pages and set within a cover design by Tschichold.

▲ **Nigel Kneale, *The Quatermass Experiment*, Harmondsworth, Penguin Books, 1959. Jacket design by Penguin Books.**
Kneale's series of horror thrillers concerning the mutation of a heroic British astronaut, Caroon, into an organic but no-longer-human thing, originated in a television play of 1953. *Quatermass II* was screened in1957, after which Penguin published the plays in book form.

▲ **Nigel Kneale, *Quatermass II*, Harmondsworth, Penguin Books, 1960. Cover illustration by Bryan Kneale.**
Nigel Kneale's brother, Bryan (b. 1930), began his career as a painter before beginning to make sculpture at the end of the 1950s. His anthropomorphic and vegetal forms have an affinity with the *Quatermass* books, but the cover drawing, while sufficiently evocative of anxiety, does not show its source.

▲ **Nigel Kneale, *Quatermass and the Pit*, Harmondsworth, Penguin Books, 1960. Cover illustration by Bryan Kneale.**
By showing the colonization of greater areas of the front cover of successive books, this series illustrates how slowly Penguin gave way to pictorial covers. In 1959, they published Colette's *Gigi* with the first "tie-in" cover to a film, and sweeping changes in 1961 radically altered the image of the covers.

▲ **James M. Cain, *Serenade*, New York, Penguin Books, 1947. Cover design by Robert Jonas.**
Allen Lane's dislike of the "bosoms and bottoms" of American pulp-fiction may have been partly allayed by this crisp, semi-abstract design by Robert Jonas, a prolific designer for a number of American paperback houses. The top and bottom bands of colour have a distant affinity with the English Penguin style.

▲ **Barbara Jones, *The Isle of Wight*, Harmondsworth, King Penguin, 1950. Cover design by Clifford Barry.**
For this collection of new topographical views, the artist Barbara Jones wrote her own text but although the cover could be mistaken for her own fine illustration work, it is actually by another hand. King Penguins often had detachable wrappers reproducing the design on the boards beneath.

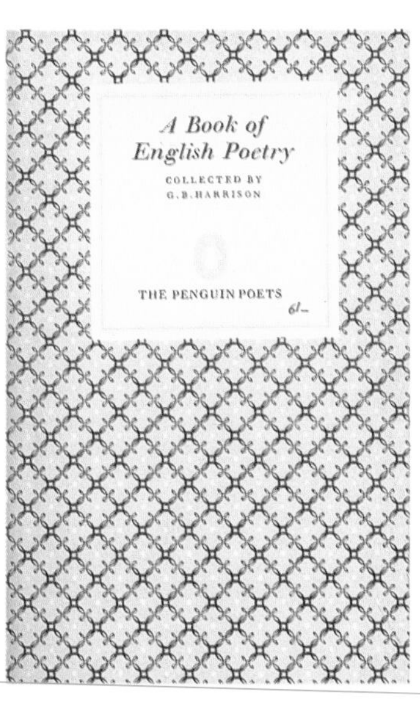

▲ **G. B. Harrison, editor, *A Book of English Poetry*, Harmondsworth, Penguin Books, 1950. Pattern design "Aurora" by Elisabeth Friedlander.**
First issued in 1937, this was one of several Penguin stock titles to be redesigned inside and out. Friedlander (1903–84) left Germany as a refugee and came to England in 1939. She had a long and fruitful relationship with Penguin from 1948 onward.

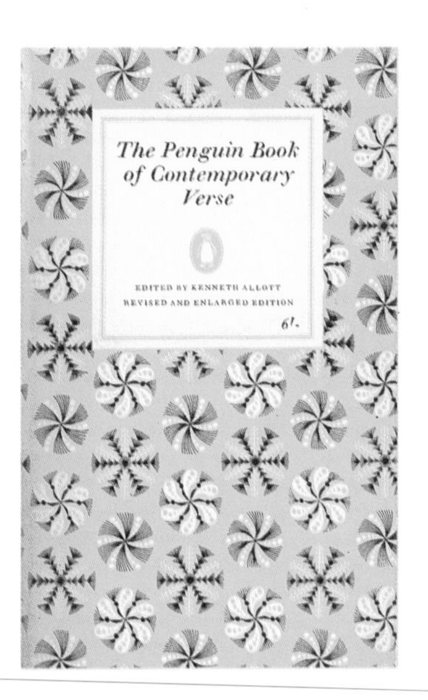

▲ **Kenneth Allott, editor, *The Penguin Book of Contemporary Verse*, Harmonds-worth, Penguin Books, 1962. Pattern design by Stephen Russ.**
The crisp vivacity of the pattern reveals Russ's training with Edward Bawden and Eric Ravilious at the Royal College of Art in the 1930s. Pattern papers were frequently used by publishers in Britain from the 1920s to the 1950s, and Penguin kept this tradition alive.

▲ **Antoine de Saint-Exupéry, *Night Flight*, New York, Penguin Books, 1945. Cover design by Edgard Cirlin.**
According to legend, Cirlin (1913–73) avoided military call-up when he said he made jackets – the military authorities believing that he was in the essential garment industry. For *Night Flight*, Saint-Exupéry, best known for *The Little Prince*, published in English in 1944, drew from his experiences in commercial aviation.

Kitchen-sink Novels

1956 was a significant year in which the "kitchen-sink" painters, a group of left-wing realists whose depiction of everyday reality gave them their name, were officially chosen to exhibit at the Venice Biennale. It was also the year in which left-leaning realism turned deliciously sour with John Osborne's play, *Look Back in Anger* at London's Royal Court theatre, which created the archetypal figure of the "angry young man" found, in the play, in the vicinity of the kitchen sink, though seldom engaged in any useful domestic activity.

Writing and art came together in the jackets designed for the first editions of some of the classic texts of the 1950s, for example the expressionist jacket for Alan Sillitoe's *The Loneliness of the Long Distance Runner*, but this soon looked old-fashioned. As the decade progressed, photography became the preferred means of portraying gritty realism, perhaps anticipating the black-and-white films that were made from some of these texts in the 1960s. The political message was not a traditional Labour one, for John Braine wrote of *Room at the Top* (1957), "My only ambition was to get the hell out – out of being a librarian, out of local government, out of the whole system. Joe doesn't want to do away with the class system. But he would say that from now on it's achievement that counts. It shouldn't matter who your father was."

▲ Alan Sillitoe, *The Loneliness of the Long-Distance Runner*, London, W. H. Allen, 1959. Jacket design by Mona Moore.
The title story is about a Borstal (reformatory) boy who refuses to play the establishment game.

◄ Nell Dunn, *Up the Junction*, London, MacGibbon & Kee, 1963. Designer unknown.
The "junction" is Clapham Junction in South London, the setting for Dunn's short stories of working-class life, which, in a manner typical of the 1960s, she infiltrated from an upper-class background.

► Bill Naughton, *Alfie*, London, MacGibbon & Kee, 1966. Designer unknown.
Lots Road Power Station frames a setting sun on the cover of this novel, famous as a film with Michael Caine (1966).

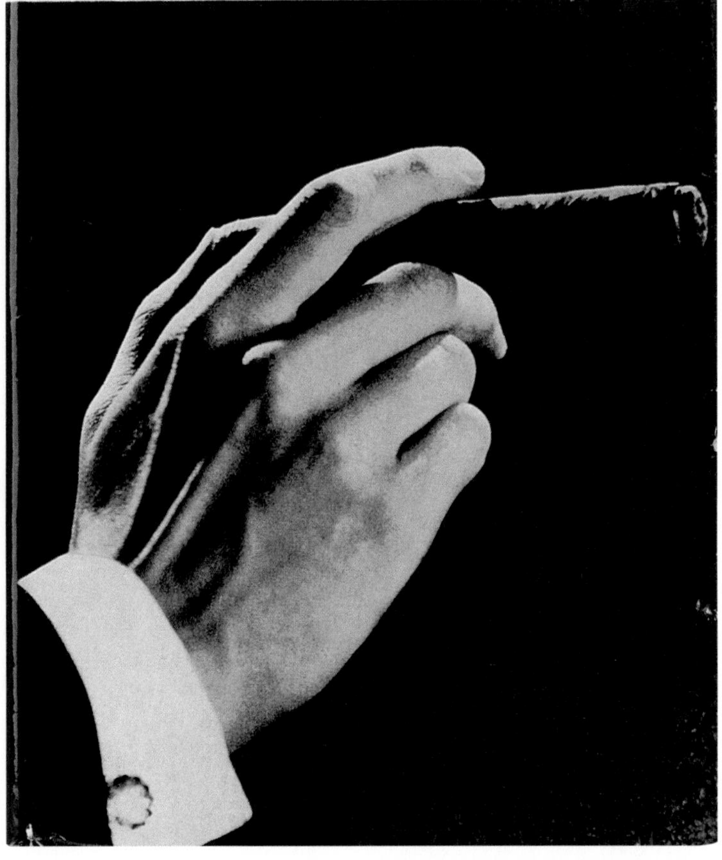

◄ John Braine, *Life at the Top*, London, Eyre & Spottiswoode, 1968. Jacket photograph by Tom Hustler.
The photographic image on the cover could be described rhetorically as a synecdoche, in which a small part is used to indicate a larger picture. The novel is the sequel to Braine's *Room at the Top* (1957), which launched the hero, Joe Lampton, as one of the archetypes of the "angry young man". It was made into a highly successful film in 1958 with Laurence Harvey and Heather Sears as the couple who marry across the class boundary.

▼ Colin MacInnes, *Absolute Beginners*, London, MacGibbon & Kee, 1957. Designer unknown.
The urban setting is a crucial component of this famous novel of the Bohemian underworld of London's Notting Hill. The quiet road, without traffic markings, the ancient-looking cars and unimproved terrace houses all give the period flavour. Like Nell Dunn, MacInnes was slumming in this milieu, since he was a great-grandson of the Victorian painter Sir Edward Burne-Jones. The novel's popularity was revived in the 1980s with the film starring Patsy Kensit.

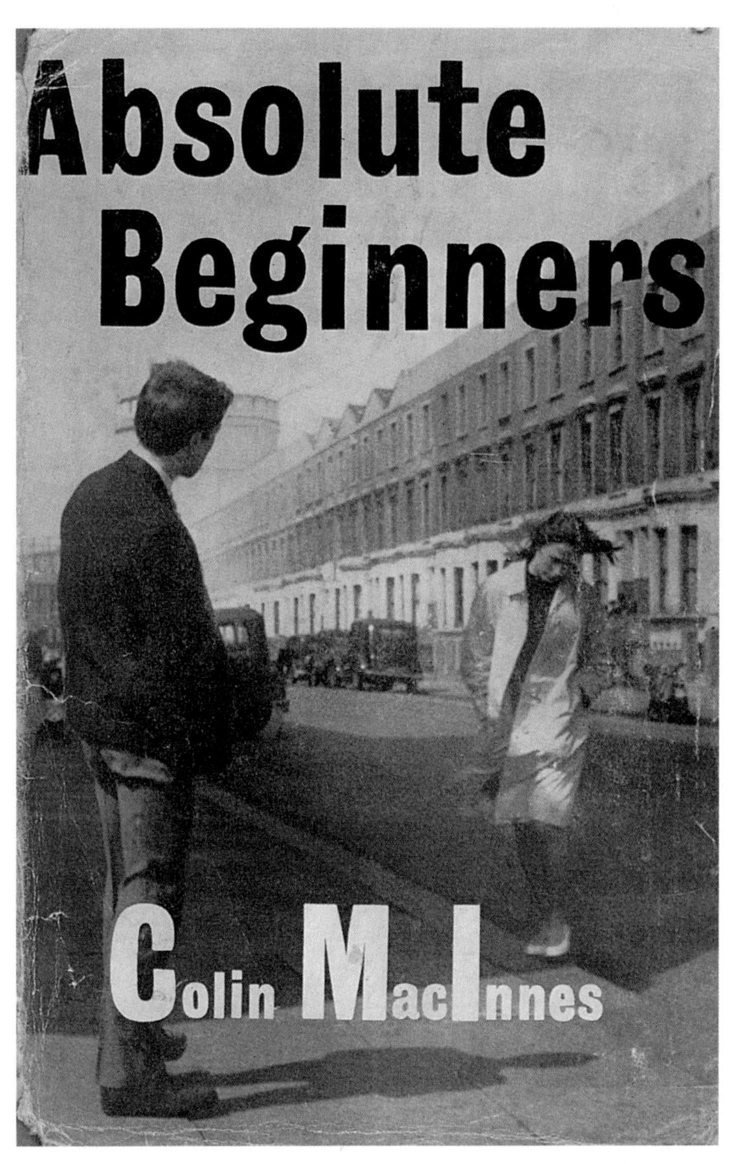

► John Braine, *The Crying Game*, London, Eyre & Spottiswoode, 1964. Jacket illustration by Salim Patel.
The cover of Braine's later novel signals an ironic approach to the conventions of social life, an important part of the author's *persona* as a writer. The graphic style is typical of the 1960s in its strong colours and flattened shapes distantly derived from the work of Aubrey Beardsley and Toulouse-Lautrec.

The disturbing novel by Vladimir Nabokov (1899–1977) of Humbert Humbert's infatuation with a "nymphet" was first published in 1955, by the Olympia Press in Paris whose "Traveller's Library" was devoted entirely to pornography, old and new, in similar plain editions. The first English edition was launched with a party at the Ritz on the night the new Obscene Publications Act was passed in parliament. Nigel Nicolson, one half of the publishing partnership, was an MP but he lost his seat at the next election mainly, he believed, because of his association with the book. The first sketch by Eric Ayers for the English hardback cover was abstract but included blobs of red and green, which were vetoed by George Weidenfeld in favour of typographic purity. The case of J. D. Salinger (b. 1919) is rather different. His book *For Esmé – with Love and Squalor* (1953) was licensed by Hamish Hamilton to the American paperback publisher Ace Books, after Penguin had refused it. The Ace cover, with a strong emphasis on squalor, so shocked Salinger that he broke off his relationship with Hamish Hamilton and has insisted ever since on total control of his book jackets.

◄ ▲ Vladimir Nabokov, *Lolita*, Paris, The Olympia Press, 1955 (2 volumes), cover design by the Olympia Press; London, Weidenfeld & Nicolson, 1959, cover design by Eric Ayers; London, Corgi, 1971, cover design by Bert Stern. When illustrated covers compete with each other, reticence can attract more attention, particularly if associated with something subversive or forbidden. *Lolita* was so successful that Nabokov could retire from his job at Cornell University. The 1971 Corgi cover, derived from the film of the book, shows how much change the 1960s had brought about in public tolerance, even though the image would hardly mean much without knowledge of the book itself. Perhaps the best comment came from Groucho Marx when he said he was going to put off reading Lolita for six years – until she was eighteen.

▼ **Vladimir Nabokov, *Lolita*, Harmondsworth, Penguin Modern Classics, 2000. Cover photograph by Virginia Woods-Jack.**
The current Penguin *Lolita* follows a recent film version, but interestingly it does not use a still from the actual film. The camera angle and close cropping of the image convey the physical presence of the model, making even the outdoor setting strangely claustrophobic. The grey band continues the established identity of Penguin Modern Classics.

► **J. D. Salinger, *The Catcher in the Rye*, Harmondsworth, Penguin Modern Classics, 1967. Cover design by Penguin.**
Salinger's control over his book designs resulted in this "classic" cover, which looks more like a European than an English or American paperback. Since Penguin paid great attention to lettering and spacing, the results are as visually pleasing as any other form of presentation. For all its subversive strength, *The Catcher in the Rye* swiftly became a school-study text.

◄ **J. D. Salinger, *Franny and Zooey*, Harmondsworth, Penguin Modern Classics, 1973. Cover design by Penguin.**
The rearrangement of the elements between this and the cover above is an interesting study in the subtleties of layout design. As well as prohibiting pictorial covers, Salinger's contracts forbade biographical blurbs (except those written by himself) and quotations from reviews of his work. As his biographer writes, "His vigilance on these matters would extend even to the remotest foreign publication of his work."

The Pulp Fiction Jacket

Pulp fiction, a phrase made famous in the 1990s by Quentin Tarantino's film (1994), describes a sensationalist writing genre belonging to the period between the wars. The writers of these titles, which originally appeared in hardback, were descended in a line from the best-selling but now often forgotten novelists of the Victorian age. They were able to come up with a reliable "product" with which readers could identify. Seldom demanding a second reading and deemed perhaps too risqué to become the staple of the lending library, these were books styled to be sold from newsagents' stands. They were not made to last, nor were they produced by "reputable" publishers, but by lesser-known houses who acknowledged no particular cultural mission. Their brightly coloured pictorial covers were disdained by the upper end of the publishing industry, but they now appear to a modern audience to have the charm of folk art, with imagery that is often accidentally archetypal in its portrayal of the emotional crux of each story. Pulp-fiction covers made the best of the limited technology of colour printing then available. The covers were often given extra lines of selling copy, like the "come on" for readers of both sexes in the caption of Michael Arlen's *The Ancient Sin*, "How he does know women."

▲ Iris Murdoch, *Under the Net*, London, Reprint Society, 1955. Artist unknown.
One of the earliest titles by a leading post-war British novelist, who was not associated with pulp fiction. Here, Iris Murdoch's book is given a jacket design in a realistic style for a cheap edition that was obviously intended to extend her readership.

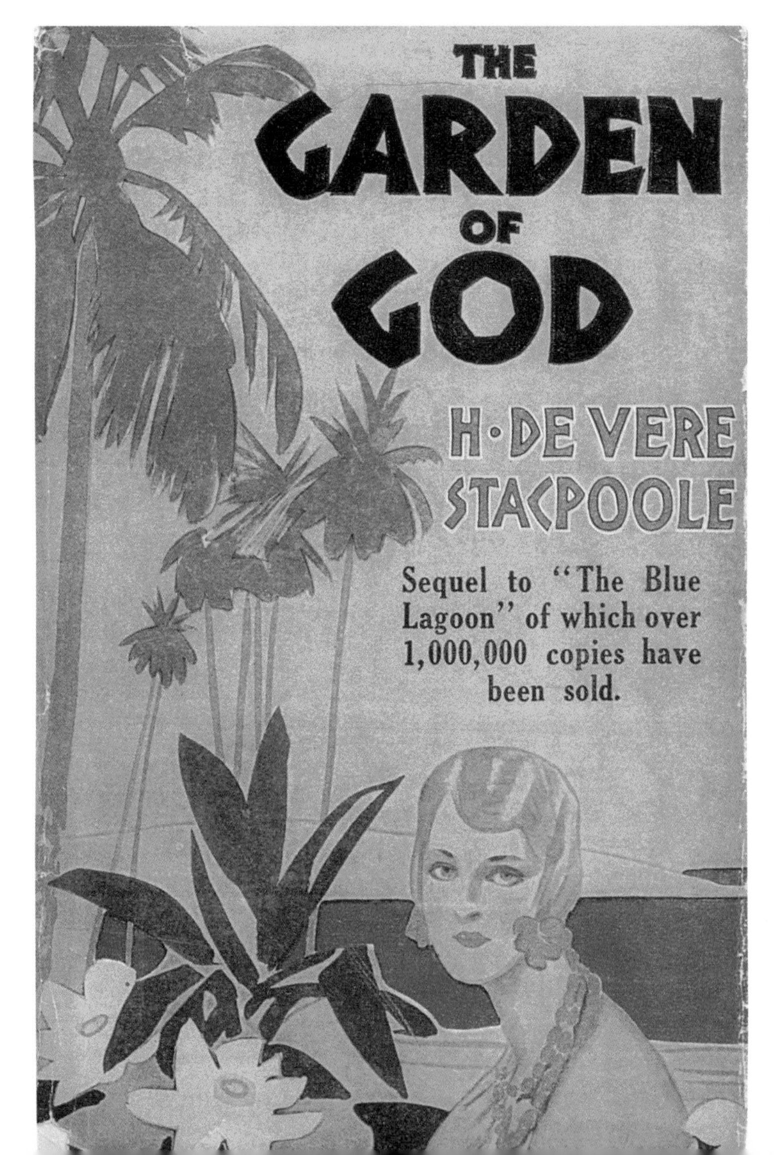

► H. de Vere Stacpoole, *The Garden of God*, London, The Leisure Library Co. Ltd, 1929. Artist unknown.
Originally published by Hutchinson in 1923, this, as the cover informs us, was the sequel to Stacpoole's most famous work, *The Blue Lagoon*. As the imagery and title suggest, Stacpoole specialized in romantic and exotic locations, in which his stories included treasure hunts, gender reversals, and hints of the supernatural.

▲ Brett Halliday, *The Private Practice of Michael Shayne*, New York, Mayflower Books, 1963. Artist unknown.
Books featuring Michael Shayne sold millions of copies. He was the Private Eye creation of Brett Halliday, one of several pseudonyms of David Dresser (1904–77). The cover illustrates the hats, the cars, and the cigarettes. Somewhere out of sight, no doubt, are the drinks and the dames.

◄ John Fleming Wilson, *The Man Who Came Back*, publisher and artist unkown.
Many pulp-fiction covers portray more than one episode of the story in simultaneous montage. Without knowing any more details of the story, it is clear that the hero has come back from the opium dens of the East and is now apparently engaged in throttling the red-headed heroine.

▼ Michael Arlen, *The Ancient Sin*, London, The London Book Co., Ltd. 1930. Artist unkown.
Michael Arlen was one of the best-known writers of romantic fiction in the Flapper age. Rebecca West described his work as "a mixture of the genuine article and advertising copy".

► Hank Janson, *Beloved Traitor*, London, Roberts & Vintner, 1960. Artist unknown.
An American-style cover for an English author with an American-style pseudonym. He was actually born Harry Hobson in Sheffield in 1908, and began his career as a musician. Women with smoking guns are among the favourite visual devices of pulp fiction.

American Graphic Artists

From the European viewpoint, American paperbacks in the 1940s were sold almost entirely on what the founder of Penguin described as "bosoms and bottoms". The covers for Pocket Books, the first major American paperback imprint, were dramatic and explicit lures for the reader. Their graphic style, however, in the hands of artists such as H. L. Hoffman (d. 1976), recognized some of the disciplines of modernism in the use of simplified form and balanced colour with well-integrated lettering, and the leading authority on American paperbacks, Piet Schreuders, claims that the period from 1939 to 1959 was one of "charming, naive, artistic, daring covers, covers used as testing grounds for new graphic forms, covers whose designs were not one hundred per cent dictated by sales departments." Penguin Books were imported from the UK in 1939 to rival Pocket Books, but Penguin editions were soon being originated in the US. The covers for these by Robert Jonas came well before any equivalent attempt to give pictorial jackets to English Penguins, and they reflected Jonas's involvement in the avant-garde, which included friendship with the artist Willem de Kooning.

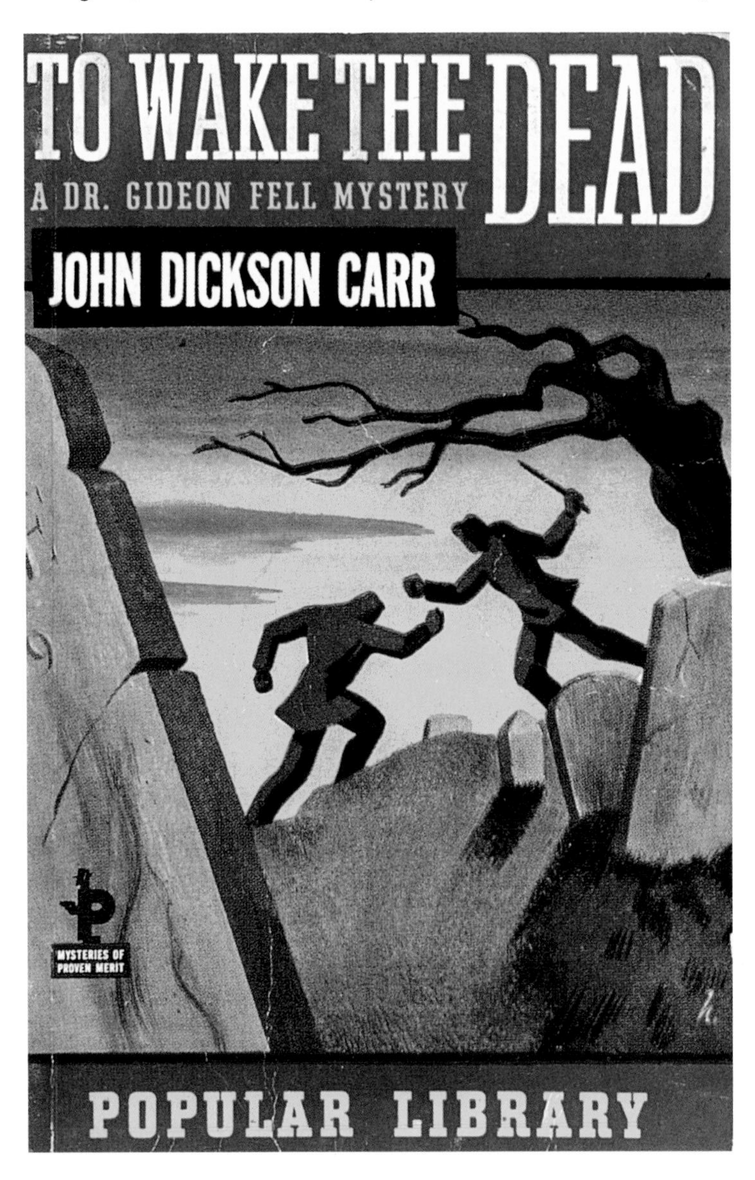

◄ John Dickson Carr, *To Wake the Dead*, New York, Popular Library, 1942. Jacket design by H. L. Hoffman.
Snappy "playbill" type and a lurid yellow sky give this jacket a graphic character that pure pulp fiction would studiously avoid. Carr (1906–77) was an English author and official biographer of Sir Arthur Conan Doyle, the creator of Sherlock Holmes. Like this master, he had a reputation for setting up apparently incredible situations, and then guiding the reader by logic and reasoning towards a solution. He is reputed to have said, "If there's one thing I can't stand, it's a nice healthy murder."

▲ Dashiell Hammett, *The Thin Man*, New York, Pocket Books, 1943. Jacket design by H. L. Hoffman.
A cast shadow out of *film noir* combines with a spider's web in a confused but suggestive design. Pocket Books favoured the picture-frame effect, with curved corners to the illustration. Hammett, also author of *The Maltese Falcon* (1930), was one of the founders of the "private eye" genre in which the lonely investigator's quest for truth is also a critique of American capitalism.

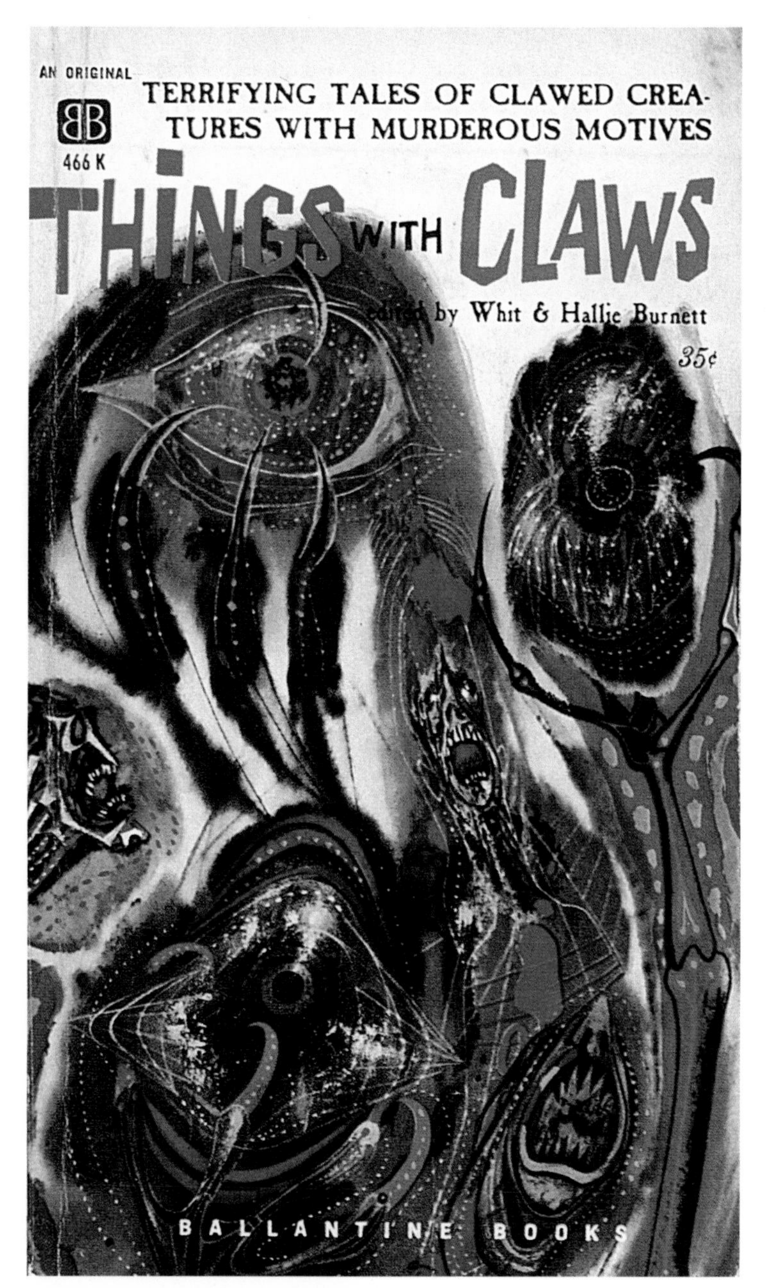

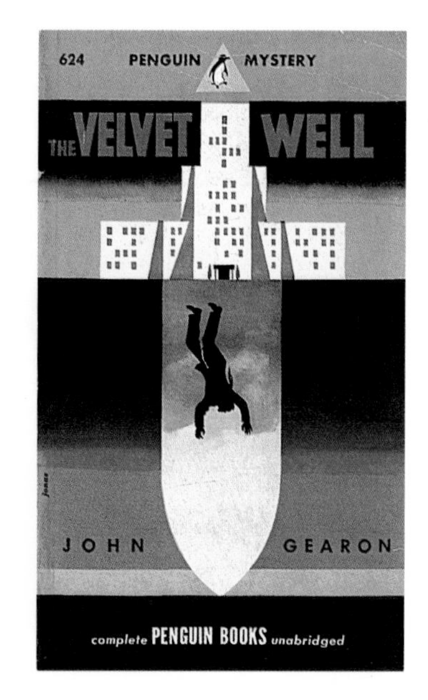

▲ Carson McCullers, *The Heart is a Lonely Hunter*, New York, Penguin Books, 1946. Jacket design by Robert Jonas.
Tennessee Williams described Carson McCullers (1917–67), as "the greatest prose writer that the South produced." Jonas's use of collage looks forward to the 1960s.

◄ Whit and Halbo Burnet, *Things with Claws*, New York, Ballantine Books, 1961. Jacket design by Richard Powers.
An effective nightmare evocation of horror of the organic unknown, where the comic-book style of the lettering seems out of place. Alien invaders were often linked in the American psyche with the threat of Communism during the McCarthy period.

▲ John Gearon, *The Velvet Well*, New York, Penguin, 1947. Jacket design by Robert Jonas.
Jonas's distinguished graphic style, typical of the 1930s, lost favour in the post-war world of mass consumption and he was forced to draw more in a more realistic way. Around 1947, as Piet Schreuders writes, "we can see the paperback industry's progression from an abstract and even surreal 'artistic' approach to… steaming realism."

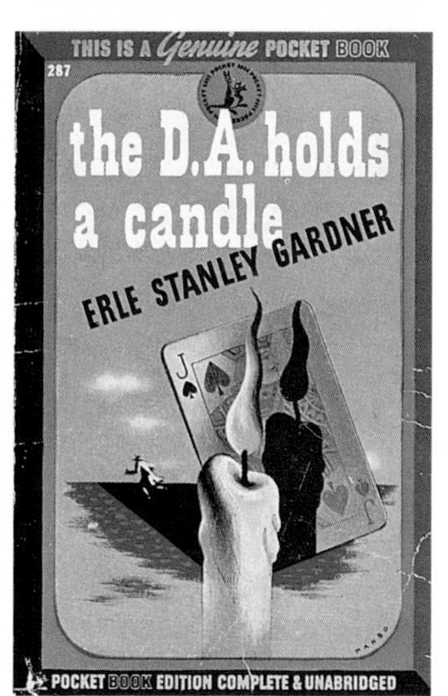

◄ Erle Stanley Gardner, *The D.A. Holds a Candle*, New York, Pocket Books, 1954. Jacket design by Leo Manso.
Pocket Books have been criticized for the way their covers were distanced from the emotional reality of the books' content. Leo Manso (b. 1914) was the chief designer for the imprint from 1943 to 1945. His designs often seem to have been influenced by the surrealist assemblages of Salvador Dali.

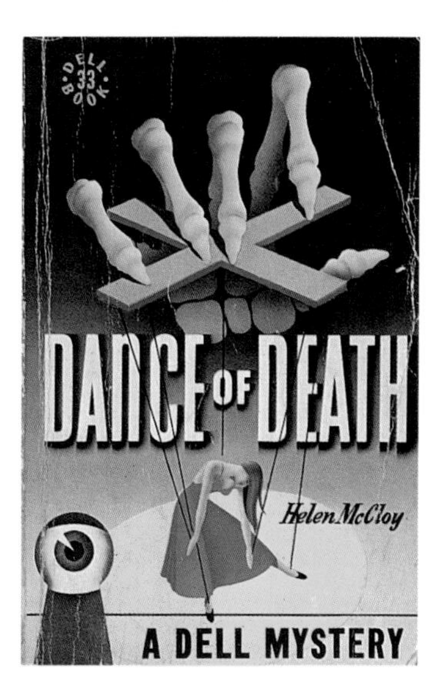

◄ Helen McClay, *Dance of Death*, Racine, Dell Books, 1944. Jacket design by Gerald Gregg.
Gerald Gregg grew up in Racine and Milwaukee, where he began working for the local publishers, Western Printing and Lithographic Partnership, effectively an equal partner in the Dell business. Gregg often asked Western's secretaries and typists to model for the beautiful women on his airbrushed covers.

One night in a sleazy hotel by the Pacific, Raymond Chandler (1888–1959) picked up a mystery magazine. An aspiring man of letters, recently fired from his job in an oil company for alcoholism, he suddenly realized, "I might be able to write this stuff and get paid while I was learning." He studied the existing masters of the thriller genre, such as Erle Stanley Gardner (1889–1970) and Dashiell Hammett (1894–1961), before writing his first success, *The Big Sleep*, in 1939.

As Chandler explained in his essay, "The Simple Art of Murder", Hammett, writing in the 1920s, had taken murder out of the drawing room and put it back in the alleys where it belonged. With this, came a special kind of detective, who was not a walking but emotionless brain like Sherlock Holmes or Hercules Poirot, but a man with his own moral weaknesses who knew that he could only have a limited success in putting the world to rights. The new detective in the words of a contemporary writer, Sara Paretsky, was someone "who operates with a passionate engagement with the world, a loner whose triumphs are always tinged with loss". Hammett created Sam Spade, and Chandler created Philip Marlowe, who revealed in world-weary tones the corruption and injustice that Chandler observed around him in California.

▲ Raymond Chandler, *Spanish Blood*, New York, The World Publishing Company, 1944. Jacket design by H. Lawrence Hoffman.
Hoffman was a prolific designer for Pocket Books, Penguin, and other American imprints. His cover evokes the mean streets and alleys that form one of the backgrounds of the thriller.

► A. A. Fair (Erle Stanley Gardner), *Beware the Curves*, London, William Heinemann, 1957. Jacket design by "Stein".
Produced at a high point of English admiration for all things American, this jacket is elegantly understated without losing its punch. The flat areas of colour associated with1930s designers are used here to convey a distinctly 1950s image, with a figure in the style of Audrey Hepburn.

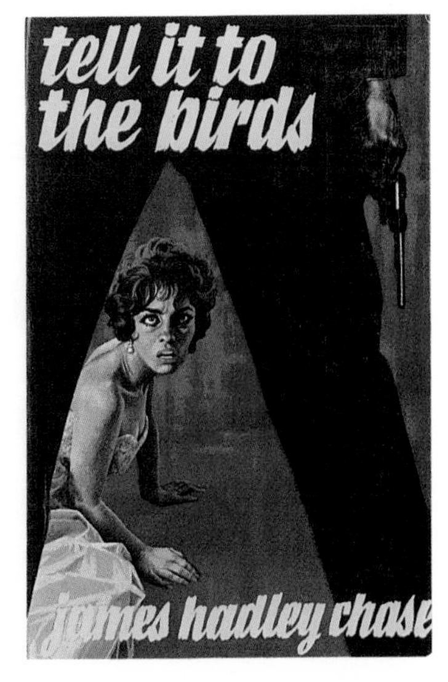

▲ ► **James Hadley Chase, *The Soft Centre*, 1964, and *Tell it to the Birds*, 1963, London, Robert Hale. Jacket designs by Barbara Walton.**
James Hadley Chase (1906–85) was born in London. He visited the US only a few times, and researched his novels from slang dictionaries, police reports, and magazines. The heightened emotion, highlighted realism, and tough but sexy imagery on these jackets would have enabled British book-buyers to identify them straightaway as American, even though they are effectively British-made. These jackets are in fact less cluttered with verbal information than their typical American pulp-fiction originals, while the insistence on lower-case lettering helps to reinforce the identity of the series.

◄ **A.A. Fair (Erle Stanley Gardner), *Bedrooms Have Windows*, London, William Heinemann, 1956. Artist unknown. James Hadley Chase, *A Lotus for Miss Quon*. London, Robert Hale, 1960. Jacket by Stephen Val Biro.**
The graphic artist Stephen "Val" Biro (b. 1921) was heavily involved in book design at the publishing firm of John Lehmann in the 1950s. While his Hadley Chase jacket conforms to the identity of the series, its design has an abstract quality, which gives it more interest than some of the other titles in the series. The image on the Erle Stanley Gardner jacket offers an original incorporation of the author's name in the perspective of a far from believable window.

The Beat Generation

▲ Jack Kerouac, *On the Road*, London, André Deutsch, 1958. Jacket design by Len Deighton.
The designer of the English edition of Kerouac's masterpiece is better known as a writer of thrillers (see pp. 82–3), but he studied illustration at the Royal College of Art in London where he was in love with all things American, and was one of a group of students who created English pop art. The use of signboard slogans in his Kerouac jacket points that way, although the drawing itself is relatively conventional.

► Jack Kerouac, *The Dharma Bums*, New York, Viking Press, 1958. Jacket design by Bill English.
The title of Kerouac's second major work reveals the importance of Eastern religions in the formation of the beat world view. The book describes modern religious wanderers in search of *dharma* or truth in place of modern consumerism. The cover image, reminiscent of the 1930s, illustrates the theme with simple symbolism, but is interestingly shrunk to a small window on the cover, allowing the lettering to dominate.

The son of French-Canadian parents, Jack Kerouac (1922–69) grew up in the textile town of Lowell, Massachusetts. He made his name with *On the Road*, first published in 1957, which became the key text of the "beat" generation, a phrase Kerouac himself is supposed to have coined. Kerouac's loosely flowing prose, written at speed, has been compared to the paintings of Jackson Pollock and the jazz playing of Charlie Parker. "Beat" is associated with music, but extends into other meanings, including "beatitude". The movement had a sense of renewal from the culture of the street and, with its emphasis on personal freedom over social conformity, found fertile ground in the United States in the second half of the 1950s, where the hopes of an open society cherished at the end of the war were being undermined by the paranoia of McCarthy's anti-Communist investigations and the increased striving for material goods. The line from the "beats" to the hippies runs directly, even though the two cultures were manifested in very different ways. Kerouac became uncomfortable with his celebrity status and his writing career soon went into decline. J. D. Salinger, three years his senior, also found public life an impossible strain and became one of America's most famous recluses, an action that did nothing to diminish the reputation of his small number of published works.

▲ Herbert Simmons, *Corner Boy*, Boston, Houghton Mifflin, 1957. Designer unknown.
Simmons, born in 1930 in St Louis, Missouri, was strongly influenced by jazz and organized "Portraits in Rhythm", a combination of original poems read to musical accompaniment in coffee houses. The blurb displayed on this jacket pushes all the beat buttons of teenage independence and revolt, young love, and the sense that America's self-image was out of date and needed adjusting to reality.

▼ J. D. Salinger, *The Catcher in the Rye*, London, Hamish Hamilton, 1951. Jacket design by Fritz Wegner.
The jacket for the English edition, which appeared in the same year as the first American publication, is the work of one of Britain's most skilful and witty illustrators, who has since specialized in children's books. Although the drawing style is gentle, almost academic, the louring figure of Holden Caulfield in the foreground, treated with indifference or fear by those around him, is an effective image for one of the most influential books of the later twentieth century.

Playing with Typography

The book cover based principally on lettering is capable of a considerable range of expression. These examples show how two-word titles, or in the case of Thomas Pynchon's *V.*, just a single letter, can be used to interpret the mood and content of the book, and reinforce the title. Lettering tends to work best when used with a limited colour range. Saul Bellow's *Herzog* uses a classic combination of red and black, together with the background colour of the paper. Yellow and black used in *Black Spring* is a well-known combination for attracting attention and signalling danger. Here, the colouring also interprets the book's title. The cover of *Catch-22* comes as a surprise, in that the story is now so strongly associated with its specific setting and imagery: the tiny black plane gives away little of the contents. Perhaps it illustrates a rule that book jackets move from the universal to the particular as the subject of the book becomes better known. The jacket for *Albert Angelo* is an example of the kind of work that satisfies a designer but results in visual confusion. The design plays with typographic overlays, which render both the title and the words underneath illegible.

▲ Saul Bellow, *Herzog*, London, Weidenfeld & Nicolson, 1964. Jacket design by John Griffiths.
An effective abstract representation of the tension in the novel, which is about a Jewish intellectual driven to the verge of breakdown.

◄ Joseph Heller, *Catch-22*, New York, Simon & Schuster, 1961. Artist unknown.
Heller's experience as a wartime bombadier in the US Air Force was the basis for the instant success of his first novel, which was backed up by a film.

◄ Henry Miller, *Black Spring*, London, John Calder, 1965. Artist unknown.
A plain design for Miller's stream-of-consciousness autobiography.

◄ B. S. Johnson, *Albert Angelo*, London, Constable, 1964. Jacket design by Philip Thompson.
This jacket, produced by manipulation of Victorian wooden poster type, is similar to the kind of exercise undertaken by art-school students in the 1950s and '60s when it formed part of the first-year training in "Basic Design". The jacket mirrors the eccentric typography of Johnson's novels, which includes blank pages, holes in pages, and black pages, a sample of which can be read beneath the title lettering.

► Thomas Pynchon, *V.*, New York, J. B. Lippincott, 1963. Artist unknown.
Artists and designers have sometimes played with the idea of lettering standing in a three-dimensional landscape, as depicted on this cover, and there is a park in Barcelona where you can walk through a poem. Thomas Pynchon's first novel includes such delights as albino alligators inhabiting the New York sewers, but these are kept for the reader to discover within.

When a novel is first launched, nobody knows whether or not it will become a classic, and if so, which aspects of the story are likely to seize the public imagination. It can therefore be a surprise to see classic titles in their original jackets, often because they are so unrevealing of the content. The two world-famous titles by George Orwell are such an example – from the impression the jackets give, they could be about almost anything. Similarly, *The Prime of Miss Jean Brodie* was given a curiously generic cover for its first publication in 1961, suggesting neither the setting in Edinburgh, nor the 1930s pre-war period, nor even the psychological tension of the plot. Perhaps only the red branches of the tree, like veins, indicate a symbolic level. Anthony Gross's depiction of *Lord of the Flies* looks surprisingly cheerful, like a jungle romp, revealing nothing of the real content of the book. The cover of *A Clockwork Orange* is interesting, since the book's image has now become so closely linked to the poster from the film made by Stanley Kubrick in 1971, with the actor Malcolm McDowell as Alex. The most compelling of the jackets on these pages is that for *Gormenghast*, drawn by the author who until this time was better known as an artist. As a cover, it leaves plenty to the imagination, for Peake's imaginary castle in many ways defies literal depiction.

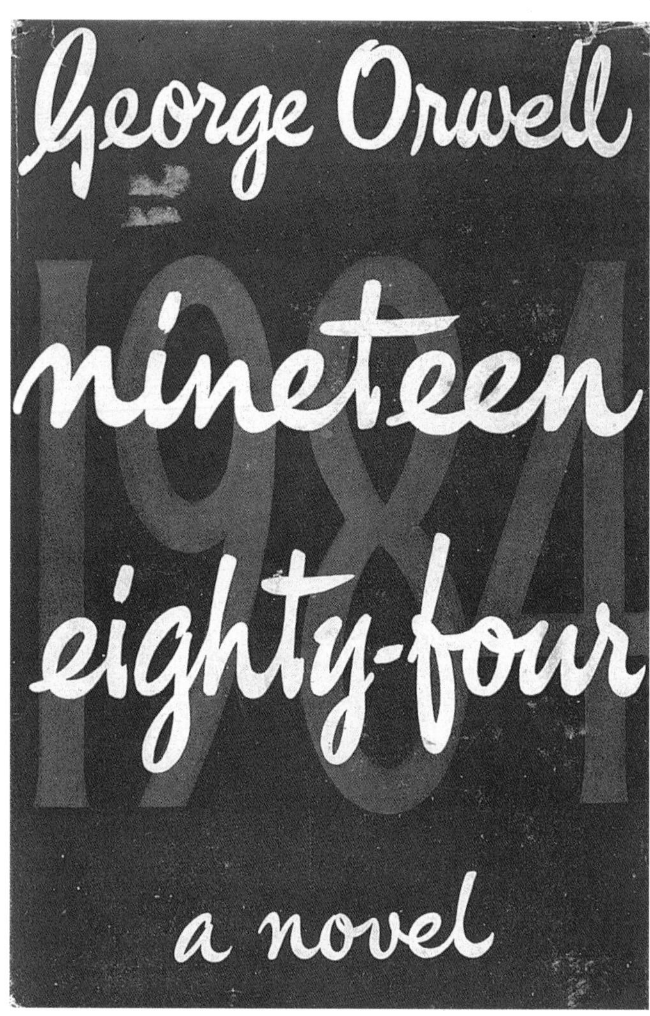

▲ George Orwell, *Nineteen Eighty-Four*, London, Secker & Warburg, 1949.
Jacket designer unknown.
Published in the year before Orwell's death, his grim vision of the future offers many possibilities for an illustrator. This jacket is deceptively jaunty, even in its austerity uniform. The same design was also printed in dark brown, the colour most evocative of the 1940s.

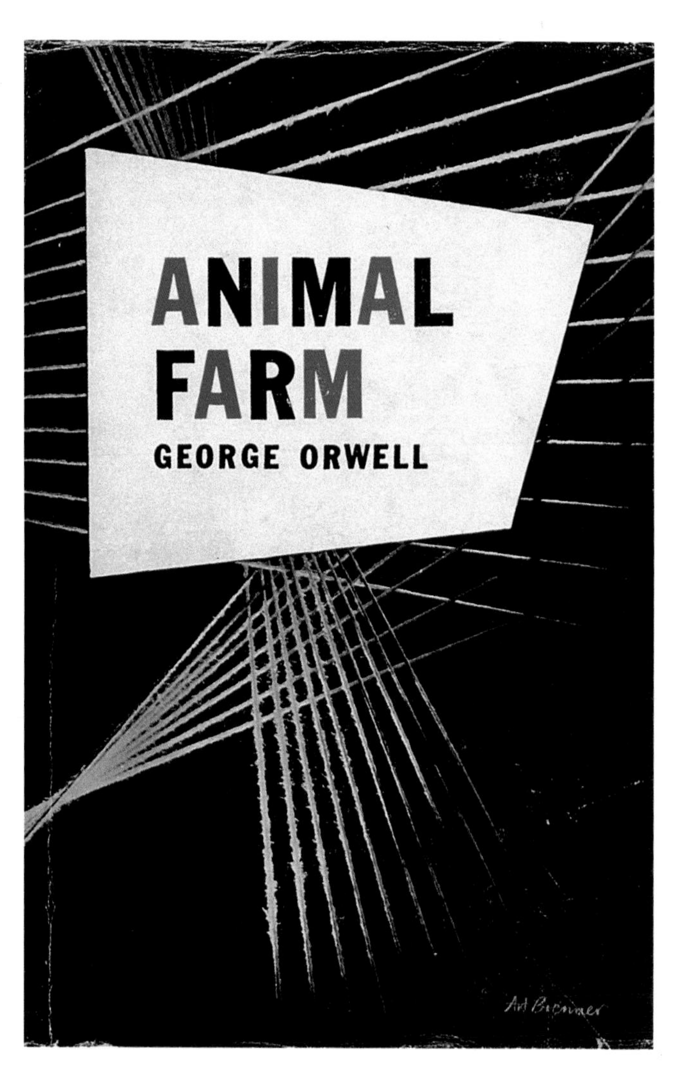

◄ George Orwell, *Animal Farm*, New York, Harcourt Brace & Co., 1946.
Jacket designer unknown.
This jacket resembles the linear abstract style of New Directions books created by Alvin Lustig (see pp. 52–3), although without the appropriateness to the theme which he always succeeded in introducing.

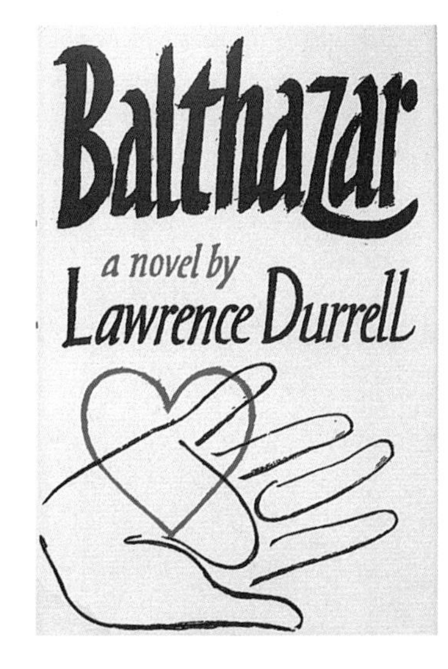

▲ William Golding, *Lord of the Flies*, London, Faber and Faber, 1954. Cover illustration by Anthony Gross.
The cover of Golding's first novel, published with a modest print-run of 3040, has Faber's own typeface, Albertus.

▲ Lawrence Durrell, *Balthazar*, London, Faber and Faber, 1958. Jacket design by Berthold Wolpe.
This volume in Durrell's "Alexandria Quartet" has a simple effective cover with Wolpe's own freehand calligraphy.

▲ Muriel Spark, *The Prime of Miss Jean Brodie*, London, Macmillan, 1961. Jacket design by Victor Reinganum.
Already famous for books such as *The Ballad of Peckham Rye*, Muriel Spark's tale of a scandalous schoolmistress in Edinburgh became her most famous work when filmed with Maggie Smith in the title role in 1969. Victor Reinganum brought his skills to this theme, but failed to create a design as enduring as the text.

► Anthony Burgess, *A Clockwork Orange*, London, William Heinemann, 1962. Jacket designer unknown.
Burgess's fantasy of the near future was well publicized, but the invented slang of the teenage gang proved offputting for many readers.

► Mervyn Peake, *Gormenghast*, London, Eyre & Spottiswoode, 1950. Jacket design by Mervyn Peake.
The central book of a trilogy, all with Peake's own pen-and-ink jackets. Their small cult-following grew in the late 1960s with a revival of interest in fantasy.

IF I DIE IN A COMBAT ZONE

BOX ME UP & SHIP ME HOME

TIM O'BRIEN

A Revolution in Print:

The 1960s and 1970s

In China under Mao Tse-tung, ranks of workers and children held their little red books of the Chairman's thoughts in the air for the cameras. In Soviet Russia and Eastern Europe, the printed words of dissident writers like Berdayev or Milan Kundera were precious enough to be circulated in multiple carbon copies as samizdats. In the affluent West in the1960s and '70s established publishers had little choice other than to catch up with Penguin Books and publish paperbacks, continuing the revolution in affordability and availability that was begun by Allen Lane in 1935.

In the bookshops, the winds of change could be seen as publishers' old backlist titles with dowdy, if nostalgic, austerity period wrappers began to share space with the latest intoxicating covers produced by young graphic designers. It was the swan song of graphic design as a studio craft, a time when skilled hands, working with watercolours, photographs, Letraset rub-down lettering, and overlays would create images to go under the blockmaker's camera and be turned, eventually, into satisfyingly substantial plastic-laminated book covers.

◀ Tim O'Brien, *If I Die in a Combat Zone*, New York, Delacorte Press/ Seymour Lawrence, 1973. Jacket design by Wendell Minor (see page 96).

Psychedelia

◄ Alfred Chester, *Behold Goliath*, London, André Deutsch, 1965. Jacket design by William Belcher.
The jacket for a novel by an American author, showing the "op art" phase of the 1960s, a genre derived from abstract paintings by artists such as Bridget Riley.

◄ *It's World that Makes the Love Go Round*, London, Corgi Books, 1968. Jacket designed by Hapshash and the Coloured Coat (Michael English and Nigel Weymouth).
The cover illustrators were famous designers of pop posters, who also had their own group. Their work was strongly influenced by art nouveau.

"All power to the imagination," said the graffiti in Paris in May 1968, and through the 1960s confusion of new music, films, and graphics, important ideas were surfacing. The Vietnam War (1954–75) added urgency to the generational revolt against post-war conformity in the United States and Europe, as the young took to the streets to protest. Assessing the situation in 1969, Theodore Roszak wrote, "If the resistance of the counter culture fails, I think there will be nothing in store for us but what anti-utopians like Huxley and Orwell have forecast – though I have no doubt that these dismal despotisms will be far more stable and effective than their prophets have foreseen." The graphic manifestation of these feelings of resistance was in some ways arbitrary. They drew on several artistic traditions of the twentieth century simultaneously, including abstraction, surrealism, art nouveau, art deco and the experiments in perception introduced into art school curricula through the influence of the Bauhaus. It was an easy style to follow. Book jackets need to make a split-second visual impact, for which bright colours and bizarre imagery were ideal.

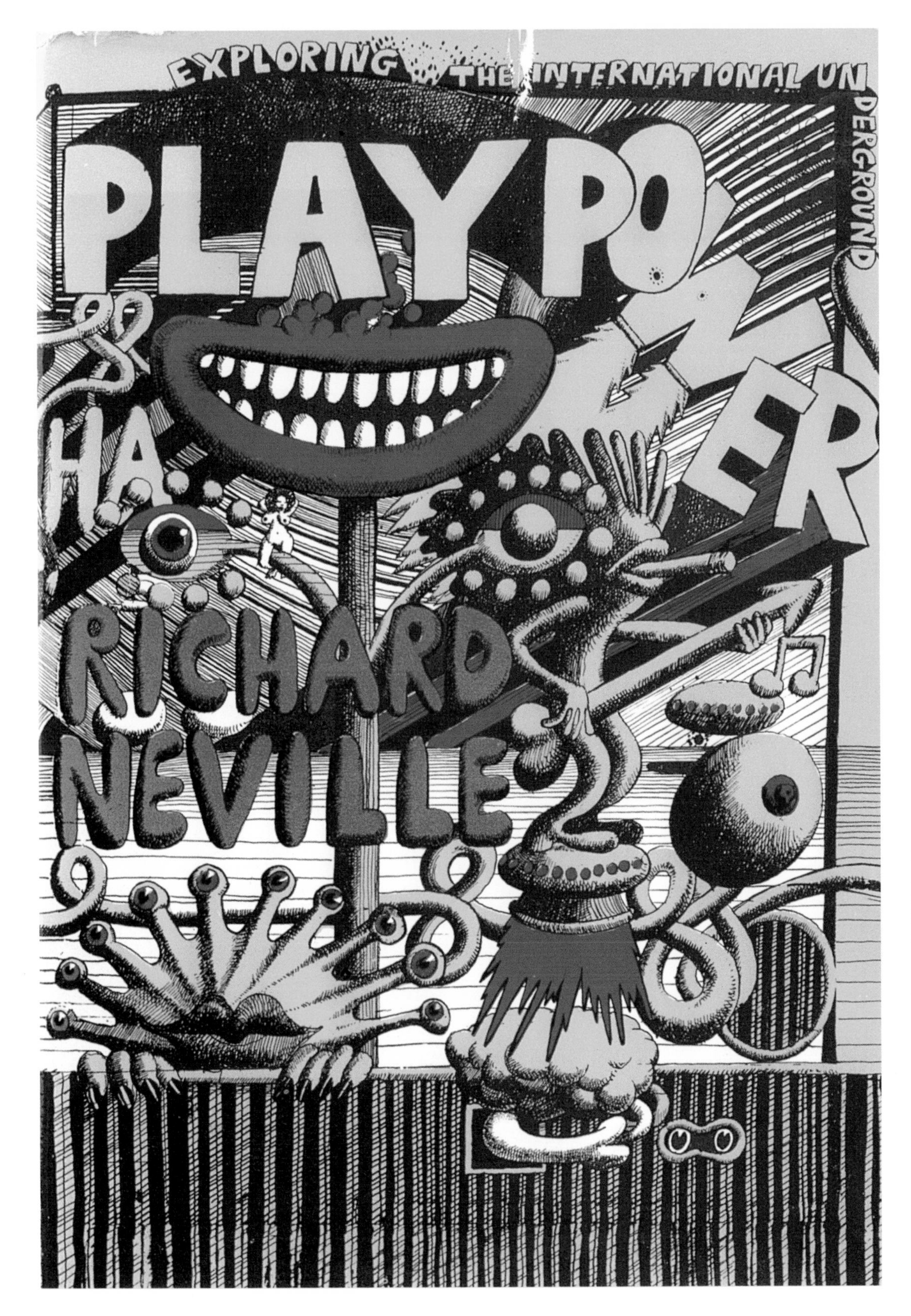

◄ John Clellon Holmes, *Nothing More to Declare*, London, André Deutsch, 1965. Jacket design by Farrell Wade.
Holmes's book is an account of the "beat generation", in the1960s style – a pop art version of art deco. The formula grew in importance until the mid-1970s.

◄ Richard Neville, *Play Power*, London, Jonathan Cape, 1970. Jacket design by Martin Sharp.
Martin Sharp was one of the creators of the "psychedelic" style, designing posters for the "legalize cannabis" campaign in 1967, "the summer of love". Richard Neville was editor of the leading underground magazine, *Oz*. The obscenity trial over the "schoolkids" issue ended in 1971 with his imprisonment and that of his fellow editors.

▼ Peter Max, *Paper Airplane Book*, Publisher unknown, 1971. Jacket design by Peter Max.
When Peter Max first designed murals for US border checkpoints, they were rejected by Customs because they were believed to show the influence of drugs. Eventually President Jimmy Carter gave them official sanction. Max, who was born in Germany in 1939, was one of the best-known artists of the 1960s. His work was to be found on postage stamps, stationery, and even on shower curtains.

Exploring the Erotic

This is the flip side of the sexual revolution, with its ability to pull away the contrived veils of illusion around sex and play on the shock and disgust that can come from knowing too much. Issued in hardback in successive years by different publishers and the work of different designers, they show how an author, rather than a publisher, creates an image for their work.

◄ Edna O'Brien, *August is a Wicked Month*, Harmondsworth, Penguin, 1967. Cover photo by Barry Lategan.
Barry Lategan's cleverly cropped photograph has a "come on" character, as has the illogical "sell" line added to the book's title. "Despite" hardly seems the appropriate word in this context.

▼ Edna O'Brien, *The Love Object*, Harmondsworth, Penguin, 1970. Cover photo by Barry Lategan.
Another of Barry Lategan's sculptural nudes. The result stands on an edge between soft pornography and high art, redeemed perhaps by the abstract quality of shape that the lighting reveals.

If the 1960s discovered and fought for new sexual freedoms, it was not until the 1970s that they were taken for granted to the extent that they ceased to shock. Even by today's standards, the representation of the naked body is remarkably candid. Penguin Books were adept at giving individual authors a visual identity through the covers of their books, and Barry Lategan's photos for Edna O'Brien's novels were part of a series that made these sensuous novels with an Irish background popular. There was no attempt to illustrate the Irish content in the covers; instead, the close-ups of beautiful female torsos could be adapted to thousands of different love stories. Rising feminism would soon relegate such images to the world of soft pornography, but their restraint may indicate a certain freshness and innocence. The covers for two of Molly Parkin's novels, on the other hand, trigger a cynical mood by their graphic interpretation of the books' titles.

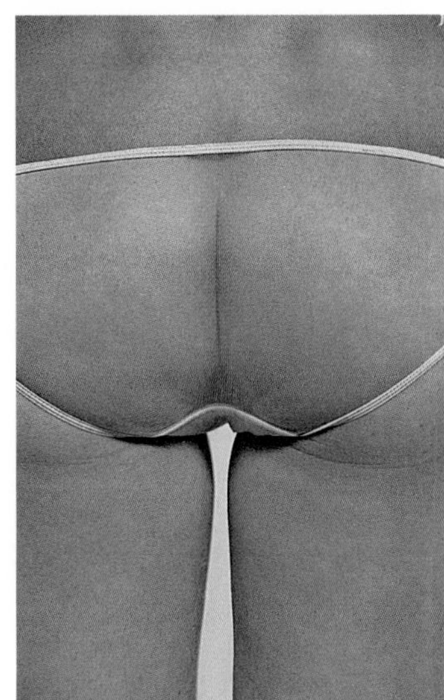

▲ ► Molly Parkin, *Uptight*, London, Blond & Briggs, 1975. Photo and jacket design by Harri Peccinotti.
After the Watergate scandal and world recession, the mid-1970s was not a time when innocence could easily be feigned. The use of back and front views for this cover creates a clinical effect, which is nevertheless effective in arousing curiosity about the novel's contents.

▼ Molly Parkin, *Full Up*, London, Michael Joseph, 1976. Jacket design by Gaynor Moore.
This cover makes an effective use of black-and-white photography with an additional colour reserved for lettering. The mixed imagery of the photograph plays successfully with the inferences of the book's title.

Not many best-selling authors have begun their careers as graphic designers, but Len Deighton was particularly versatile (see his illustration for Jack Kerouac's *On the Road*, page 70). His studies at the Royal College of Art, London, were supplemented by a variety of jobs, including railway lengthman, assistant pastry cook, airline steward, magazine proprietor, waiter, and manager of an East End clothing factory. Born in 1929, Deighton had an early literary success with *Funeral in Berlin* (1964), a story about an attempt to smuggle an East German biologist out of East Berlin. The *New York Times* described it as "a ferociously cool fable of the current struggle between East and West."

Deighton succeeded in creating a new type of spy story, with a nameless working-class hero, set down, as the critic Julian Symons wrote, 'in a world of terrifying complexity in which nobody is ever what he seems.' Deighton handed the design of his book jackets to his friend, Raymond Hawkey – with whom he went to college – who used a variety of techniques, particularly with photography, to give the books a fresh and original look. Hawkey is himself well known as a writer of thrillers, and his novel *Side-Effect*, 1979, was described by *The Times* as 'fast-moving as any Ian Fleming and with a great deal more persuasive and thrilling detail.'

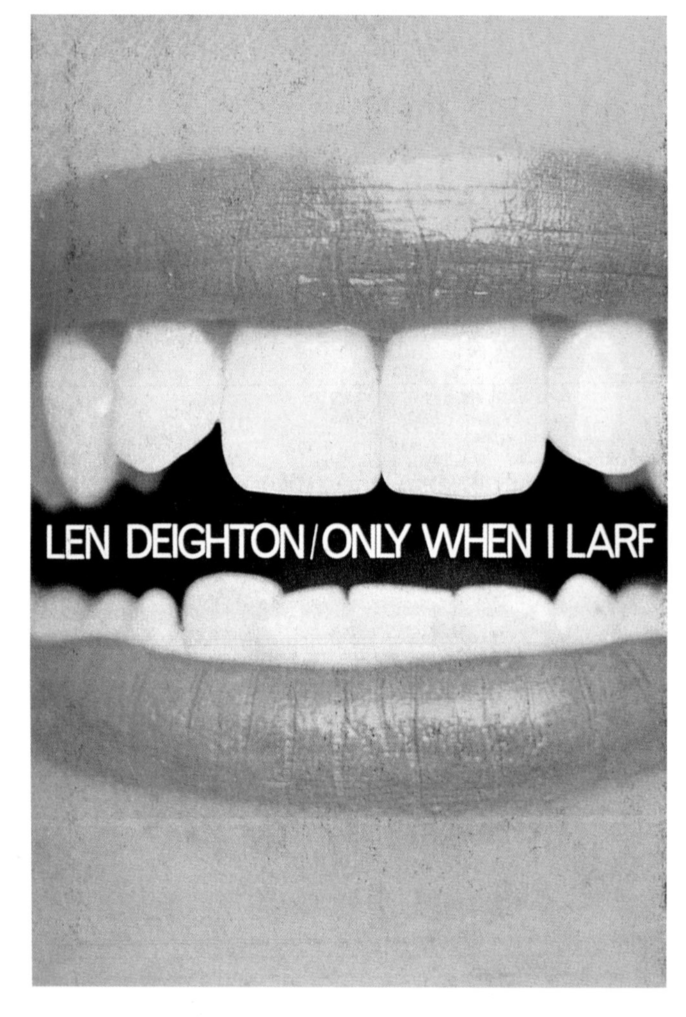

▲ Len Deighton, *Billion Dollar Brain*, London, Jonathan Cape, 1966. Jacket design by Ramond Hawkey.
An early attempt to capture the idea of the computer in graphic terms, including the lettering style of the title which mimics the machine-readable punch-card letter forms of early computers. The hard-selling promotional copy is as much the focus as the author's name or the book title.

► Len Deighton, *Only When I Larf*, London, Michael Joseph, 1968. Jacket design by Raymond Hawkey.
A brilliant use of a photographic image, which is almost too close for comfort. In 1969, Deighton added to his list of occupations by directing a film based on the book.

▲ **Len Deighton, *Bomber*, London, Jonathan Cape, 1970. Jacket design by Raymond Hawkey.**
A simple image for a book subtitled "Events Relating to the Last Flight of an R. A. F. Bomber over Germany on the Night of June 31, 1943."

▲ **Len Deighton, *An Expensive Place to Die*, London, Jonathan Cape, 1967. Jacket design by Raymond Hawkey.**
A complex multiple photograph, owing something perhaps to Richard Chopping's still-life designs for the *James Bond* series (see pages 48–9).

◄ **Len Deighton, *Funeral in Berlin*, London, Jonathan Cape, 1964. Jacket design by Raymond Hawkey.**
The spy's hold-all is a graphic metaphor for the novel's complex packing of different parts and characters.

Ivan Chermayeff and Tom Geismar

Ivan Chermayeff (b.1932) is the elder son of the well-known architect Serge Chermayeff, one of the 1930s leaders of the Modern movement in the UK. A year after working as assistant to Alvin Lustig in 1955, the year of the distinguished designer's untimely death, Chermayeff founded a design partnership with Tom Geismar (b. 1931). (The partnership originally also included Robert Brownjohn, designer of film titles for the first Bond films.) Chermayeff and Geismar's work has no mannerisms of style, yet is usually recognizable through its wit and visual freshness, which depend on a thorough understanding of the problem involved, and a delicate balance between freedom and control. They are best-known as designers of corporate logos, with a client list that includes Mobil, Xerox, Chase Manhattan Bank, and the American Bicentennial. In addition, they have designed public art, exhibition installations, and street furniture. Their printed design work, in the form of books and posters, has also been a consistent theme. Book jackets have played a part in this, demonstrating the versatility of their thinking, the captivating quality of their imagery, and the clean visual presentation that makes their work distinctive while allowing them freedom to adapt to clients' needs.

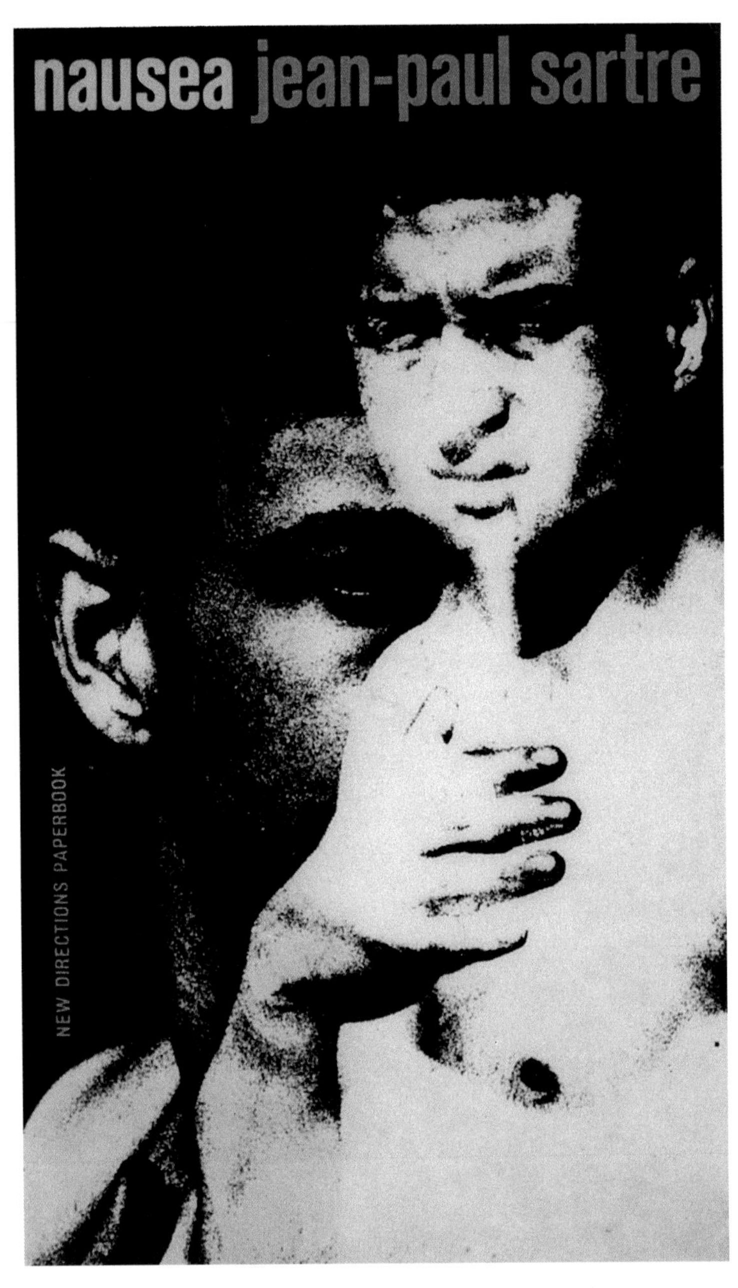

▲ Jean-Paul Sartre, *Nausea*, Norfolk, Conn., New Directions, 1959. Jacket design by Chermayeff and Geismar.
The overlaid photographs are well-judged to create the disoriented and anxious atmosphere of Sartre's first novel, which was originally published in France in 1938. The information about the author and title are kept under firm control on the top line, and although the cover is basically monochrome, it is full of tonal variety.

► Ngaio Marsh, *Dead Water*, New York, Little, Brown & Co., 1963. Jacket design by Chermayeff and Geismar.
A striking example of work by Chermayeff and Geismar, which, in its translation of words into images, approaches conceptual art. The sense of the heaviness of an object floating in water could hardly be better conveyed, and the design also has an abstract simplicity and coherence, in which the lines of type correspond to the two layers of the image.

▲ Frederick J. E. Woodbridge, *An Essay on Nature*, New York, Columbia University Press, 1961. Jacket design by Chermayeff and Geismar.
A brilliant graphic shorthand to illustrate the title of the book. The idea of handwriting is transferred from the ink bottle, with its leaf-sprig pen, to the script lettering above.

► Henry Miller, *The Wisdom of the Heart*, Norfolk, Conn., New Directions, 1960. Jacket design by Chermayeff and Geismar.
An example of the richness attainable in a simple image. The head and the heart are often seen as opposite forces, but here they are uneasily conflated by graphic means. A red heart would have been a cliché, but a black one not only is visually more coherent but also suggests deeper levels of ambiguity.

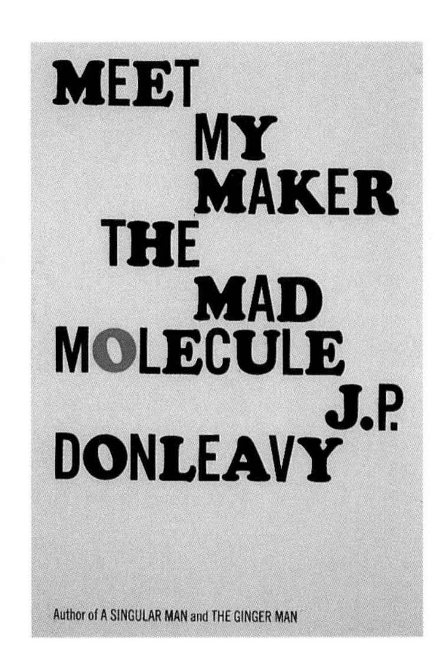

▲ Gore Vidal, *Julian*, New York, Little Brown & Co., 1964. Jacket design by Chermayeff and Geismar.
Vidal's fictional reconstruction of the court of the Roman Emperor Julian the Apostate is backed by meticulous research, while, in its gossipy commentary, it emphasizes resemblances to the contemporary world. Judging from the cover, this could be the most sober kind of book, but its very simplicity seems to hint at something more subversive.

▲ J. P. Donleavy, *Meet My Maker The Mad Molecule*, New York, Little, Brown & Co., 1964. Jacket design by Chermayeff and Geismar.
Chermayeff and Geismar have made many designs that play with the meanings inherent in the way that text is presented through typography, often the best means of subliminal communication. The red "O" seems to pick out the singularity of "molecule" in the title. It is also a reminder of the firm's most widespread logo – for Mobil Oil.

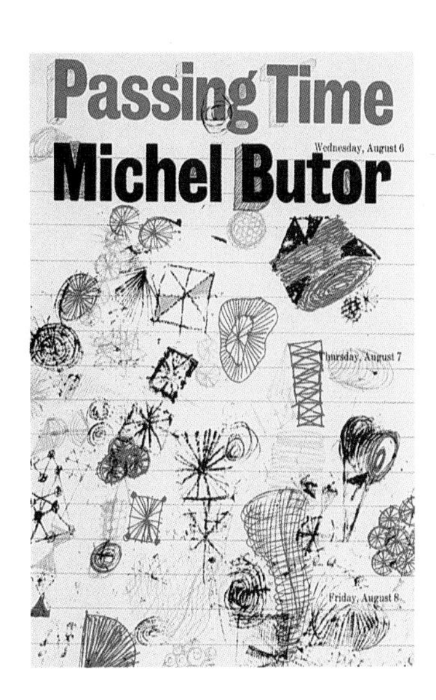

▲ Michel Butor, *Passing Time*, New York, Simon & Schuster, 1960. Jacket design by Chermayeff and Geismar.
As in several of their posters, Chermayeff and Geismar have produced something that looks like a rough rather than a finished product, whose informal multiplicity immediately singles it out for attention in the bookshop. In this novel, Butor (b.1929) adopts the collage method of writing of James Joyce's *Ulysses*.

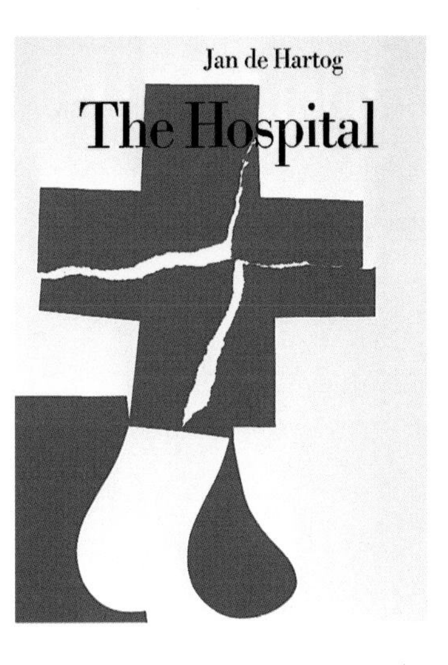

▲ Jan de Hartog, *The Hospital*, New York, Atheneaum, 1964. Jacket design by Chermayeff and Geismar.
A shattered red cross and implications of drops of blood convey that this is no ordinary medical drama. The book is in fact a report on the overcrowding and scandalous conditions in a hospital in Houston where Hartog and his wife (the daughter of J. B. Priestley) worked as volunteers.

Paul Rand

Paul Rand (1914–96) broke away from an Orthodox Jewish family in Brooklyn to become the man who, more than any other individual, shaped American post-war graphic design. He discovered modern design on the magazine racks and in the New York public libraries, and asked his mother (only once) if he could study at the Bauhaus in Germany. In fact, half the Bauhaus staff arrived in the US by the late 1930s anyway.

Rand always worked within a commercial context and thrived on it, designing advertising, packaging, and magazines. As he said, "You can be a great manipulator of form, but if the solution is not apt, it's for the birds." Rand produced many book jackets in the course of a varied career: Steven Heller, editor of the *AIGA Journal of Graphic Design*, in his book about Rand, described the covers as, "not so much mini-posters as small playthings. Perhaps in another life he would have been a toy maker because he loved the magic of combining shapes, colours and objects into sculptural cartoons."

Rand's work has the same casual perfection resulting from practised professionalism that is found in the work of a few other American designers in the period spanning from 1940 to 1970, in what now seems a golden age before techniques of colour reproduction became so cheap and easy that the designer's special skill of interpretation was valued less.

◄ Nicholas Monserrat, *Leave Cancelled*, New York, Alfred A. Knopf, 1945. Jacket design by Paul Rand.
Rand was skilled at giving tactile immediacy to the printed surface, as in the real-life punch holes of this cover for Alfred Knopf, one of Rand's most trusting clients. The design interprets the story of lovers separated by war in terms of a Cupid shot down while on active service.

▲ Philip Roth, *Goodbye Columbus and 5 Short Stories*, New York, Meriden Books, 1959. Jacket design by Paul Rand.
There is an audacious message in the lipstick print (getting the right lips took Rand days to achieve) and in the implied American flag, which is suggested by the red and blue colouring and the stars. The design makes effective use of hand lettering to unify all the written information.

◄ David Karp, *Leave Me Alone*, New York, Alfred A. Knopf, 1957. **Jacket design by Paul Rand.**
Rand enjoyed using collage techniques with cut and torn paper to make an abstract pattern that would work on its own but would also click together with the book's title and content.

▼ Albert Camus, *Caligula and 3 Other Plays*, New York, Alfred A. Knopf, 1968. **Jacket design by Paul Rand.**
The effect of coloured shadows against a white stage is suggested here in almost subliminal terms, creating an image that will work for a book of varied content. Rand designed a number of covers for literary and critical classics, including the Wittenborn Schulz "Documents of Modern Art" series.

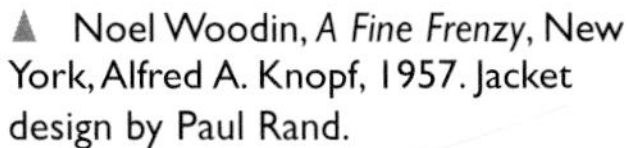

▲ Noel Woodin, *A Fine Frenzy*, New York, Alfred A. Knopf, 1957. **Jacket design by Paul Rand.**
The message of the blurb is in complete agreement with the image. The naive lopsidedness is an equally necessary part of the equation, while the lined paper background brings this cover back to the nature of books themselves. Rand restyled the Knopf logo of a Borzoi dog, as seen here, with daring minimalism.

► Mark Harris, *Wake up, Stupid*, New York, Alfred A. Knopf, 1959. **Jacket design by Paul Rand.**
Collage plus cartoon, plus handwriting equals modernism without pain. The image is set dancing in a slightly unstable way, against simple blocks of colour, with perhaps a nod to Henri Matisse's collages.

From the time of Sherlock Holmes, British writers have specialized in crime fiction. It can provide the thread on which a number of other issues can be strung, involving social observation and a philosophical view of the world. A writer of crime fiction or thrillers can also describe a detailed specialist world whose secret knowledge draws the reader further in to the story. Dick Francis's writing, for example, mirrors his first career as a steeplechase jockey between 1948 and 1957. Agatha Christie succeeded in drawing on the world of archaeology in which her husband, Max Mallowan, worked, and Dorothy Sayers launched her career by describing a London advertising office in the late 1920s. Others have given their fictional detective a specialism, like Ruth Rendell's Chief Inspector Wexford, who quotes from literary classics, while Colin Dexter's Inspector Morse, lugubriously pursuing the psychopaths of Oxford, is famous for his love of opera.

Crime fiction is a gift for the jacket designer, allowing for the depiction of some suggestive aspect of the story in a context that will set the mood of suspense in order to draw in the reader. Some covers are in danger of glamorizing murder, even if the novels themselves are not.

▲ Bruce Hamilton, *Too Much of Water*, London, Cresset Press, 1958. Jacket design by "HW".
Bruce Hamilton (1900–74) was the epitome of the English amateur author of detective fiction. He had a distinguished career as a teacher in Barbados from the age of twenty-six, publishing a series of novels and plays on crime themes from 1930 onward. The jacket makes dramatic use of contrast of scale between the liner and the falling figure, giving the title an added suggestiveness.

◄ Ruth Rendell, *Wolf to the Slaughter*, London, John Long, 1967. Jacket design by William Randell.
The illustrated jacket of Ruth Rendell's fifth book looks old-fashioned by standards of the time. However, design was no longer needed to promote an author described as "incomparably better than Agatha Christie".

► Dick Francis, *Proof*, London, Pan Books, 1985. Art direction and design by Gary Day-Ellison, photography by Colin Thomas.

The theme of horse racing runs through the novels of Dick Francis, although, as with all good detective fiction, this is only a device around which to build character and plot. As Judith Rascoe has written of Dick Francis, "you don't have to know anything about racing to be his devoted reader," although by the end you certainly will.

◄ P. D. James, *Unnatural Causes*, London, Faber and Faber, 1967. Jacket designer unknown.

A career civil servant, P. D. James (b. 1920) launched her writing career in 1962 with *Cover her Face*. Needing to continue a daytime job until retirement, she would write for two hours every morning before going to work. The cover of this title is a map collage, highlighting Dunwich on the Suffolk coast in England, and has a section of text as a "come-on", which is not unlike the use of text in the famous Gollancz yellow jackets (see pages 22–3).

▲ P. D. James, *Shroud for a Nightingale*, London, Faber and Faber, 1971. Jacket designer unknown.

An appropriately gruesome image for an author who has been described as having "a keen, cunning mind and positively bloody imagination".

The Paperback Explosion: Penguin

The early designers at Penguin were chiefly concerned with the inside of the book. As late as 1956 a director declared, "The most familiar feature of the Penguin look is, of course, the avoidance of pictorial covers. In America, the lurid cover is considered essential for securing mass sales of paper-backed books." Penguin, he affirmed, was standing out for good taste. A group of new appointments around 1960 changed the situation, especially when Germano Facetti become Penguin Art Director and a group of new freelances including Derek Birdsall, Alan Fletcher, and F. H. K. Henrion began to contribute designs. Tony Goodwin hired the young Alan Aldridge as head of a new Fiction Art Department in central London and Penguin entered the 1960s with new graphic styles and extensive use of photography. Despite the success of this approach, the old guard wanted to pull back, and in 1967 Goodwin and Aldridge both left. In its many different series, Penguin continued to strike a balance between company identity and the individualism of each title, hovering (in their own minds at least) somewhere over the heads of their competitors.

▲ Stanley Ellin, *Dreadful Summit*, Harmondsworth, Penguin Books, 1964. Jacket design by Germano Facetti.
A cover using a version of the new grid for Penguin Books designed by Romek Marber. Its typographic correctness and abstract restraint of image was soon superseded by less disciplined alternatives.

◄ Raymond Chandler, *Playback*, Harmondsworth, Penguin Books, 1975. Jacket design by James Torney.
A postmodern relaunch of Chandler reflecting the 1970s obsession with pre-war Hollywood stars such as Humphrey Bogart. There is no price because at the height of inflation in the 1970s it was too risky to print the price on a book.

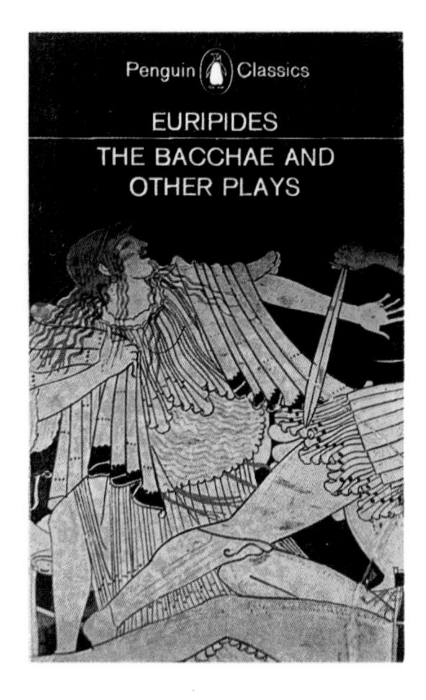

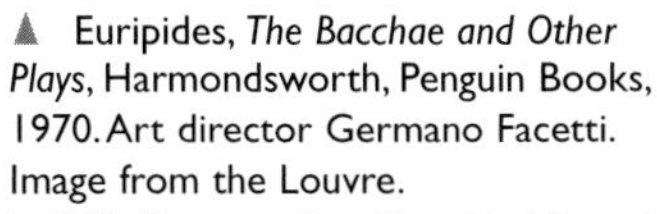

▲ Euripides, *The Bacchae and Other Plays*, Harmondsworth, Penguin Books, 1970. Art director Germano Facetti. Image from the Louvre.
In 1963, Germano Facetti restyled Penguin Classics, with Helvetica type and old master or museum images bled to four sides with the title overlaid. Many students expanded their knowledge of art as well as of literature by reading this series.

▲ Elias Canetti, *Auto da Fé*, Harmondsworth, Penguin Books, 1965. Jacket illustration by Malcolm Carder.
A transitional Penguin cover for a distinguished series, playing up the "classics" more than the "modern" in a version of the Marber grid. *Auto da Fé*, inspired by the burning of the Palace of Justice in Vienna in 1927, was first published in 1935.

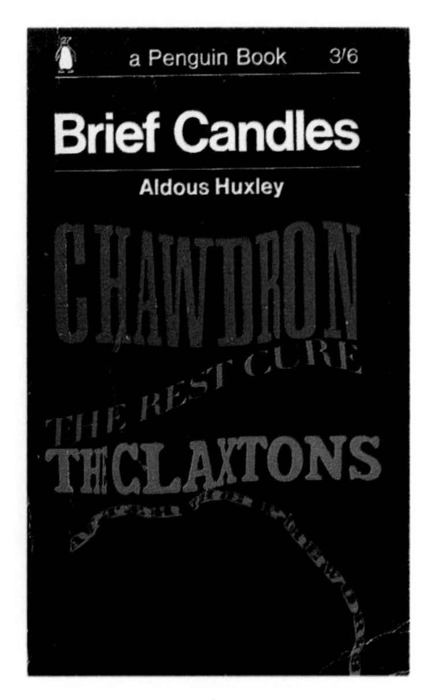

▲ Aldous Huxley, *Brief Candles*, Harmondsworth, Penguin Books, 1966. Jacket design by Alan Spain and Nelson Christmas.
The touch of psychedelic distorted lettering reveals the impact of Alan Aldridge on the Penguin fiction list in the mid-1960s. The all-black background was adopted for science fiction titles at this period.

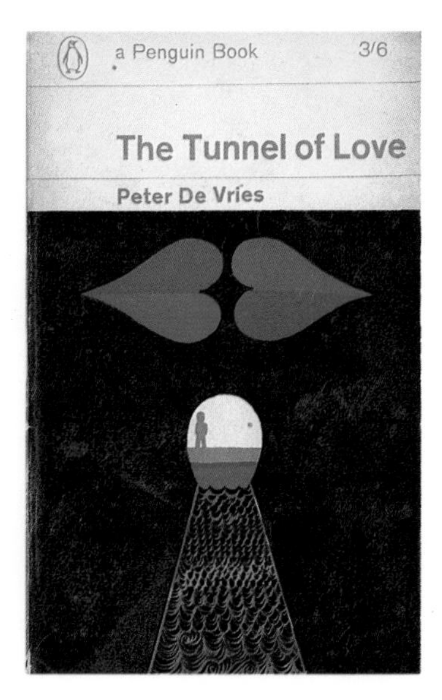

▲ Peter De Vries, *The Tunnel of Love*, Harmondsworth, Penguin Books, 1964. Jacket illustration by Alan Aldridge.
Within the Marber grid, Aldridge has an illustration whose dream-like subjectivity is at odds with the tough rationalism of Penguin's design policy, and anticipates the romantic rebellion to come. Aldridge was closely involved with the Beatles and his later airbrushed style typified the 1960s.

▲ Simone de Beauvoir, *She Came to Stay*, Harmondsworth, Penguin Books, 1966. Jacket design by Gianetto Coppola.
Derived perhaps from the pop art paintings of Peter Blake, this illustration is successful in suggesting the content of the story about the generation gap, while retaining a graphic integrity in the use of flat colour.

▲ Edna O'Brien, *Girls in their Married Bliss*, Harmondsworth, Penguin Books, 1967. Jacket design by Alan Aldridge.
A distressed Penguin inside his logo looks away in distaste at this unleashing of imagery by Penguin's *enfant terrible*. A true child of the '60s, Aldridge liked to portray as many undressed women as possible but as he wrote, "Problems: covers with naked tits sent the sales up but upset the authors. Anthony Powell wrote me a nasty letter." Edna O'Brien seems unlikely to have minded.

▲ L. Woiwode, *What I'm going to do, I think*, Harmondsworth, Penguin Books, 1972. Jacket design by Tony Meeuwissen.
While the graphic designer rigidity of the early 1960s, with its manic protection of identity, has disappeared from this cover, in its place came something like a return to the older Penguin tradition of restraint, echoing the reversal from '60s experiment to the cooler, often nostalgic style of the 1970s which now allowed for differentiation in a bookshop display.

▲ Evelyn Waugh, *The Ordeal of Gilbert Pinfold*, Harmondsworth, Penguin Books, 1972. Designer Peter Bentley (Bentley/Farrell/Burnett).
Political reaction and cynicism in the aftermath of the 1960s brought a new popularity for the work of Evelyn Waugh, which was beginning to be televised at the time. Peter Bentley's series of covers shows the self-conscious historicism of a new generation of illustrators returning to the craft skills of hand-drawn imagery.

The Paperback Explosion: Other Publishers

During the war, nine publishers banded together in the British Publishers' Guild, specifically to try to beat off the paperbacks, but the lead taken by Penguin had become so strong that even the most conservative could hardly ignore the irrevocable change. Paperback cover designs were usually anonymous, but they provided the opportunity for young designers to experiment with new ideas in a fast-moving market, which was influenced by film and television rather than by traditional book illustration. Penguin was the first in the field and, because of their good salesmanship, stayed in the lead at the upper end of the market. Soon, however, other imprints were providing competition. Pan Books was founded by Alan Bott in 1944, and several publishers with major fiction lists, such as Heinemann, Collins, and Macmillan, also published in paperback. By the mid 1960s, many publishers launched their own "trade paperback" imprints and, by 1972, there were 34,556 paperback titles in print in Britain and over 114,000 in the US. Following the Albatross and Penguin lead, paperback imprints were frequently named after birds or animals, if possible beginning with "P", or at least given some other catchy series title – that is, apart from the prosaic but distinguished "Faber Paper Covered Editions".

◄ Gavin Lyall, *Shooting Script*, London, Pan Books, 1967. Designer unknown.
The fourth book by an author who fitted into the pattern established by Ian Fleming and John Le Carré, although readers have found more of an echo of Raymond Chandler in his tales of espionage. The design of the cover mimics the style of the Bond film credits and plays on the idea of gambling and chance.

▲ Simon Raven, *The Feathers of Death*, London, Panther Books, 1964. Designer unknown.
The first novel by an author who has been said to combine aspects of Graham Greene, Lawrence Durrell and Arthur Conan Doyle. Originally issued in 1959, *The Feathers of Death* was issued in paperback in the year of publication of his unforgettably titled book, *The Rich Pay Late*, which was the first of a long series. The cover is a filmic come-on, with fashionable typesetting all in lower case.

▲ L. P. Hartley, *The Shrimp and the Anemone*, London, Faber and Faber, 1963. Cover design by Shirley Tucker.
First published in 1944, this was the first of the Eustace and Hilda trilogy. Hartley's subtle anxieties about class and gender in English Edwardian society have maintained a steady readership, aided by the film of his 1953 novel, *The Go-Between.*

▲ Wilson Harris, *Palace of the Peacock*, London, Faber and Faber, 1968. Cover design by Berthold Wolpe.
Described as "a weird river journey of a crew already dead through the British Guyana jungle," this book, first published by Faber in hardback in 1960, puzzled readers. Berthold Wolpe gave it one of his most exuberant designs.

▲ Jean Bruce, *Shock Tactics*, London, Corgi Books (Transworld Publishers), 1966. Designer unknown.
A work by Jean Alexandre Brochet, written under his pseudonym and translated from French. The cut-out photograph and the jarring colours are remarkably close to devices favoured by graphic designers in the 1990s.

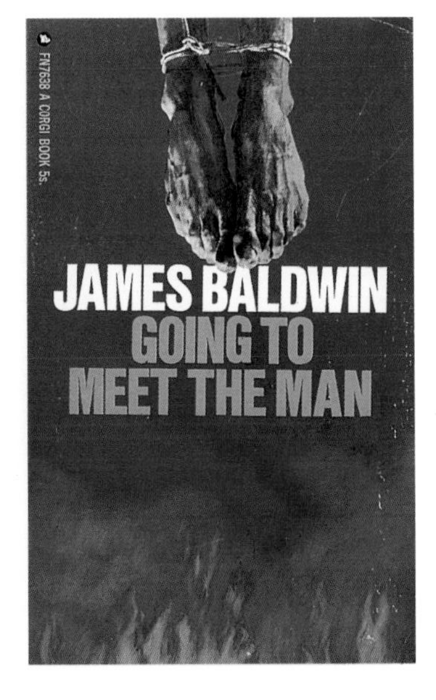

▲ James Baldwin, *Going to Meet the Man*, London, Corgi Books (Transworld Publishers), 1967. Designer unknown.
Baldwin was one of the most important writers on racial problems in the US, of whom it was written, "black people reading Baldwin knew that he wrote the truth." This book of short stories, first published two years earlier, was presented with uncompromising imagery.

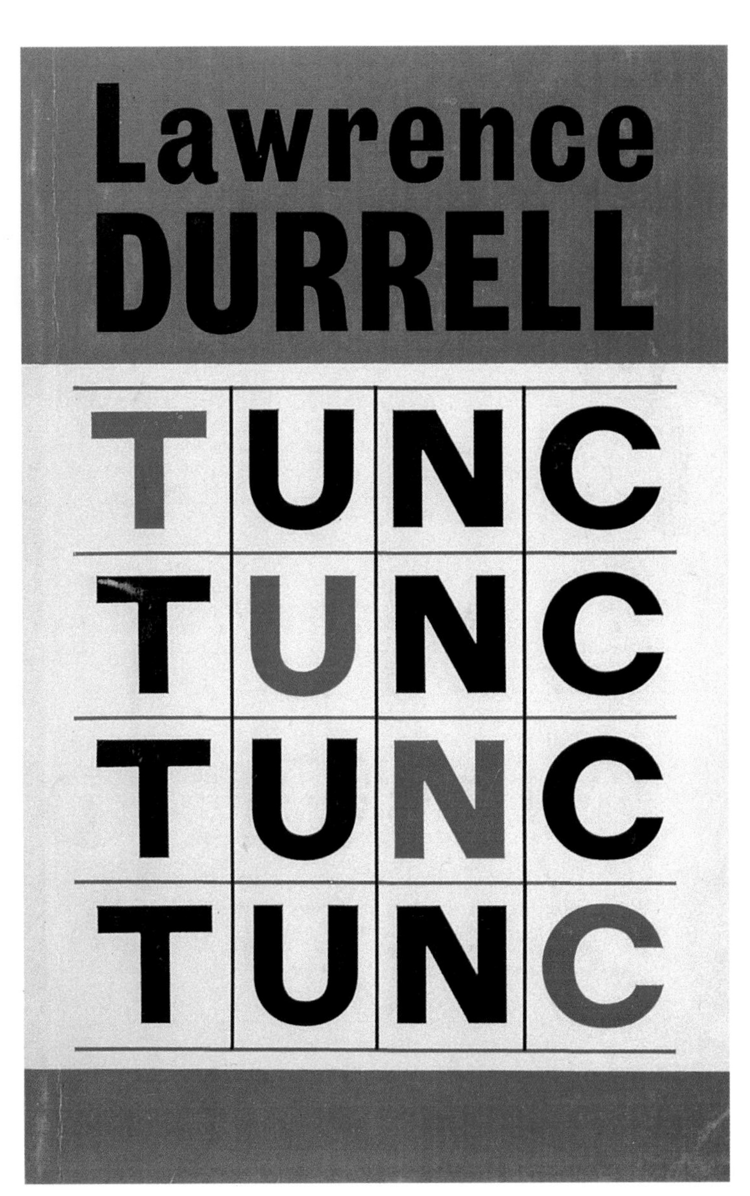

▲ Lawrence Durrell, *Tunc*, London, Faber and Faber, 1969. Cover design by Shirley Tucker.
Durrell's first major novel after the completion of the *Alexandria Quartet* deliberately mocks and subverts the modernism found in his earlier books, while dealing with the theme of the castration complex. The cover, in the sober manner of Berthold Wolpe, gives away nothing of this content.

The stand-off between the so-called "free" world and its certainly far-from-free counterpart in central Europe and the Soviet Union ended with the fall of the Berlin Wall in 1989 and the rapid unravelling of a whole economic and political system based on ignorance, fear, and deprivation. When the Cold War is remembered, it is likely to be in terms of the novels of John Le Carré (b. 1931), an English former diplomat who was serving as consul in Hamburg at the time that his first novel, *The Spy Who Came in From the Cold*, was published in 1963, soon after the creation of the Berlin Wall. No simple heroics would serve to describe the contest between the two opposing systems, whose agents were so often double-crossing their own employers. Le Carré, who was shocked by the disclosures of spying by his former colleagues such as Kim Philby, saw his work as "a moral search... a quest for some kind of truth about England". A sinister irony in visual presentation perfectly matched the content of his books.

Frederick Forsyth (b. 1938) was equally motivated by events to become a writer, in his case discovering as a reporter during the Biafran War (1967–70) that the British government were backing the wrong side. This realization led to his resignation as a journalist and the need to make an alternative income.

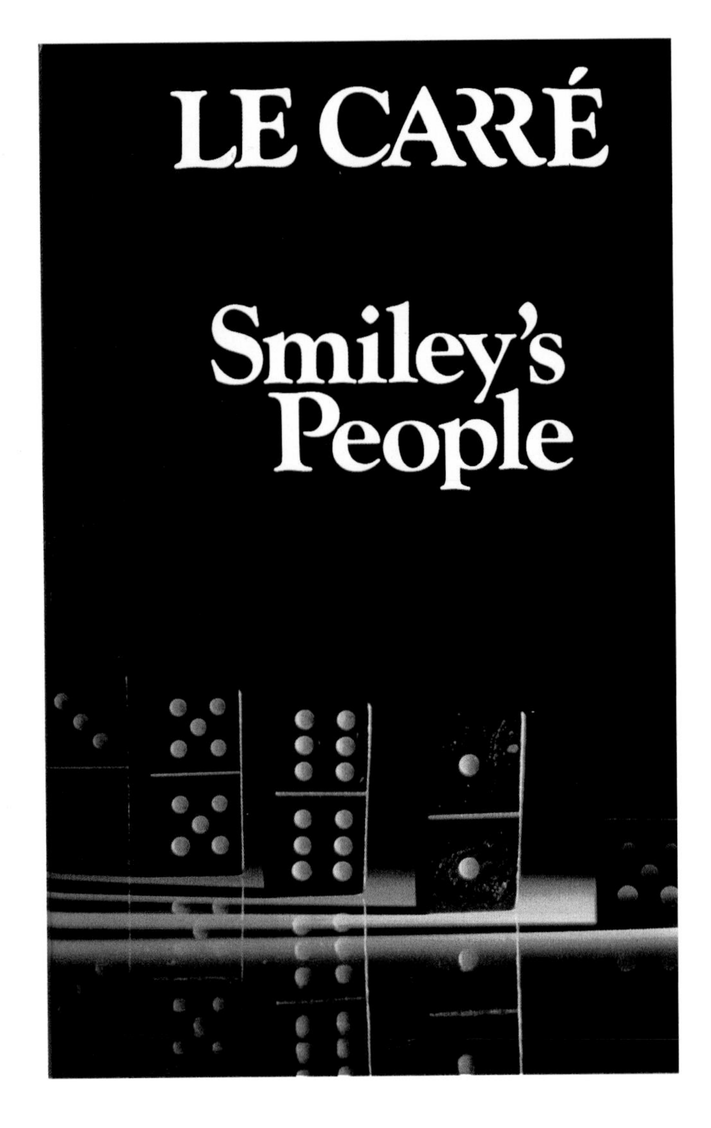

◄▲ John Le Carré, *The Spy Who Came in From the Cold*, London, Victor Gollancz, 1963; *Smiley's People*, London, Hodder & Stoughton, 1974; *Tinker Tailor, Soldier, Spy,* London, Hodder & Stoughton, 1980. Designers unknown.
Le Carré's initial reputation was sustained through the trilogy of novels about the spy, George Smiley.

► John Le Carré, *A Small Town in Germany*, London, Pan Books, 1969. Designer unknown.
The deserted square by night indicates the setting of this novel in Bonn, the city that provided the background to the topical issue of Britain and the Common Market.

▼ Thomas Hinde, *Ninety Double Martinis*, London, Hodder & Stoughton, 1963. Jacket design by Victor Reinganum.
More a psychological study in paranoia than a cold-war novel as such, this work by Sir Thomas Wiles Chitty, under his regular pseudonym, has a particularly evocative jacket by Reinganum.

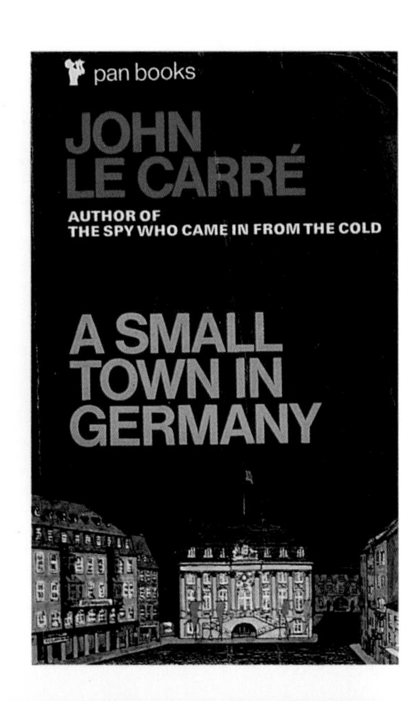

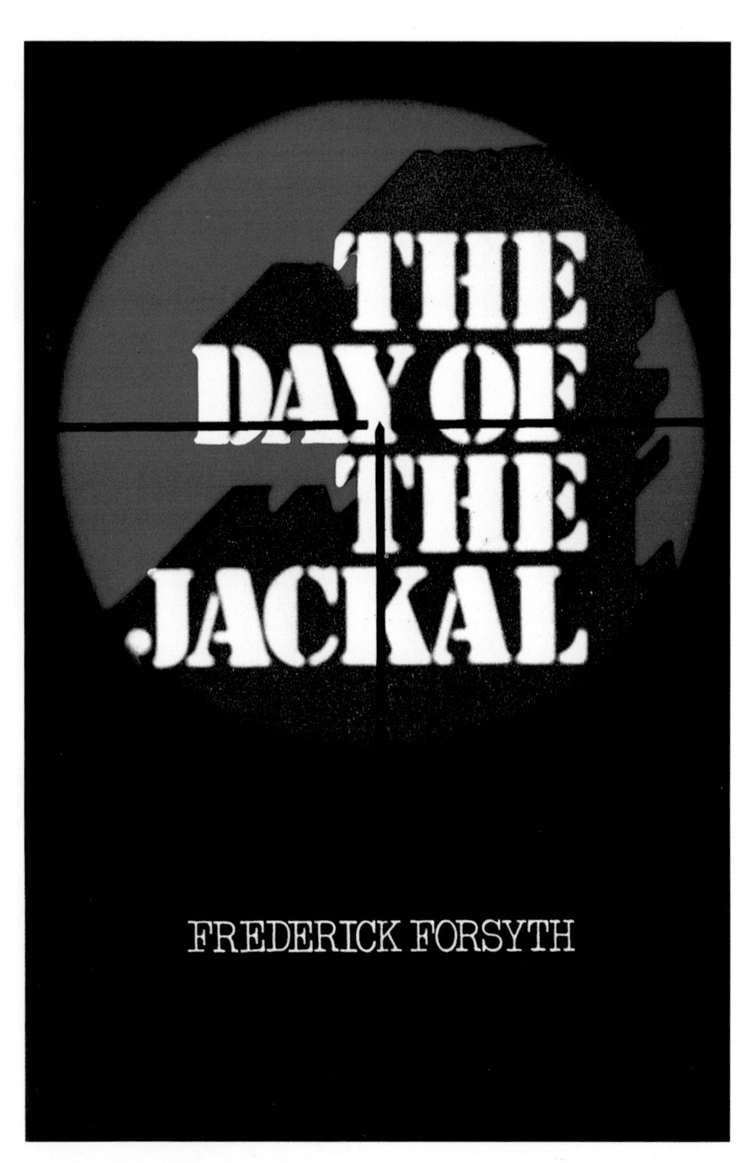

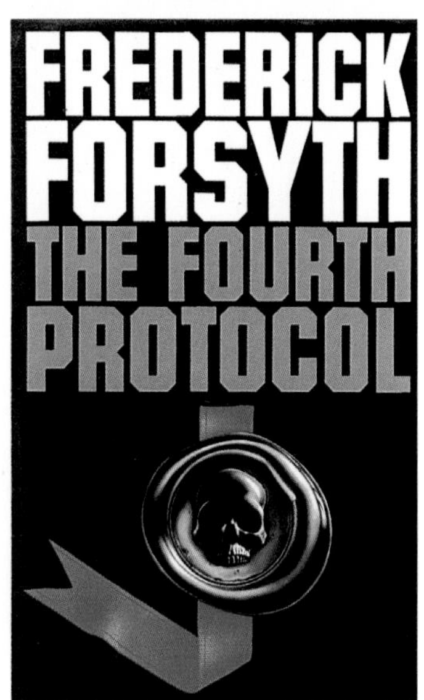

▲ Frederick Forsyth, *The Day of the Jackal*, London, Hutchinson, 1971. Designer unknown.
Gunsights indicate the theme of the book, an assassination attempt on General de Gaulle, as President of France, planned by "The Jackal". Forsyth wrote the book in one month, and its detailed knowledge and psychological realism confounded critics who thought that a non-event in the real world would be boring. As one critic wrote, "the point was not whodunnit but how, and how close would he get."

◄ Frederick Forsyth, *The Fourth Protocol*, London, Hutchinson, 1984. Jacket design by Raymond Hawkey, illustration by Harry Wilcock.
Black backgrounds for dark subjects dominate cold-war fiction.

The Times They Are a-Changin'

Post-war America was a divided culture, split on issues of race, economic status, social and political conformity, and materialism. Books of the late 1950s such as William H. Whyte's *The Organization Man* and Vance Packard's exposé of advertising, *The Hidden Persuaders*, showed that capitalism could be as corrosive of moral values as Communism. The Vietnam War was the focus for protest, seeming more futile the longer it went on. Tim O'Brien's *If I Die in a Combat Zone*, a fictionalized treatment of his experiences as a soldier in Vietnam between 1968 and 1972, was described by Annie Gottlieb in the *New York Times* as "a beautiful, painful book, arousing pity and fear for the daily realities of modern disaster". The protest took many forms,including underground magazines and music, as well as fiction. Ironically, the welcome given to these messages of dissent was so great that their authors became part of a new élite and were rewarded with material goods. The ironies of the fashion for revolution among those whose security need never be troubled by it were exposed by Tom Wolfe in *Radical Chic*, indicating the beginning of a backlash against the naivety of the 1960s.

▲ Tom Wolfe, *Radical Chic & Mau-Mauing the Flak Catchers*, London, Michael Joseph, 1971. Jacket design by Graham Rogers.
These two essays by Tom Wolfe (b. 1931), one of the founders of the "New Journalism", launched the term "radical chic", exemplified by "white liberals at a party nibbling caviar while signing checks for the revolution with their free hand". First published in New York by Farrar, Straus, & Giroux in 1970, it caused Wolfe to be "publicly excommunicated from the orthodox" of the liberal left.

► Tim O'Brien, *If I Die in a Combat Zone*, New York, Delacorte Press/ Seymour Lawrence, 1973. Jacket design by Wendell Minor.
The joky rhyming title mirrors the irony of the song "What are we fighting for?" which featured largely at the Woodstock open-air pop festival in 1968. The anti-nuclear symbol on the soldier's helmet reinforces the ambiguity of what the author described as the difficulties of "trying to do the right thing in the world".

◄ **Bob Dylan, *Tarantula*, London, Macmillan, 1971. Jacket design by Michael Jarvis, photo by Jerry Schatzberg.**
This stream of consciousness text that "defied meaning and lacked the emotion of true poetry", according to Anthony Scaduto, indicated that Dylan was best at doing what he was famous for: writing songs and performing them on guitar and harmonica. At his best, in George Melly's words, he described "a complicated universe where cause and effect, greed and exploitation, revolution and reaction are part of our fibre." The cover plays with Dylan's light and dark sides.

▼ **Wiliam S. Burroughs, *Exterminator!*, New York, Viking Press, 1973. Designer unknown.**
Burroughs (1914–97), best known as the author of *The Naked Lunch* (1959), once held a job as a vermin exterminator, and in this novel a writer kills off all his characters and destroys their worlds. The exterminator and all his victims are versions of Burroughs himself in a grim metaphorical structure by the author described as "the grand old man of the seamy underbelly". The cover is striking in its minimalism, with a typeface typical of the art deco revival of the 1970s.

Exterminator!
by William S. Burroughs

► **Thomas M. Disch, *334*, London, McGibbon & Kee, 1972. Jacket design by Michael Hasted.**
The cover indicates the content: a New York housing project of the future where the characters live in boredom and poverty in a rundown environment. Though described as holding up "a slightly distorted mirror to contemporary life", it was scarcely removed from the experience of the many who were unable to share in America's material prosperity.

Poetry

Very few poetry books sell in large numbers and buyers of poetry are less likely to be lured by an attractive jacket into an impulse buy, as readers of general fiction may be. The overall feeling of a poetry book is nonetheless important to the experience of reading, for it allows the designer to interpret the mood and ethos of the work, even if it is being issued with a standard house style. Poetry therefore continues to allow opportunities for thoughtful cover design, ranging from the modern classic lettering by Berthold Wolpe for Sylvia Plath's *Ariel* (1965), to the googly graphics of Adrian Henri's *Tonight at Noon*, issued three years later.

Wolpe created one of the most recognizable house styles of the post-war period, based mainly on lettering and plain colours. He was born in Offenbach in Germany in 1905 and studied under the leading type designer Rudolf Koch before leaving for England in 1935 to escape Nazism. The jacket for Ted Hughes's *Lupercal* is set in Wolpe's typeface Albertus. It has a Germanic character in its clear derivation from the pen-drawn letter, and was widely used by printers and designers well into the 1960s. After his time working on Gollancz jackets in the later 1930s at the Fanfare Press, Wolpe joined leading poetry publisher Faber and Faber in 1941 where his style was continued by his colleague and successor, Shirley Tucker.

▲ **Adrian Henri, *Tonight at Noon*, London, Rapp & Whiting, 1968. Jacket design by Lawrence Edwards.**
Adrian Henri, who performed poems to jazz in the clubs of Liverpool, launched this collection at the height of the "Mersey Poets" craze.

► **Alex Comfort, *Haste to the Wedding*, London, Eyre & Spottiswoode, 1962. Designer unknown.**
Poems by an anarchist doctor, who ten years later achieved fame as the author of *The Joy of Sex*.

► **Thom and Ander Gunn, *Positives*, London, Faber and Faber, 1966. Jacket photograph by Ander Gunn.**
Thom Gunn, well known as a poet in the 1950s, wrote verse captions for photographs in an unusual collaboration.

▲ **Sylvia Plath, *Ariel*, London, Faber and Faber, 1965. Jacket design by Berthold Wolpe.**
Published two years after her suicide, this collection included five poems written in the last week of Plath's life. The poetry list at Faber and Faber first achieved eminence when T. S. Eliot was the editor, and has continued to include many of the best British poets ever since.

LUPERCAL
LUPERCAL
LUPERCAL
LUPERCAL
LUPERCAL
LUPERCAL
LUPERCAL
LUPERCAL
• TED • HUGHES •

◄ **Ted Hughes, *Lupercal*, London, Faber and Faber, 1960. Jacket design by Berthold Wolpe.**
Set in Wolpe's Albertus type, the cover plays a simple typographic game, drawing attention to the letter forms rather than to any inherent meaning in the title. Ted Hughes was already recognized from the publication of *Hawk in the Rain* (1957) as a significant young poet concerned with the natural world.

▼ **Derek Walcott, *Selected Poems*, New York, Farrar, Straus & Giroux, 1964. Designer unknown.**
The first collection of poems by the Caribbean author who in 1992 was awarded the Nobel Prize for Literature. His poems, based on traditional English verse forms, are full of allusion and have been described as "almost Elizabethan in their richness".

► **Leonard Nimoy, *You & I*, California, Celestial Arts Publishing, 1973. Designer unknown.**
The author's portrait on this otherwise insignificant book of poems indicated that the author was none other than the actor who played the character Spock in the original series of *Star Trek*. Although Nimoy titled his 1975 autobiography *I am not Spock*, he said, "I wouldn't even have a career if it weren't for Spock."

With hindsight will we view the 1970s and '80s as a uniquely disturbed time in the history of the world, or merely average? The fiction of this period ranges over a great many issues, some of them inseparable from the timeless condition of mankind, such as *Carrie*, Stephen King's study of psychic power and possession, and others more germane to their period, such as Edward Abbey's novel of environmental protest. The shock value of these books comes not from specific external events, of the kind that wars or espionage provide, but from a general sense of anger or anxiety about the state of the world. Thomas Pynchon's *Gravity's Rainbow*, for example, is a reflection on the collapse of the Newtonian world view with its assumptions of order and rationality, and the crisis that expanding technology has generated in a world which can no longer adapt to sustain it. In the psychologically inward-looking novels of Iris Murdoch, a similar view is expressed. The covers of these novels reflect the continuing influence of the art nouveau revival from the late 1960s. Circles, whole or interrupted, are a recurrent graphic theme in these examples.

▼ Julian Barnes, *Metroland*, London, Jonathan Cape, 1980. Jacket design by Craig Dodd.
Pure typography, mixing futurism with nostalgia, for Barnes's first novel, which has been described as "a vision of decadence in short trousers".

▲ Alasdair Gray, *Lanark*, Edinburgh, Canongate, 1981. Jacket design by Alasdair Gray.
Gray trained at Glasgow School of Art, which features in this, his first novel.

▲ Edward Abbey, *The Monkey Wrench Gang*, Philadelphia, Lippincott, 1975. Designer unknown.
A classic of the environmental movement.

◄ Thomas Pynchon, *Gravity's Rainbow*, New York, Viking, 1973. Designer unknown.

▼ Ian McEwan, *First Love, Last Rites*, London, Jonathan Cape, 1975. Jacket design by Bill Botten.
In the title story, illustrated on the cover with Beardsleyesque elegance, two young lovers destroy a rodent.

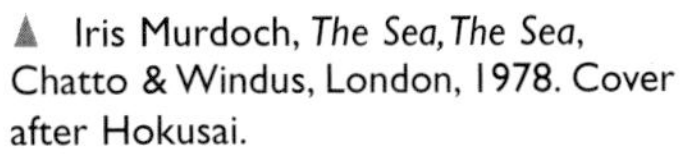

▲ Iris Murdoch, *The Sea, The Sea*, Chatto & Windus, London, 1978. Cover after Hokusai.
A famous image borrowed for one in a series of varied Murdoch jackets.

► Martin Amis, *The Rachel Papers*, London, Jonathan Cape, 1973.
Amis's first novel was described by Karl Miller as 'a crusadingly nasty adolescent unburdening himself in print.'

Counter Culture

With increasing material plenty in the post-war West, social problems were expected to wither away. However, a void was left when the struggle for existence disappeared. In the 1960s, drug addiction became a major theme, while sex was spoken of more freely than ever before in literature, nearly always in terms that involved a link with violence and exploitation. No author has lived the experience of this void more fully than Hunter S. Thompson, nor written about it more compellingly. As one of the group that created "New Journalism", he talked from first-hand experience, but without prejudice. Hell's Angels, high on drugs, sex, and speed, embodied for him "the puerile spirit of the nation's fantasy life", reflecting "the poverty of spirit that spawned them". Many readers missed the satire of accepted values which underlay Thompson's apparent glorification of violence and disorder. Jim Carroll's innocuously named *The Basketball Diaries* is also an account of drugs based on personal experience, but is more effective as a warning than an encouragement. As Steven Simels has written, it is "a virtuoso performance for those who still tend to romanticize the counterculture."

▲ ► Hunter S. Thompson, *Fear and Loathing in Las Vegas*, 1972, jacket illustration by Ralph Steadman; and *Hell's Angels*, 1966, jacket design by Joseph del Gaudio. New York, Random House. While Thompson's first book was based on reportage of a recent phenomenon, his second and most famous performance in "Gonzo journalism" more radically questions what kind of truths modern America can sustain.

► Jim Carroll, *The Basketball Diaries*, Bolinas, Tomboctou, 1978. Jacket photograph by Rosemary Klemfuss. A portrait of the author by his future wife provides a simple and understated image for the book.

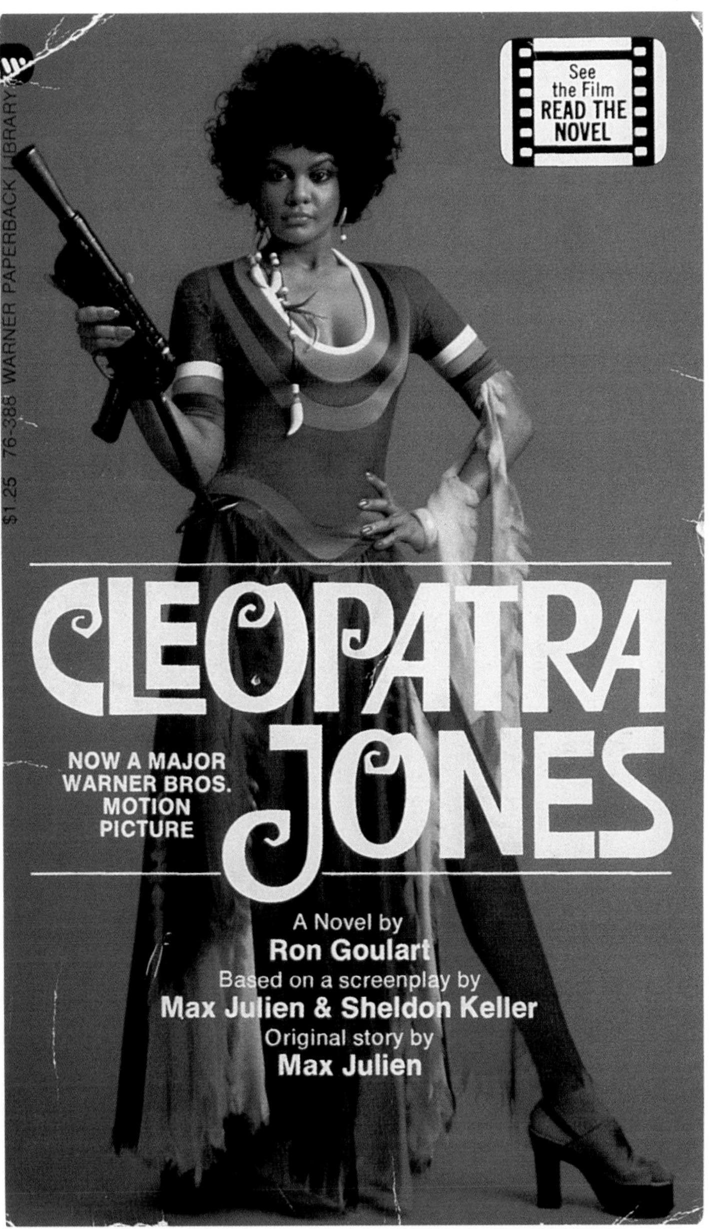

▲ Ron Goulart, *Cleopatra Jones*, New York, Warner Paperback Libary, 1973. Designer unknown.
A book tie-in with a successful film, by an author described by Martin Amis as sharing with Kurt Vonnegut, "something fundamental – a satiric ear for America, refined and intensified in the free fall of sf".

◄ Morton Cooper, *Delinquent!*, New York, Avon Publications, 1958. Designer unknown.
An unsophisticated piece of illustration, evidently intended to excite curiosity without necessarily implying disapproval. The pack ice of American convention was beginning to break up.

▼ Clarence L. Cooper, Jr, *Weed*, Illinois, Regency Books, 1961. Jacket design by W.A. Smith.
Published in the early stages of the drug culture, the imagery of this cover is restrained. Graphically, the cover is a good example of the integration of text and image.

► Iceberg Slim, *Pimp*, Los Angeles, Holloway House Publishing, 1967. Designer unknown.
The subject matter is rendered with an apparent sympathy for all those involved, a characteristic of the counter-culture's search for blame in the structures of society rather than the behaviour of the individual.

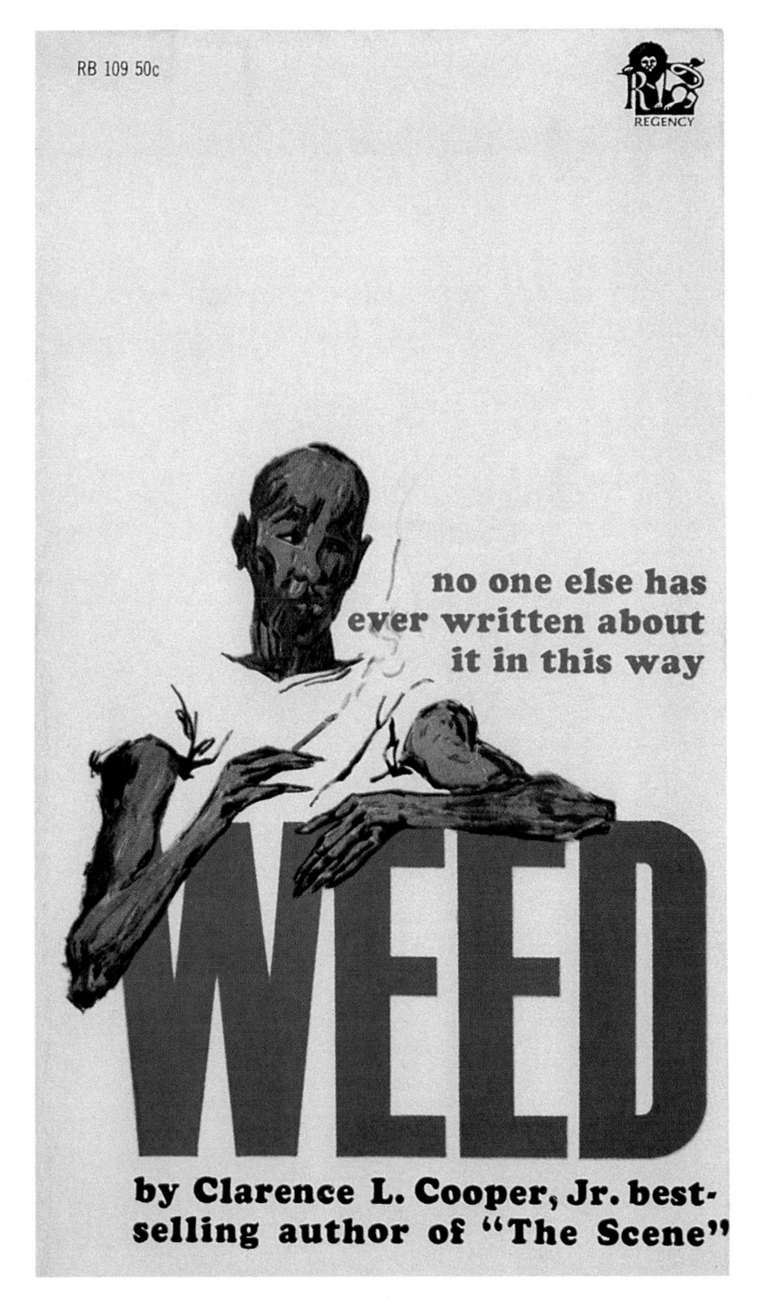

Prolific and amazingly consistent in quality and reliability, Agatha Christie (1890–1976) began her writing career with *The Mysterious Affair at Styles* (1920), written as a result of a challenge from her sister. She remained a prolific writer throughout her long career, remarking, "Oh, I'm an incredible sausage machine." Nonetheless, the writer Francis Wyndham reflected on the "animated algebra" of her plots, in which the solution is buried in the material, deftly concealed, until the final denouement, which "too complicated to grasp, is suddenly reduced to satisfactory simplicity" with the effect of "comfortable catharsis". While she was adding new titles to Collins's hardback list, Agatha Christie's earlier books were much in demand from addicted readers. Some titles were issued by Penguin in their standard green format, and some by Pan, before Collins set up its own Fontana paperback imprint. While she was still writing, the covers sustained the illusion that even the older stories were taking place in the present. Gradually, the "period" aspect became more apparent, although the meticulously drawn and threateningly surreal Fontana covers by Tom Adams current in the 1970s, are a memorable exception. Following the success of television dramatizations of *Poirot* with David Suchet, replete with white modernist houses and period cars, covers for the current series of HarperCollins reprints have an unequivocally nostalgic approach.

▲ Agatha Christie, *Passenger to Frankfurt*, London, Collins, 1970. Cover design by Collins.
A late work, not involving either of her famous detectives, Hercule Poirot or Miss Marple, both of whom, unlike their creator, had retired. The cover is simple and subdued, as if for a travel book.

◄ Agatha Christie, *Sparkling Cyanide*, London, Collins Crime Club, 1945. Cover design by Collins.
A rather crude image from the company who were Agatha Christie's publishers throughout her long career, showing just how much more sophisticated cover design would become over the next three decades.

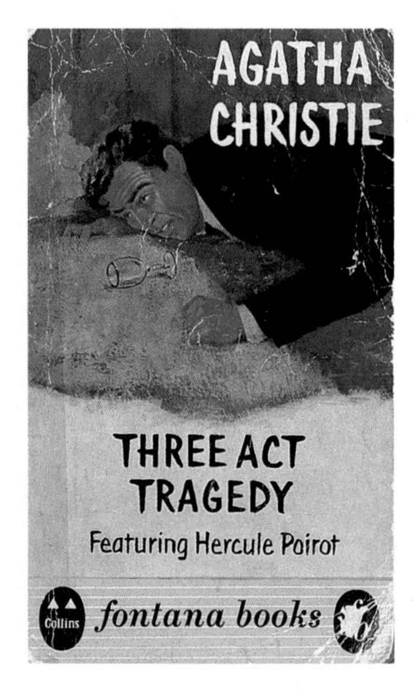

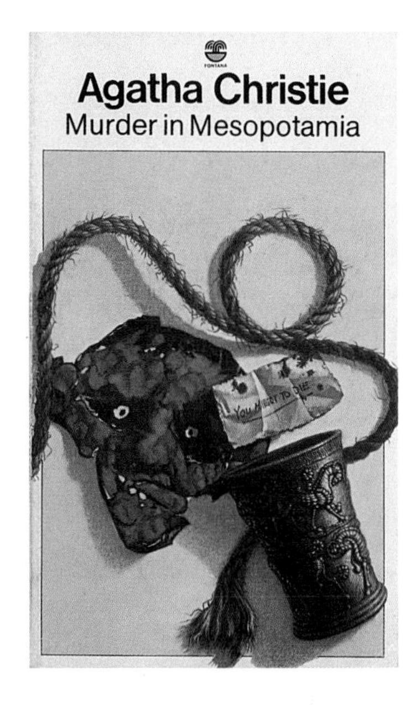

▲ **Agatha Christie, *Three Act Tragedy*, London, Fontana, 1957. Cover design by Fontana.**
A typical Christie country-house murder story, in which the vicar is killed with a poisoned cocktail. It was first published in 1935, and updated by the cover designer who may have thought that clerical dress for the figure might detract from the story's saleability.

▲ **Agatha Christie, *Murder in Mesopotamia*, Fontana Books, London, 1978. Cover design by Tom Adams.**
"We very much doubt if the author has ever given us a better story," wrote the *Evening News* when this was published. Christie's husband, Max Mallowan, was an archaeologist, and his excavations gave the setting and detail for the story.

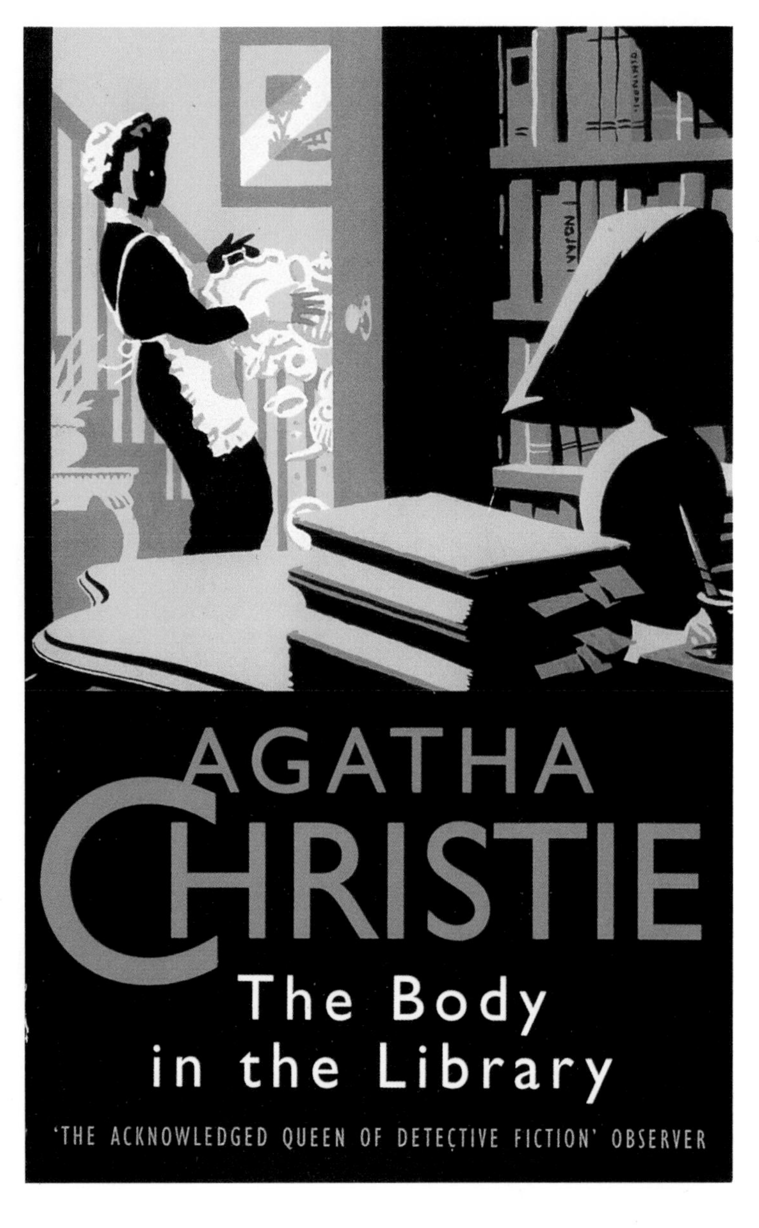

▲ **Agatha Christie, *The Man in the Brown Suit*, London, Pan Books, 14th printing 1965. Cover design by Pan.**
The rights to this early story, originally a Bodley Head story of 1924, were evidently not controlled by Collins and Fontana, thus it could be issued in paperback by Pan.

▲ **Agatha Christie, *Towards Zero*, New York, Pocket Books, 1969. Cover design by Pocket Books.**
Pocket Books issued a large range of Agatha Christie's stories in the US, often with altered titles. This stylish 1960s cover is very different to the claustrophobic look that English designers gave to the books.

▲ **Agatha Christie, *The Sittaford Mystery*, London, Fontana, 1971. Cover design by Tom Adams.**
One of Tom Adams's finest nightmare dreamscapes, in a cover format that gives it an uninterrupted field. The story, first published in 1931, involves a mystery death at a séance.

◄ **Agatha Christie, *The Body in the Library*, London, HarperCollins, 1994. Cover design by HarperCollins.**
Published at the height of the popularity of the television *Poirot* series, this 1942 story involves Agatha Christie's other detective, Miss Marple, a typical maiden aunt, who the author declared was her favourite of the two.

Granta
COLSON WHITEHEAD
The Intuitionist
PAPERBACK ORIGINAL

Design in the Digital Age:

The 1980s and 1990s

Book publishing is a domain where Hermes and Athene rule together. The goddess of wisdom must embrace the mercantile trickster, for they cannot live without each other. The book cover is the marriage broker, and is continually driven to seduce and deceive, even if in the most charming and learned ways.

During the 1980s and 1990s, the old world of publishing was strained to the point of collapse, as firms with a strong individual tradition of patronage and commissioning were absorbed into multinational conglomerates, and the book trade sought to make more money out of fewer titles. At the same time, book production became increasingly mechanized, and fewer specialists were needed to turn a manuscript into a printed book. The cover certainly remains an important link in the whole publishing operation, but the opportunities for individualism and enterprise tend to be squashed by the need to second-guess the market on the basis of design elements that have already been seen to succeed. One encouraging sign is that a few small imprints have been created or have revived themselves with management buy-outs, showing that publishing still has space for imagination and risk-taking. It is not surprising that these are some of the firms which produce the most interesting covers.

Colson Whitehead, *The Intuitionist*, London, Granta, 1999. Cover design by Peter Dyer, photo by Steve Wiley (see page 126).

Faber and Faber

Starting in 1981, Faber and Faber commissioned more than 200 book jackets a year for their list in a comprehensive makeover that has entered publishing legend. The work was put in the hands of an outside design consultancy, the Pentagram Design Partnership, under the direction of John O'Connell. The company was given a new logo, a double "f" ligature, and house rules were set down to give distinctive looks to different kinds of book. The book trade was shocked by the expense, but as the former Penguin art director, David Pelham, wrote "Even today there are hardback houses which still tend to consider design as something of an indulgence. I think it is particularly remarkable that Fabers approached such a progressive design group in the first place." He added that the investment was already paying off, and although twenty years later Faber has made substantial changes, the style – managed by a new generation at Pentagram – has remained consistent. The "look" was originally built around the idea of the panel of lettering, which allowed for a greater freedom for an image, like Penguin's all-over covers, while retaining recognition. The images behind were a mixture of drawing and photography, the latter often manipulated in illustration software, which came into use around 1990, while the text on poetry titles was nostalgically framed in a pattern made of ff logos.

ff
James McClure
The Song Dog
A Kramer and Zondi Mystery
'The best crime novel I've read all year.'
Independent

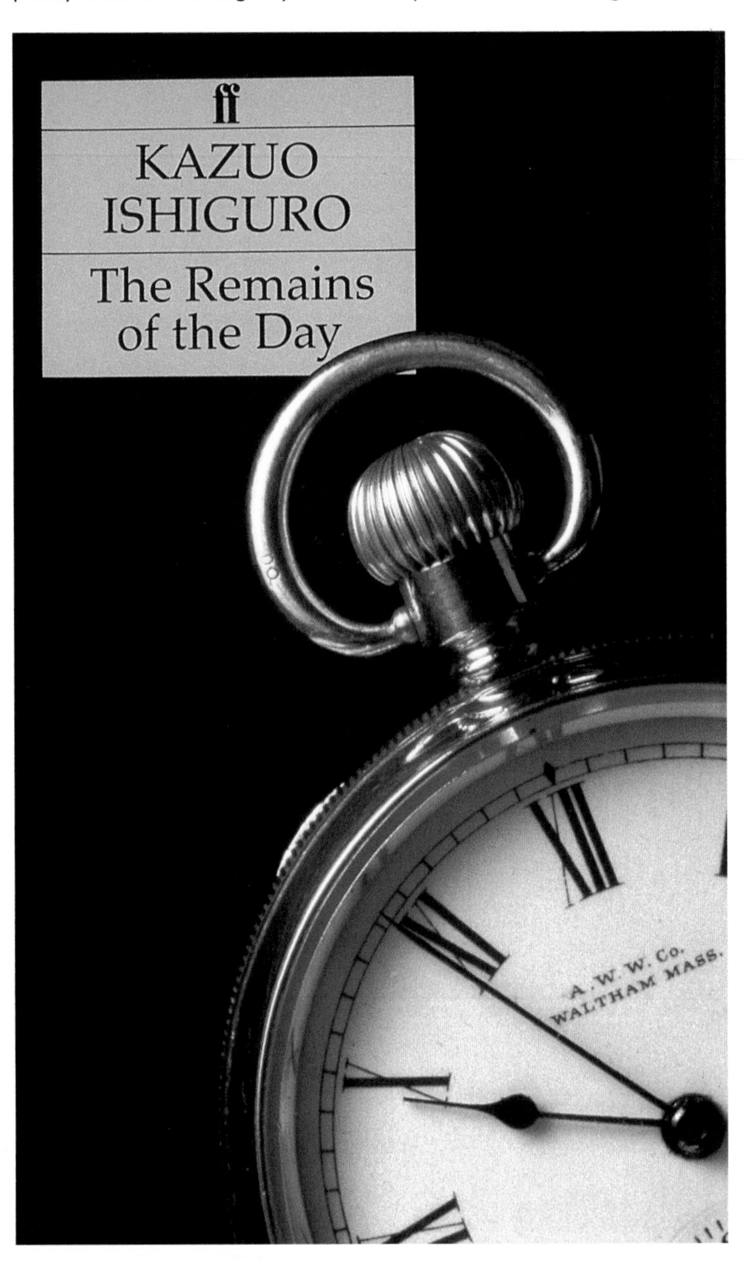

◄ James McClure, *The Song Dog*, London, Faber and Faber, 1993. Cover design by Pentagram.
First published in New York two years earlier, this story is no simple mystery, but is part of a series featuring a Zulu detective and his Afrikaner partner. The relationship between these two, which McClure deliberately does not idealize, was said to have assisted in bringing apartheid to an end.

▲ Kazuo Ishiguro, *The Remains of the Day*, London, Faber and Faber, 1989. Cover design by Pentagram.
A good example of Pentagram's style of visual synechdoche, in which a detail stands for the whole atmosphere of the story. The fine but archaic watch represents the butler's tale of lost time and unvoiced regret, made famous in the 1993 film by Merchant Ivory, starring Anthony Hopkins.

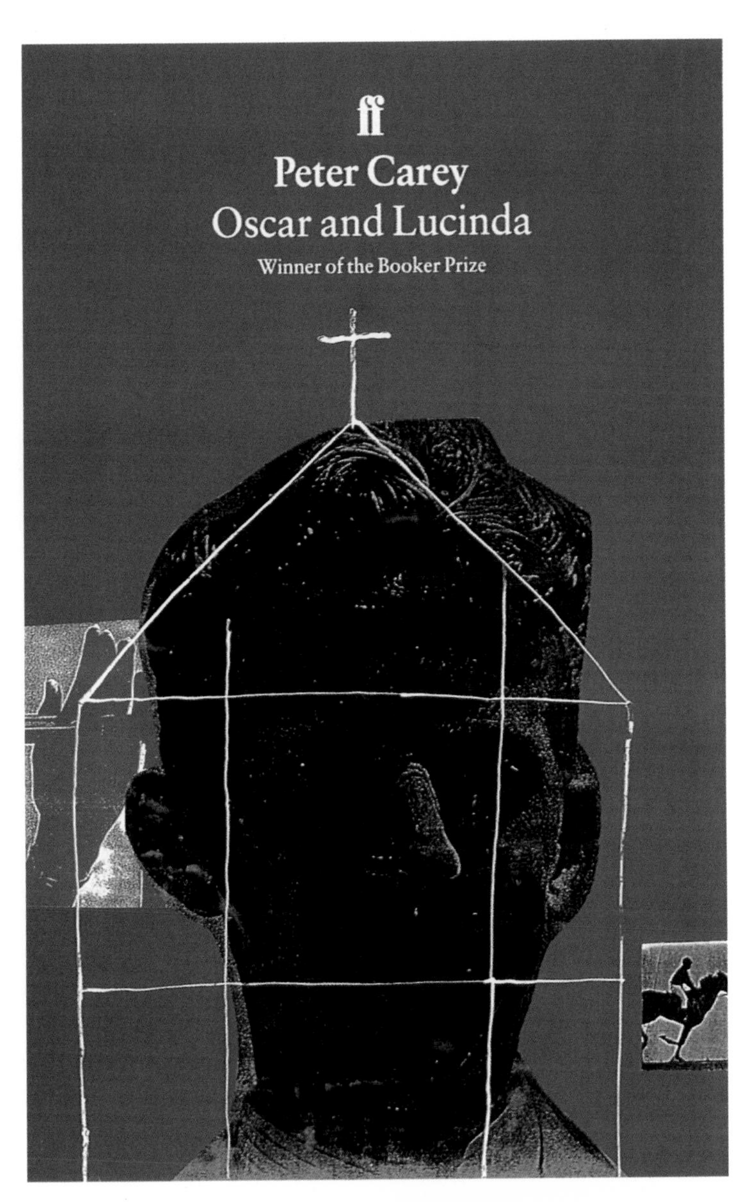

▲ Peter Carey, *Oscar and Lucinda*, London, Faber and Faber, 1995. Cover design by Pentagram.
The third novel by an Australian author which explores "the perfect irrationality of human behaviour" through the unlikely pairing of two Victorian gamblers.

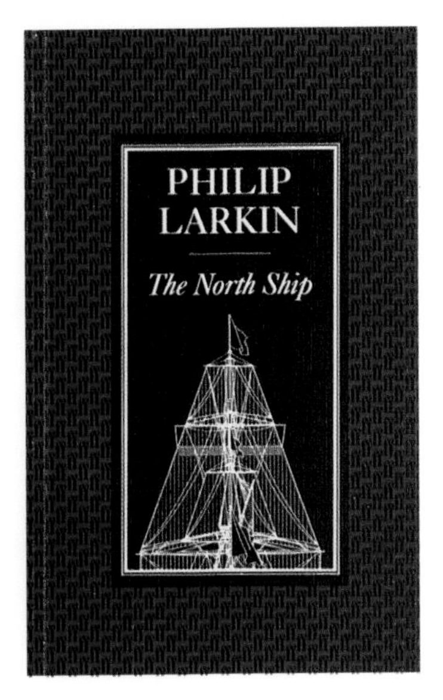

▲ Philip Larkin, *The North Ship*, London, Faber and Faber, 1986. Cover design by Pentagram.
Artful cropping of images, as seen here, contributes much to the Faber/ Pentagram style.

▲ Paul Muldoon, *Meeting the British*, London, Faber and Faber, 1987. Cover design by Pentagram, illustration by Charlotte Everest-Philips.
The small vignette in the title panel for books in Faber's renowned poetry list makes effective use of illustration.

◄ William Golding, *Lord of the Flies*, London, Faber and Faber, c1990. Cover design by Pentagram, illustration by Paul Hogarth.
An unequivocally nasty image, by a veteran illustrator, which dominates the all-white cover.

◄ Kinky Friedman, *Greenwich Killing Time*, London, Faber and Faber, 1997. Cover design by Pentagram.
A murder story with a New York setting, characterized by cynical commentary and unlikely simile. It was first published in 1986. The Faber identity has become quite loose in this example.

Picador

Picador was launched in 1972 by Sonny Mehta as a specialized list within the Pan group. At the time, bookshops tended to have one wall devoted exclusively to Penguins, with all other paperbacks jumbled together. Picador titles were deliberately larger than standard paperbacks of the time, and the company distributed special "spinner" display stands for them, giving an immediate recognition factor. David Larkin was the original art director, followed in 1978 by Gary Day-Ellison, a designer just out of college, who operated a policy of seeing aspiring illustrators personally and allowing them plenty of freedom. He says that he aimed to display the best talent in visual arts, allowing the artists to propose their own treatments, or encouraging them to try something different in a creative relationship of give and take. He was helped by the freedom he was given, as he believes that cover approval committees usually dilute the best concepts. Picador Classics grew from the success of the main Picador list and rivalled Penguin Modern Classics. Literary agents needed to be persuaded to sell rights to Picador rather than to Penguin, and Day-Ellison made a series of mock-up covers to sell the idea. The covers, which had a standard black stripe, had a greater artistic range and freedom compared with Penguin covers, which used paintings from galleries rather than purpose-made designs.

▲ **Samuel Beckett, *The Beckett Trilogy*, London, Picador, 1979. Art direction and design by Gary Day-Ellison, illustration by Russell Mills.**
Gary Day-Ellison encouraged Russell Mills to experiment with a set-up photographic shot, based on the Beckett character who obsessively moves pebbles from one pocket to another. His close collaboration with Mills produced fresh and original ideas.

► **Michael Ondaatje, *Coming Through Slaughter*, London, Picador, 1984. Art direction by Gary Day-Ellison, design by Gary Day-Ellison and Vaughan Oliver, photograph by Robert Golden.**
This, as the cover image goes a long way to telling, is a biography of New Orleans jazz musician Buddy Bolden, whose breakdown at an early age meant that he never made any recordings. The photo was set up to convey the content while hiding the musician's face, since no actual photograph of him survives.

◄ Robert Musil, *Young Törless*, London, Picador Classics, 1979. Art direction and design by Gary Day-Ellison, illustration by Robert Mason.
Within the basic series style of Picador Classics, Day-Ellison allowed a wide margin of freedom of image and lettering as seen here.

◄ Ian McEwan, *First Love, Last Rites*, London, Picador, 1982. Art direction and design by Gary Day-Ellison and Vaughan Oliver, illustration by Russell Mills.
Five areas of one large painting were each used for a title in a McEwan series.

▼ Oliver Sacks, *The Man who Mistook his Wife for a Hat*, London, Picador, 1986. Art direction and design by Gary Day-Ellison, illustration by Paul Slater.
The striking title of this well-known popular book of case studies on defective brain functions demanded an adaptation of René Magritte's painting, "The Betrayal of Images", which shows a pipe, inscribed *Ceci n'est pas une pipe* linked to one of his equally famous images of bowler hats. The artist's estate sent a lawyer's letter, believing this to be a genuine Magritte image.

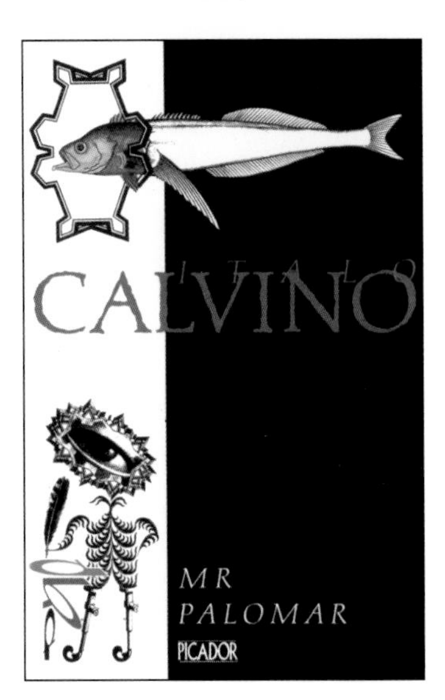

▲ Italo Calvino, *Mr Palomar*, London, Picador, 1983. Art direction and design by Gary Day-Ellison, illustration by The Brothers Quai.
The illustrators are identical twins, Timothy and Stephen.

▲ F. Gonzalez-Crussi, *Notes of an Anatomist*, London, Picador, 1986. Art direction and design by Gary Day-Ellison, illustration by Robert Mason.
Essays by a pathologist, with a painting by one of Day-Ellison's favourite artists.

Harvill Press

◄ Giuseppe di Lampedusa, *The Leopard*, London, Harvill, 1960. Jacket design by Hans Tisdall.
A Tisdall jacket is usually recognizable from the calligraphic lettering and sharply drawn colour separations. The use of the spine and back of this example are a good demonstration of his graphic humour. The author (1896–1957) wrote the book in the last year of his life as a lament for the past glory of his native Sicily. Published in Italy in 1958, it became a worldwide success with Luchino Visconti's film of 1963, starring Omar Sharif and Claudia Cardinale.

The Harvill Press was founded in London in 1946 by Manya Harari and Marjorie Villiers to specialize in foreign literature in translation. It had its first great publishing successes at the end of the 1950s, with Boris Pasternak's *Doctor Zhivago*, Giuseppe di Lampedusa's *The Leopard*, and Joy Adamson's personal account of raising lion cubs in Kenya, *Born Free*. The two novels, heavy with longing for the past, were by previously unknown authors, but both became successful films in the 1960s. The emblem of the rampant leopard, taken from Hans Tisdall's jacket for Lampedusa's book, has become the logo for Harvill Press, which regained its independence in 1995 as the result of a management buy-out from HarperCollins, led by the imprint's publishing director from 1984 onward, Christopher MacLehose. The list has remained true to its original intention by continuing to specialize in European and other foreign language fiction, a publishing area that has revived from a low point in the mid-1980s. Libanus Press, itself a remarkable enterprise based in Marlborough, an English market town, has provided much of Harvill's cover design. It was founded by Michael Mitchell who started to print by hand when working as a dentist, before becoming a full-time publisher and designer. The Libanus covers have a classic typographic quality, which is varied by the work of other designers who have given Harvill titles a sharper-edged "street" quality.

► George Perec, *A Void* (*La Disparition*), London, Harvill Press, 1995. Jacket design by Libanus Press, cover illustration by Stephen Raw.
The cover reminds the reader that no words containing the letter "e" appear in the book, a challenge to the translator from a French author (1936–82), who followed this with *Les Revenants*, in which "e" is the only vowel. Writing of this kind, which uses its linguistic eccentricity to reinforce a message about its content, is called "lipogrammatic".

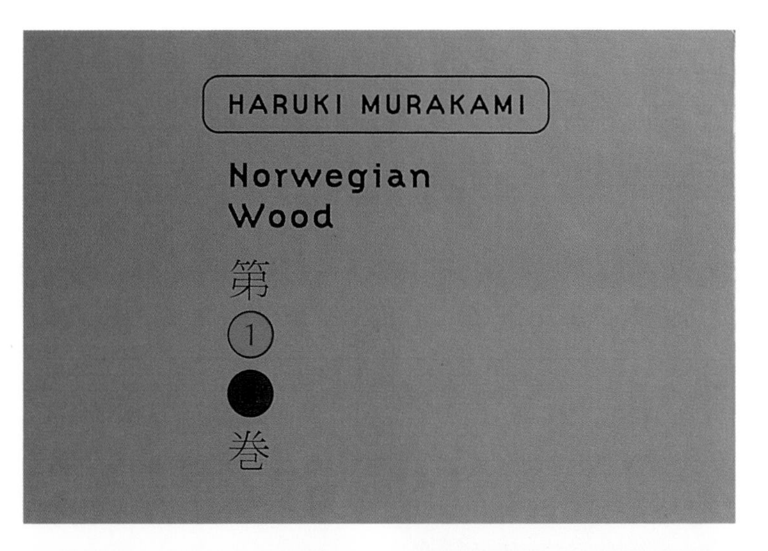

◄ Haruki Murakami, *A Wild Sheep Chase*, London, Harvill Press, 2000. Jacket design by James Keenan, photograph by Véronique Rolland.
Murakami's work has been described as "a mixture of science fiction, hard-boiled cool and metaphysics", a formula that could be applied to much of the most successful new writing of the late twentieth century. The isolation of a slightly distorted image on a brightly coloured background is a favourite visual device to accompany this genre.

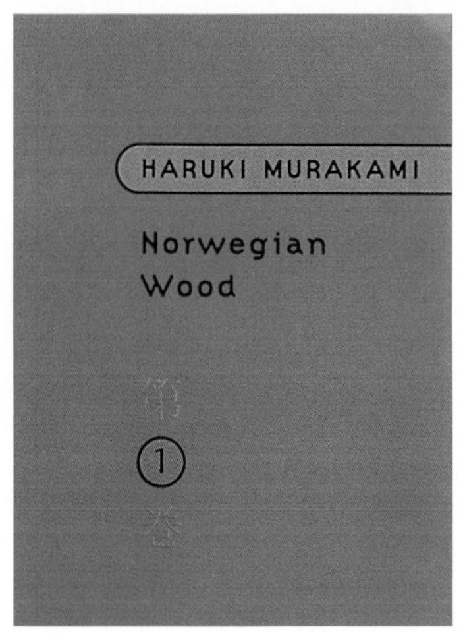

▲ Haruki Murakami, *Norwegian Wood*, London, Harvill Press, 2000. Jacket design by Libanus Press.
Orignally published in Japan by Kodansha in 1989, this two-volume novel is presented in a slipcase, with attention to detail rarely found in book production today. The title, taken from a Beatles song, reflects the author's attachment to the pop culture of the West, which led him to open a jazz bar in Tokyo in 1974.

▼ Dermot Healy, *Sudden Time*, London, Harvill Press, 2000. Jacket design by Crush, photograph by Tim Kavanagh.
This novel about Irish people in London deals with fragmentation through its language, and as Gordon Burn wrote in the *Times Literary Supplement*, "Healy's great achievement is the way he allows his characters to find their coherence in confessed incoherence." The cover design successfully evokes the stream of consciousness.

Bloomsbury

In an age of mergers that swallowed up some of the most distinguished names in London publishing, Bloomsbury was a newcomer, "founded in 1986 on the principle of publishing books of the highest quality to the mass market." Having survived the early 1990s recession, the company was floated in 1994 and its paperback and children's lists were established, the latter making publishing history with a book by an unknown author, J. K. Rowling, called *Harry Potter and the Philosopher's Stone*, first published in 1997 after one of the in-house editors recognized its potential. The *Harry Potter* series reached four titles by the summer of 2000, with a Warner Brothers film in prospect, and was hailed as the rebirth of the traditional book for children. Bloomsbury expanded into the US in 1998, supported by a £6.1 million rights issue, and has been active in digital publishing, with the *Encarta World English Dictionary* launched in 1999, and a recent deal to create the world's first on-line business reference service in partnership with the Economist Group. The three cover designs by William Webb illustrated here create a family style, chiefly characterized by widely spaced lettering, but the list as a whole indicates that current marketing policy places little value on brand-recognition of a publisher (which risks monotony) and prefers instead to treat each book as an individual item in the market.

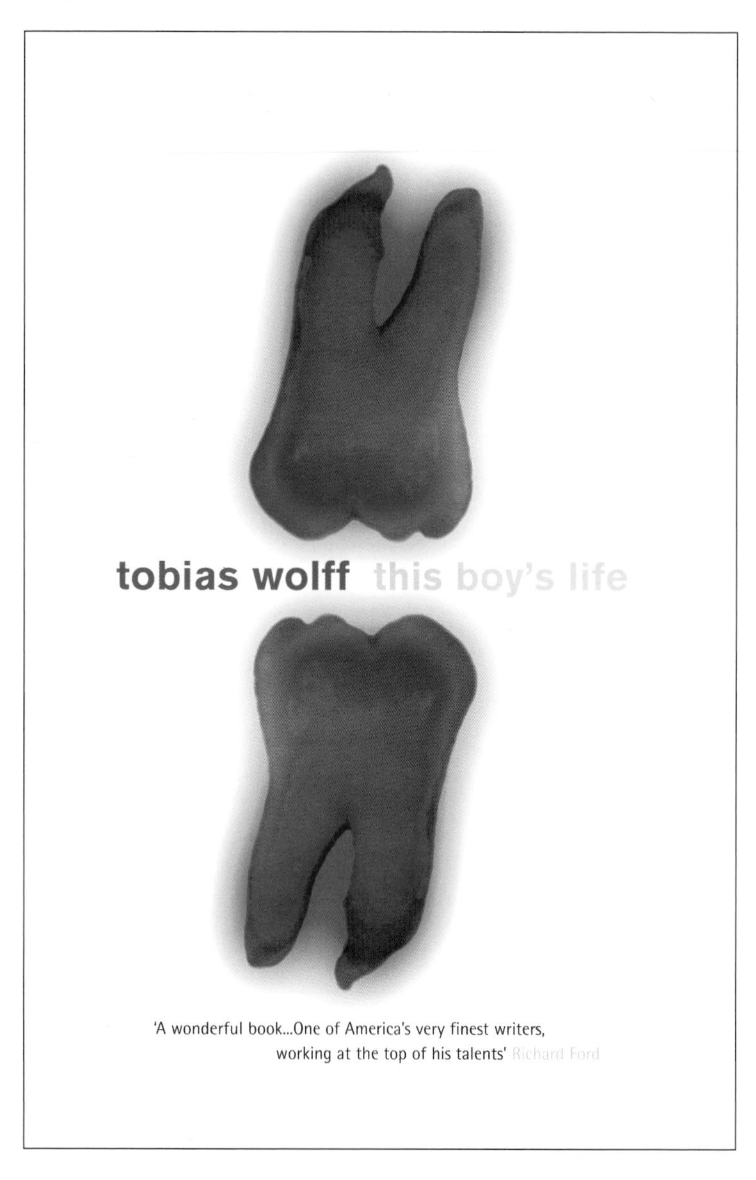

◄ Lesley Glaister, *Honour Thy Father*, London, Bloomsbury, 1999. Cover design by William Webb, photo by Mark Pennington.

First published by Secker & Warburg in 1990, this novel explores the boundaries between opposite states, such as love and hate, madness and sanity, danger and safety, laughter and tears, revealing how such distinctions become illusory with experience. Including a laudatory sound-bite on the cover has almost become an essential aspect of the design brief.

▲ Tobias Wolff, *This Boy's Life*, London, Bloomsbury, 1999. Cover design by Andy Vella, photo by Science Photo Library.

The author, born in Birmingham, Alabama in 1945, declared that this novelized version of his life, first published by Atlantic Monthly Press in 1989, would have been "too much like a novel" if it had been written as autobiography. The child's teeth are a well-chosen image, composed into a simple but effective design.

◄ Rupert Thomson, *Soft*, London, Bloomsbury, 1998. Cover design by William Webb.

A cover whose design seems to be a postmodern reflection on the designer's own computer-screen image, with its diagonally braced picture boxes, presents a novel about a soft drinks company trying to launch a new product. The book has been described as "a hard-edged satire that simply turns upside down the corruption typically seen in a large corporation."

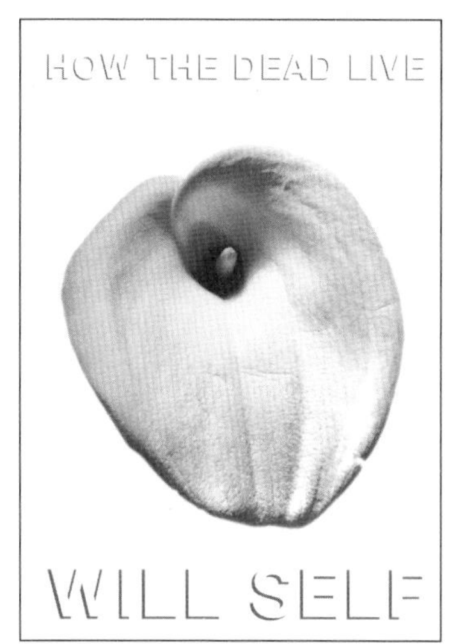

◄ Will Self, *How the Dead Live*, Bloomsbury, 2000. Jacket design by Nathan Burton, photo by Michael Wildsmith.

The cover is appropriately chilling in fashionable white for this title in which the dead don't go to heaven but to a North London suburb called Dulston. Will Self's novel includes many references to his famously disordered lifestyle, which has helped to spread his literary fame. The complexity of language leads readers to compare him to James Joyce, but for some this is no advantage.

◄ Jay McInerney, *How It Ended*, London, Bloomsbury 2000. Jacket design by William Webb, photo by Peter Zeray/Photonica.

A clever juxtaposition of text and image that has abstract design quality while also giving a strong indication of content, all wrapped in candy colours. McInerney claims to like Evelyn Waugh, P. G. Wodehouse, Mark Twain, *Don Quixote*, *Tom Jones*, *The Ginger Man*, and *Ulysses*.

Few critical labels have been more widely and loosely applied than "postmodern". Defined by Marxists as a vigorous stage in the senescence of capitalism, and by art historians as a return to ornament and historicism, postmodernism implies more than just the reaction against modernism. Its ancestors include Lawrence Sterne and James Joyce, both of whom played with the reader's knowledge and expectations of what a story should consist of. With the spirit of play normally comes a distancing from emotional engagement and politics, typical of the aftermath of the 1960s, with all its utopian schemes. *American Psycho* by Bret Easton Ellis exemplifies the amorality of postmodernism, introducing a hero with no saving graces whose crimes are never uncovered. William Gibson, inventor of "cyberpunk", introduces the dimension of computers and information technology. He had to walk out of Ridley Scott's film *Bladerunner* because, he explained, "it looked like the inside of my head." Tom Wolfe is surely one of postmodernism's godparents, with his exposure of the venal world of modern art in *The Painted Word* and a demolition of modern architecture in *From Bauhaus to Our House*. In his novel *The Bonfire of the Vanities*, Wolfe exposed how, in the words of *Time* reviewer R. Z. Sheppard, "a culture geared to profit from the immediate gratification of egos and nerve endings is not a culture at all, but an addiction."

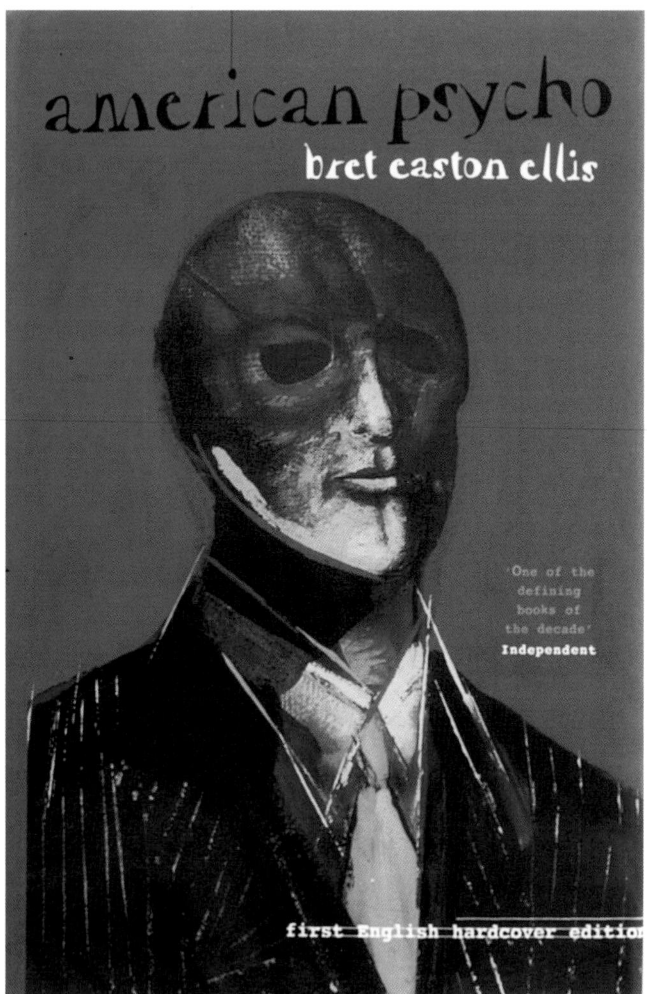

▲ Bret Easton Ellis, *American Psycho*, New York, Simon & Schuster, 1991. Designer unknown.
An appropriately sinister evocation of the anti-hero, Patrick Bateman, who tortures and mutilates random victims from New York's underclass, while maintaining a respectable persona as a businessman. The tale is described by its author as a satirical black comedy on the lack of morality in contemporary America.

◄ Bret Easton Ellis, *Less than Zero*, New York, Simon & Schuster, 1988. Jacket design by George Corsillo.
A sassy but mercifully unexplicit cover for a novel of teenage drugs and sex in Los Angeles, which, in the words of Alan Jenkins, "reproduces with numbing accuracy the intermittent catatonic laws of a psycho-physical system artificially stimulated beyond normal human endurance."

▲ William Gibson, *Virtual Light*, New York, Viking, 1993. Jacket design by Stuart Hunter.
"Technology has already changed us, and we have to figure out a way to stay sane," says William Gibson, whose first novel, *Neuromancer* (1984), outstripped postmodernism in seeing a future dominated by computers. *Virtual Light* is set in a city of the future called "The Sprawl", a concept not far removed from several American cities of today.

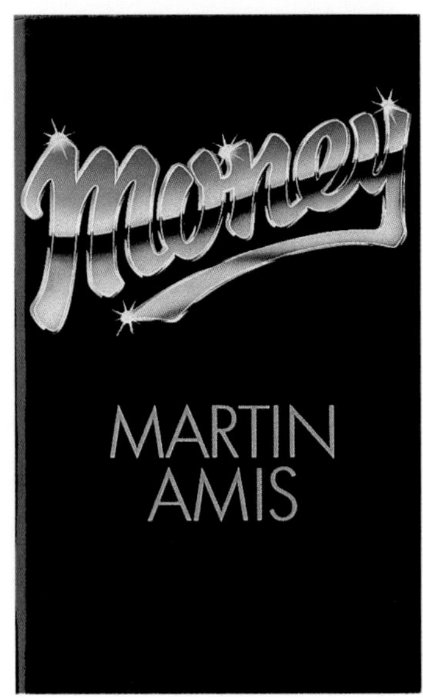

► Martin Amis, *Money*, London, Jonathan Cape, 1984. Jacket design by Mon Mohan and Dick Jones.
Martin Amis made his name with *The Rachel Papers* (1973). *Money* was considered offensive to women and led to a feminist boycott. The cover reflects the nostalgia of postmodernism for the glamour of the 1930s.

◄ Douglas Coupland, *Generation X: Tales for an Accelerated Culture*, New York, St Martin's Press, 1991. Jacket design by Judith Stagnitto.
Coupland's first novel, published in his thirtieth year, won him the description of "the Jack Kerouac of his generation" – a lost generation "with too many TVs and too few job opportunities."

▼ Tom Wolfe, *The Bonfire of the Vanities*, New York, Farrar, Straus & Giroux, 1987. Jacket design by Fred Marcellino.
A retro cover for Wolfe's first proper novel, indicating a return to realism and an abandonment of literary experiment.

Penguin: New Designs

In publishing, the skill of survival is to keep the identity fresh but still recognizable. Pressure always exists to move downmarket, and as the former Fontana art director, Mike Dempsey, wrote in 1980, "many paperback houses have put pressure on their art departments to produce so-called 'selling covers', dripping with gold blocking, resulting in a marked drop in design standards, but they still end up on the remainder shelf looking like old tarts." Penguin has let its design standards go surprisingly loose from time to time, but has kept in mind how corporate identity made its name and fortune long before the phrase itself existed. The structure of the Penguin list still reflects series divisions which were established in the immediate post-war period, such as Penguin Classics and Penguin Modern Classics, whose high editorial standards have made them standard student editions. The formula of using modern or old master paintings in colour, combined with a simple title, first introduced by Germano Facetti in the 1970s, still remains a distinctive quality of these Penguin series, providing a valuable piece of authentic visual context to accompany the text, as well as broadening the visual education of readers. In 2000, Penguin undertook their most recent large-scale redesign, adopting a refreshingly simple and classic formula, using well-chosen images with understated typography, very much in the family tradition.

▼ F. Scott Fitzgerald, *Tender is the Night*, London, Penguin Modern Classics, 1986. Cover design by Penguin, photograph by Cecil Beaton. Cecil Beaton made his early reputation photographing his two tolerant elder sisters, Nancy and Baba, with the bobbed hair of the 1920s flapper that evokes the mood of Scott Fitzgerald's book, first published in 1934. The last-but-one series identity for Penguin Modern Classics is a counterchange with the black label of Penguin Classics.

▼ J. D. Salinger, *The Catcher in the Rye*, London, Penguin Modern Classics, 1994. Cover design by Penguin. Salinger's restrictions on the cover design of his books (see page 63) offer a challenge that most graphic designers would be pleased to take up, but which few marketing departments would voluntarily embrace.

▲ Emily Brontë, *Wuthering Heights*, London, Penguin Classics, 1995. Cover design by Penguin, detail of "The Moreland Path" by Henry Bright. A Turneresque watercolour of appropriate date for the text evokes the atmosphere of one of the world's best-known novels. The composition of the serpentine path carried up into the swirl of smoke and cloud is especially suitable for adaptation as a cover.

► Leo Tolstoy, *War and Peace*, London, Penguin Classics, 1982. Cover design by Penguin, detail of "The 1812 Retreat – The Battle of Borodino" by Vereschagin. The framing of the detail on the front cover is typical of the traditional turn in cover design in the early 1980s.

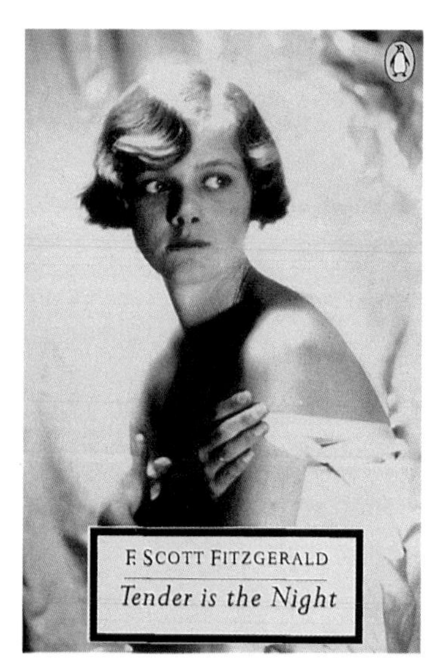

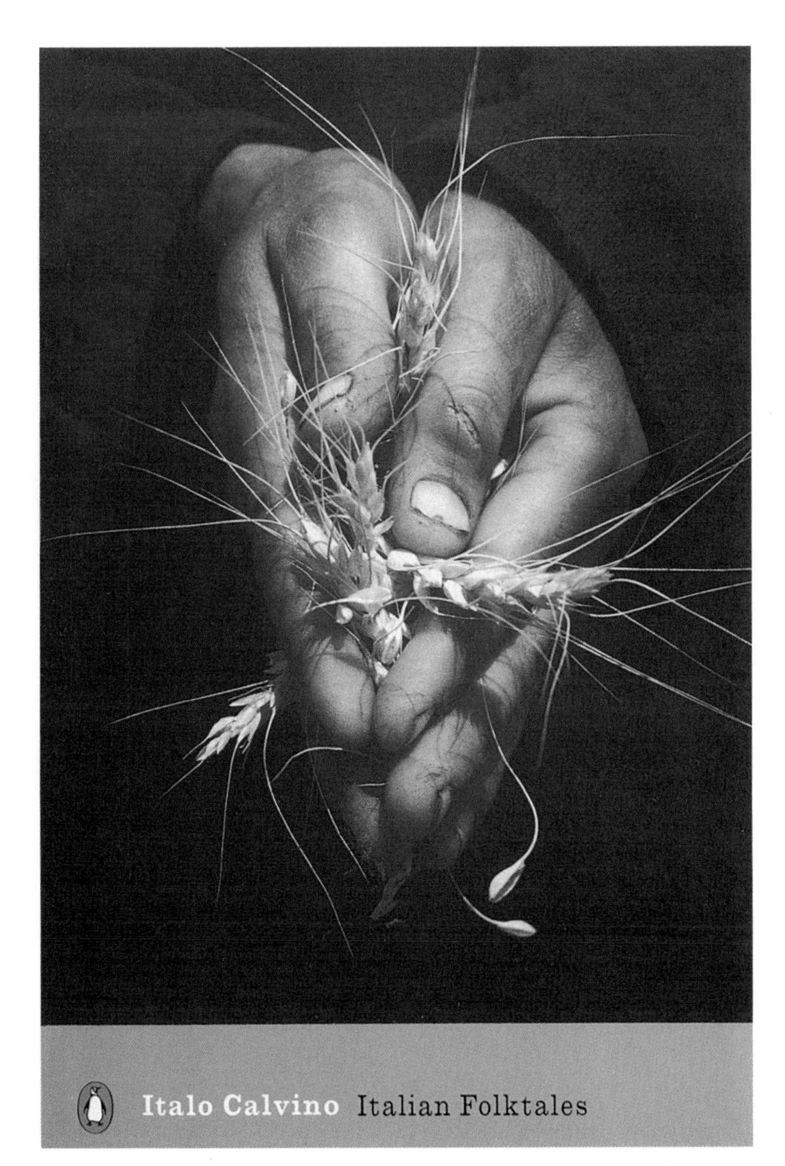

◄ Martin Amis, *Money*, London, Penguin, c2000. Cover design by Douglas Brothers.
For modern fiction, the Penguin brand identity may be more of a liability than an asset, and this cover sports the Antarctic bird discreetly in one corner of a typical 1990s "photoshop" montage.

▼ George Orwell, *Homage to Catalonia*, London, Penguin, 1987. Cover design by Penguin, illustration by Christopher Corr.
Gill Sans Bold lettering refers to the period in which this classic of the Spanish Civil War was written. The knowing naivety of Christopher Corr's illustration is representative of a trend in hand-drawn illustration in the 1980s.

▲ Italo Calvino, *Italian Folktales*, London, Penguin Modern Classics, 2000. Cover design by Penguin, photograph by Albert Watson.
Calvino's methodical collection of stories was undertaken to emphasize their structural similarities. The image evokes the agrarian background from which the stories emerged, with a hint of magic.

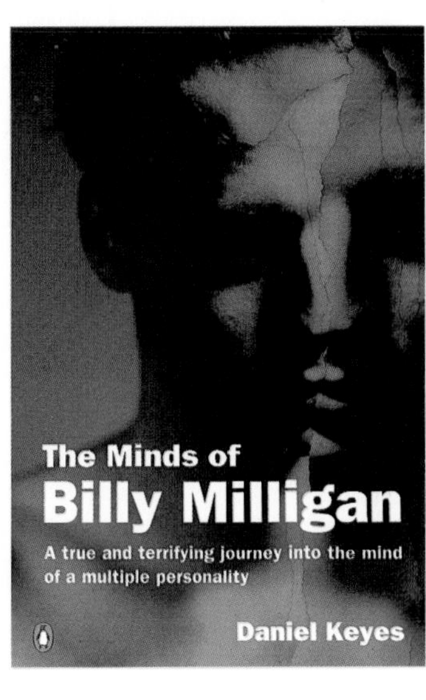

► Daniel Keyes, *The Minds of Billy Milligan*, London, Penguin, 1993. Jacket design by Penguin, photograph by Richard Ivey.
Written by a doctor and psychiatrist, the book describes a real-life case of multiple personlatiy disorder, written with the agreement of 'several of Milligan's selves.'

Pocket Canons

◄ *Jonah*, introduced by Alasdair Gray, Edinburgh, Canongate, 1999. Cover photo by Minden/Robert Harding Picture Library.
The whale (which actually occurs in the text as "a great fish") is the one thing everyone knows about the book of Jonah.

▼ *Ruth*, introduced by Joanna Trollope, 1999, photo by Brian David Stevens/ Refocus. *Ecclesiastes*, introduced by Doris Lessing, 1998, photo by Michael Wildsmith. *Exodus*, introduced by David Grossman, 1999, photo H. Skodvin/ Millennium. Edinburgh, Canongate.

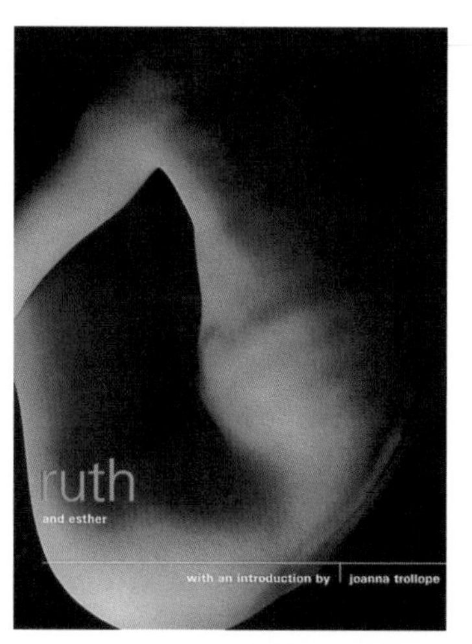

Canongate is "the youngest and hippest publisher of the lot", to use the phrase from the *Big Issue*, the magazine sold by the homeless on the streets of British cities. The Edinburgh imprint became independent after a management buy-out in 1994, at a time when, despite continuing economic recession, there was a strong feeling of cultural independence in Scotland, which came to fruition with the establishment of a Scottish Assembly at the end of the decade. Canongate explained, "when you're small, the energy makes up for the lack of capital," and have proceeded to justify this claim. Perhaps only a publisher in a country with a strong Bible tradition and no fear of appearing overly pious would have thought of launching the Pocket Canons, a series of reprints of individual books of the Bible with introductions by authors and media figures on the meaning and significance of the texts. The series was an immediate success, helped no doubt by the strong visual appeal of the covers. They were all designed by Angus Hyland at Pentagram and have no overt theological content. The *Guardian* called it "the most radical repackaging of the Bible for decades – brilliantly simple"; and the Scottish author A. L. Kennedy commented, "Few with faith in literature, humanity, or altogether higher powers would ask for more."

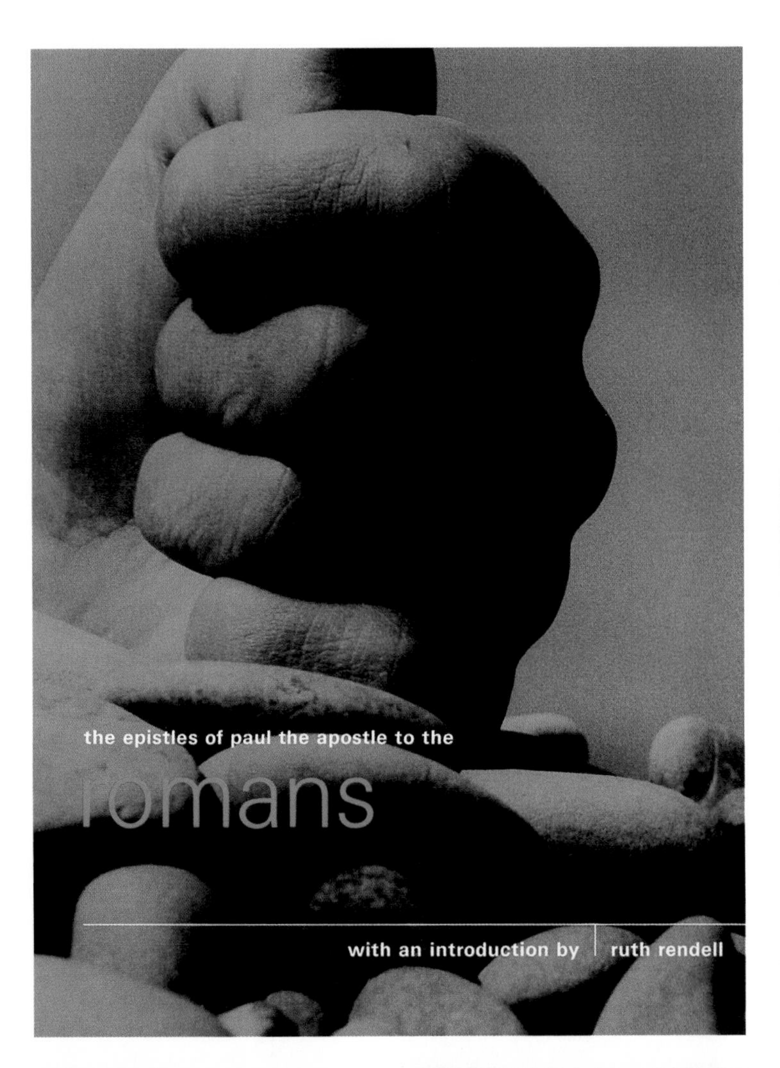

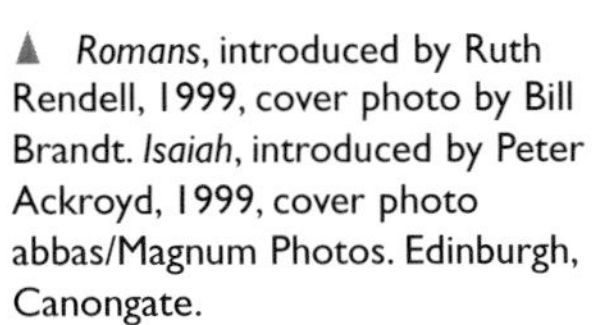

▲ *Romans*, **introduced by Ruth Rendell, 1999, cover photo by Bill Brandt.** ***Isaiah*, introduced by Peter Ackroyd, 1999, cover photo abbas/Magnum Photos. Edinburgh, Canongate.**
Most books of the Bible offer opportunities for dramatic imagery. Bill Brandt's image of a clenched fist for Romans is a timeless image, presumably chosen to indicate the imposition of Roman rule on the early Christian world.

▲ *Revelation*, **introduced by Will Self, Edinburgh, Canongate, 1998. Cover photo by Renni Burri/Magnum Photos.**
The recent public promotion of the work of the Magnum Photo agency, through books and exhibitions, has fed a fashion for period black and white photography. Black and white photos printed on colour presses, as they now mostly are, succeed in achieving a depth of tone lacking from older reproductions.

▲ *Corinthians*, **introduced by Fay Weldon, 1998. Cover photo George by Rodger/ Magnum Photos.** ***Luke*, introduced by Richard Holloway, 1998. Cover photo Didier Gallard/Special Photographers Company. Edinburgh, Canongate.**
Comfortable feelings of alienation characterize the Pocket Canon covers: each image is striking in itself and displays a family likeness. The introductions offer the musings of a well-known writer.

▲ *Proverbs*, **introduced by Charles Johnson, Edinburgh, Canongate, 1998. Cover photo by Richard Waite/Special Photographers Company.**
Images of pebbles were high fashion in 1998. The internet has become a boon to picture researchers looking for cover images, as many agencies and archives are able to display their stock which might have previously been more difficult to access.

Black Sparrow Press

The Black Sparrow Press, based in Santa Rosa, California, was started by John Martin in the mid-1960s. He was working in an office supplies firm, but had a desire to publish the works of one author in particular, Charles Bukowski. As a hard-drinking postal worker, Bukowski was an equally unlikely figure, but Martin offered him $100 a month if he would leave his job and write poetry full time. This was a visionary act, and it paid off since Black Sparrow made Bukowski's name as both poet and novelist. Black Sparrow books all have distinctive covers, reminiscent of the best of the 1920s avant-garde in their use of plain colours and sans-serif lettering, producing a commentary on the title or the content in a direct manner. These are all designed by the founder's wife, Barbara Martin, who says, "It's simply a visual matter – how colours relate to one another and how the type, design elements and space work on the page." She admits an influence from Percy Wyndham Lewis, the English avant-garde artist whose works have been reissued by Black Sparrow. The use of overlapping lettering and diagonal layouts was achieved by a variety of technical means in the past, including metal type and Letraset. Barbara Martin still resists using computers and shows how the specific limitations of the older methods were a good discipline and could stimulate creativity.

◄ Charles Bukowski, *The Captain is Out to Lunch and the Sailors Have Taken Over the Ship,* Santa Rosa, Black Sparrow Press, 1998. Cover design by Barbara Martin.
The illustration and typography are well matched in this four-colour design.

▼ Charles Bukowski, *Bone Palace Ballet,* Santa Rosa, Black Sparrow Press, 1997. Cover design by Barbara Martin.
This cover has a cartoon-like image displaying great vitality, which is set against a subtly balletic typography.

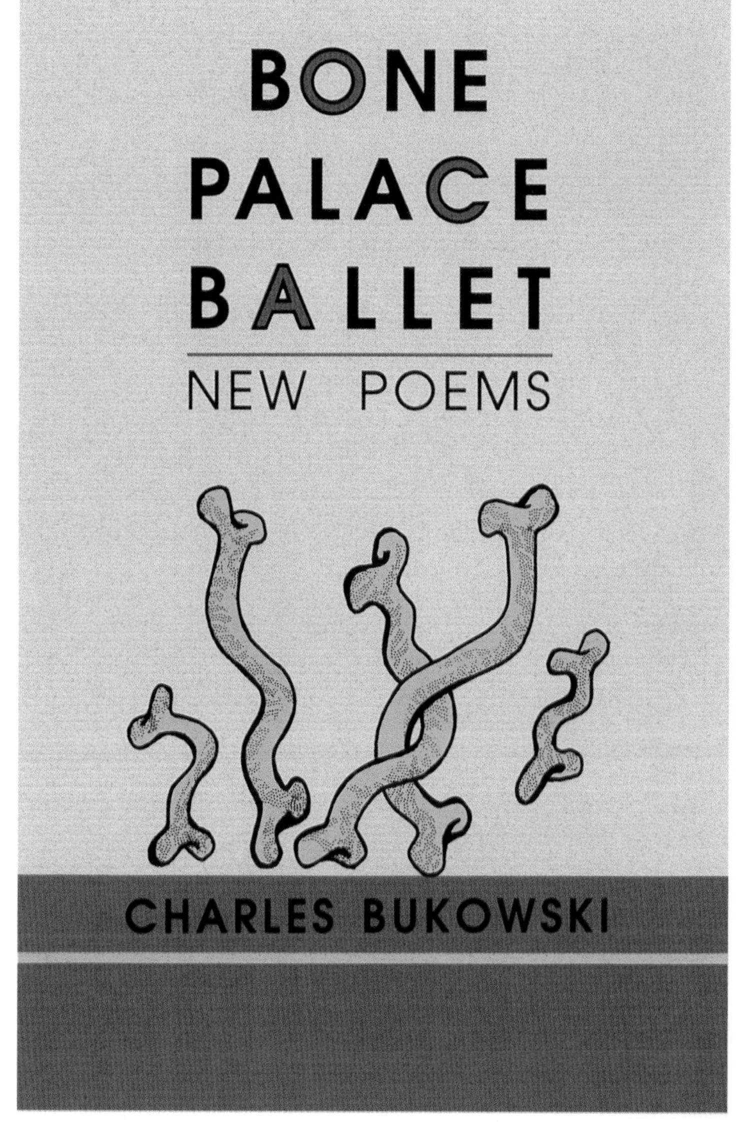

▲ Charles Bukowski, *Post Office*, Santa Rosa, Black Sparrow Press, 1971. Cover design by Barbara Martin.
This cover teases, entertains, and informs all at once by the simplest of means.

► Charles Bukowski, *Betting on the Muse*, Santa Rosa, Black Sparrow Press, 1996. Cover design by Barbara Martin.
A well-chosen action photograph is linked to the lettering by the technique of overlapping the title and author's name with the image.

◄ Charles Bukowski, *Mocking Bird Wish Me Luck*, Santa Rosa, Black Sparrow Press, 1972. Cover design by Barbara Martin.
Pure lettering is often highly effective in jacket design, although it needs to work through oblique suggestion to indicate the content of the book. The contrast in spacing between the title and the author's name here contributes to the dynamism of the design as much as the variation in colour and the unorthodox word break do.

▼ Charles Bukowski, *Women*, Santa Rosa, Black Sparrow Press, 1978. Cover design by Barbara Martin.
The classical quality of the two framed panels on this cover is disrupted by the naive yet disturbing drawing, which pushes at the corner of the frame.

Andrzej Klimowski

Born in London to Polish emigré parents in 1949, Andrzej Klimowski studied at St Martin's School of Art, but unexpectedly returned to Poland in 1973–80. There he specialized in poster design and made films in a political climate where graphic communication was not merely oil for the wheels of capitalism, but a way of maintaining hope of a better future than Communism could provide. It is appropriate that Klimowski, on his return to London, should have had a success with the cover designs for Milan Kundera's books, a writer (b. 1929) whose work was suppressed after the Russian invasion of Czechoslovakia in 1968, and who eventually found refuge in France in 1975. The dark ironies of intellectual life under an oppressive regime are reflected in his consistent and powerful use of black and in his surreally inspired collaged images, in which bodies are fragmented, often with their heads obscured. The juxtaposition of photography (vintage or fake-vintage) with enlarged sections of engravings is similar to practices of surrealist collage, and creates an effect of alienation. Klimowski added to his reputation with a wordless graphic novel, published by Faber and Faber, *The Depository, A Dream Book* (1994), and for some years designed many Faber covers within the format established by the Pentagram Partnership.

▲ Milan Kundera, *The Farewell Party*, London, King Penguin, 1984. Cover design by Andrzej Klimowski.
Kundera's third novel was first published in 1976. The cover design illustrates the central theme, of a young girl's attempt to seduce her guardian so that she can feel the triumph of her will over circumstance. The composed lines of the figure have an abstract quality in the shallow space and are claustrophobically blocked by wooden planking.

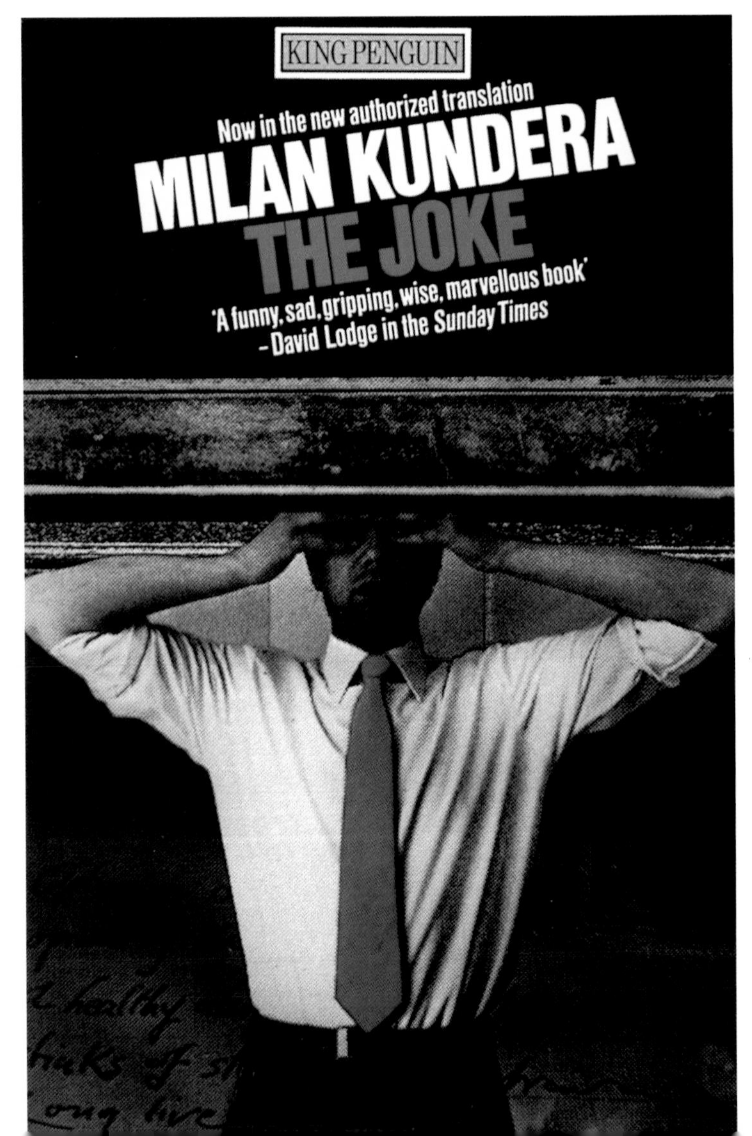

► Milan Kundera, *The Joke*, King Penguin, London, 1984. Cover design by Andrzej Klimowski.
When Milan Kundera published this, his first book, in Prague in 1967, its subversive message was so popular that three editions sold out within days. The following year, the suppression of the "Prague Spring" meant that the book was removed from libraries and banned. It was first published in English in 1992. Klimowski's covers for this and *The Farewell Party* are evidently intended as a pair.

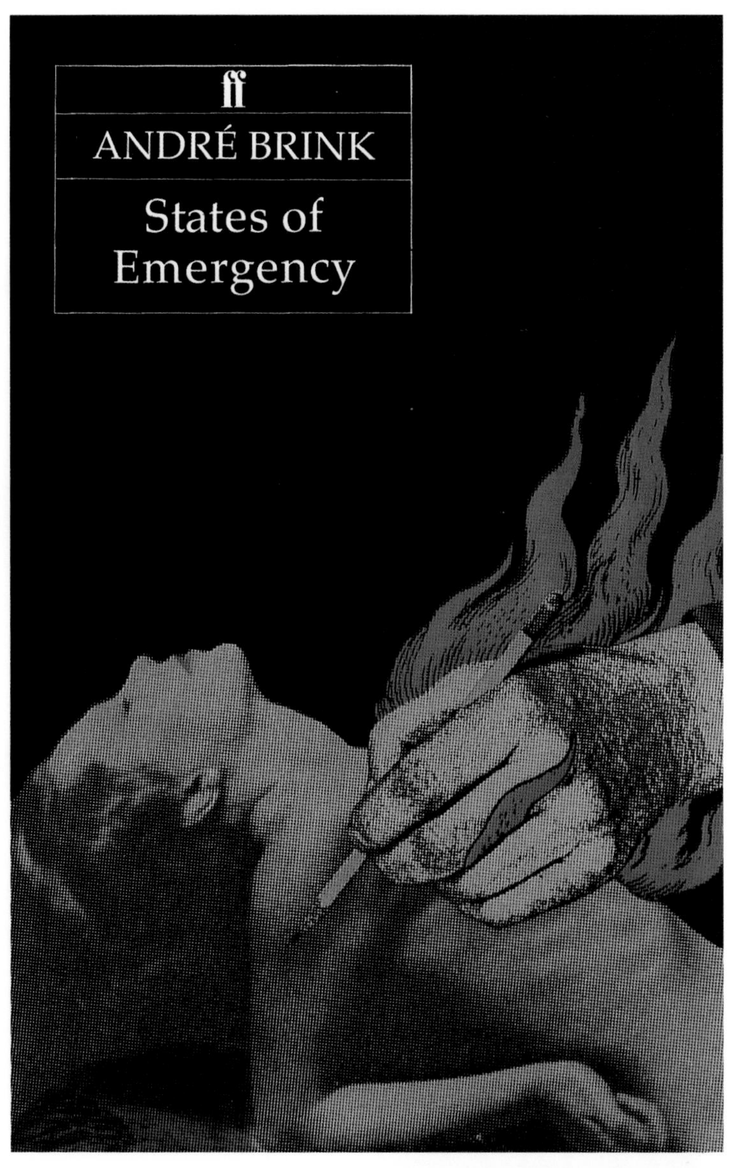

◄ Milan Kundera, *Life is Elsewhere*, London, Faber and Faber, 1986. Cover design by Andrzej Klimowski.
A typical example of Klimowski's layering of collaged images, which gives the effect of a seventeenth-century allegory or emblem.

▼ Rachel Ingalls, *The End of Tragedy*, London, Faber and Faber, 1987. Cover design by Andrzej Klimowski.
A further example of the headless torso and armless hand in Klimowski's oeuvre. It illustrates a book of horror stories by an American writer living in London, which was first published by Faber and Faber in 1987.

▲ André Brink, *States of Emergency*, London, Faber and Faber, 1988. Cover design by Andrzej Klimowski.
In this novel by a South African author, a writer finds that neither love nor art offers an escape from the reality of racism, violence, and death. The plot is driven by the death of Jane Fergusson, who sends him a manuscript before setting fire to herself. These elements are depicted in the design, but symbolically rather than realistically.

► Mario Vargas Llosa, *Who Killed Palomino Molero?*, Faber and Faber, 1987. Cover design by Andrzej Klimowski.
The novel concerns a military officer's assignment to provide prostitutes for the troops in the Peruvian jungle, a subject with humorous and grim aspects.

Granta

Granta is the title of a magazine, taking its name from one of two names of the river that flows through the ancient university city of Cambridge. (The river is also known more prosaically as the Cam.) After running for years as a university-based magazine, Granta widened its scope in the 1980s under the editorship of Bill Buford and became internationally known, especially for its new fiction, while the link to the university was effectively abandoned. The Granta book imprint was founded in 1997 as an independent company, publishing both new titles and reprints, with authors that included Jenny Diski and Iain Sinclair. The year of New Labour's election must have seemed a good moment to launch this enterprise, at a time of expansion in the economy generally, and in book retailing in particular. Granta is one of several new imprints which have demonstrated that larger publishers are likely to miss opportunities in fiction, and that readers like the cultural *cachet* that comes from an apparently small and independent list. The Granta covers shown here are typical of book design at the very end of the twentieth century. They have small-scale title lettering, linked to dominant, brighter-than-life colours and single, clearly recognizable photographic images, interpreting the content of the books, which are often treated by computer to enhance their impact. There is no attempt at a dominant house identity, just a small tag in the top right-hand corner of the front cover, which is repeated on the spine.

▲ Colson Whitehead, *The Intuitionist*, London, Granta, 1999. Cover design by Peter Dyer, photo Steve Wiley.
Elevators, as illustrated on the cover, feature strongly in this novel which was described by *The Face* as being "about the darkness and dreams of big cities, about the gloom of lift shafts and the joy of elevators, about the dangers of perfect solutions and corporate hijacking."

▼ **Steven Heighton, *The Shadow Boxer*, London, Granta, 2000. Cover design by Peter Dyer, photograph by Niki Sianni.**
This Canadian novel describes a young man's hopes of a career as a writer in the big city (Toronto) and the disillusions that follow from experience as his identity begins to be transformed. He retreats to an island on Lake Superior, the scene of his childhood, and through the course of a winter's hardship learns to understand and accept the reality of history and his own identity.

▼ **Don Hannah, *The Wise and Foolish Virgins*, London, Granta, 1999. Cover design by Peter Dyer, photograph by Robert Clifford.**
Another Canadian novel, set in a small town in a tangle of dreams and hallucinations, on which *The Times* commented, "A wonderfully sinister novel, almost Gothic. . . Hannah writes with a smooth precision, making the ordinary seem anything but."

▼ **Moshin Hamid, *Moth Smoke*, London, Granta, 2000. Cover design by Peter Dyer, photograph by Spiros Politis.**
This novel is set against the background of Pakistan's controversial nuclear tests in 1998. It is a story of personal decline and heroin addiction, which has been described as "a modern riff on the poetic Sufi image of the moth's love for the candle," hence the title and the cover image.

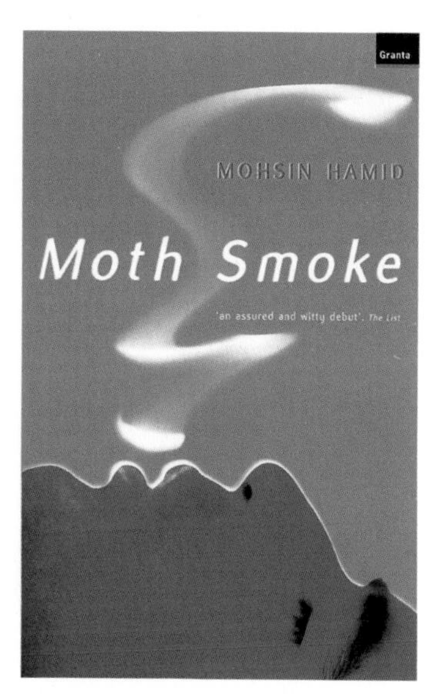

▼ **Deborah Eisenberg, *All Around Atlantis*, London, Granta, 1998. Cover design by React, photograph by The Douglas Brothers.**
A collection of stories by an American author, who was born in 1945; it was first published in the US by Farrar, Straus & Giroux in 1997. In the title story, the narrator recalls her strange and dislocated childhood in New York.

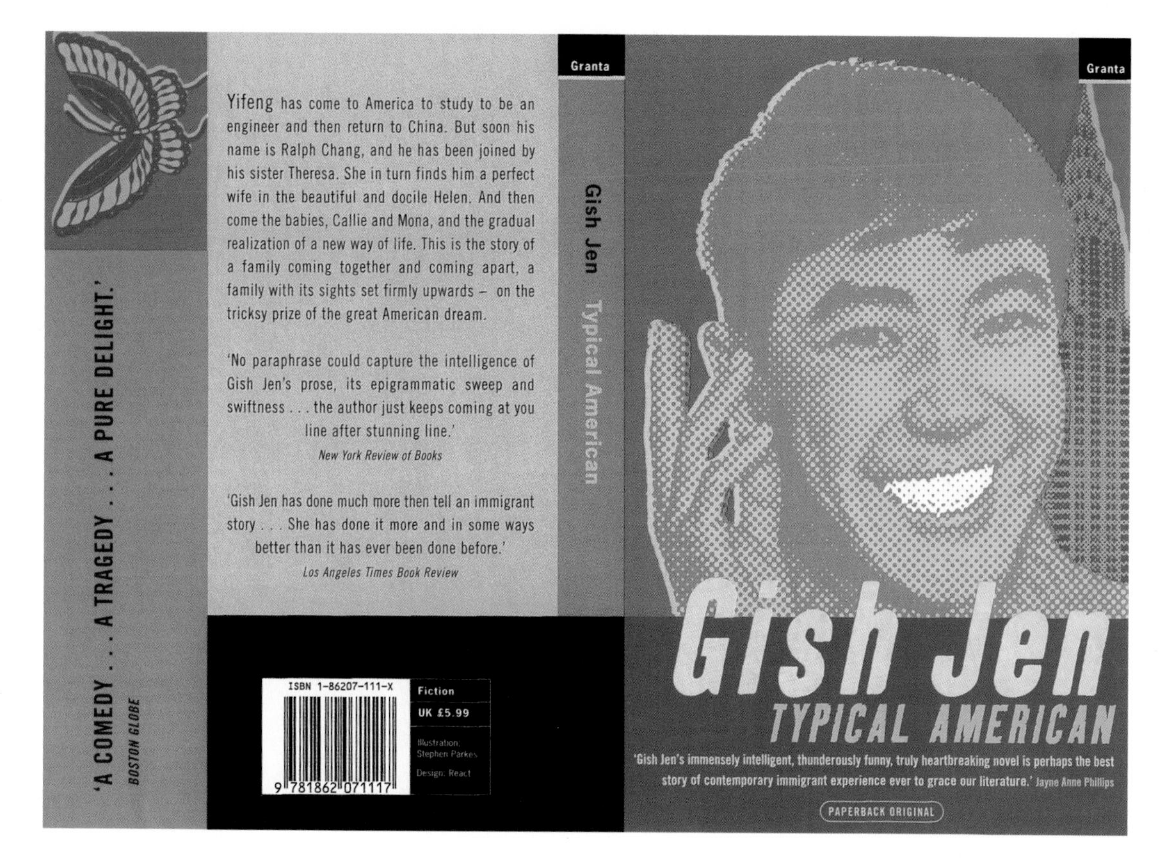

◄ **Gish Jen, *Typical American*, London, Granta, 1998. Cover design by React, illustration by Stephen Parker.**
In a novel first published in 1991, an Asian-American writer explores the position of the immigrant experiencing the freedom and the illusory promises of the New World. This "wise but sweet, hopeful but knowing" tale concludes with his success running a fast-food chicken restaurant. The cover shows how back and front are used in conjunction to present a sequence of verbal and visual information about the book.

Jeff Fisher

Jeff Fisher came to London from Australia in the 1970s and made a reputation during the boom in hand-drawn illustration that preceded the age of computers. His style is instantly recognizable, although, like all successful illustrators, he has been much imitated. A typical Jeff Fisher design includes hand-drawn lettering which is integral to the image, and clearly legible even if in a parody version of old-fashioned script. His figures are usually doll-like and slightly grotesque, and colour is used to create naive and decorative forms that have a memorable rightness. In these aspects, and in its ability to convey information with humour, his work resembles that of Edward Bawden, an artist Fisher greatly admires. His loose decorative devices of cross-hatching and squiggles owe something to the Bloomsbury Group artists, Vanessa Bell and Duncan Grant, whose decorative work was rediscovered when their home, Charleston Farmhouse in Sussex, was opened to the public in the late 1980s. Fisher's best-known work, the cover of *Captain Corelli's Mandolin*, came after a number of other successes, including jackets for a neo-traditional hardback reprint series issued by Bloomsbury in the early 1990s. It was a slightly unusual choice for a fiction title, but subsequently became inseparable from one of the most successful novels of the decade.

▲ **Ian Hamilton, editor, *Soho Square II*, London, Bloomsbury, 1989. Cover design by Jeff Fisher.**
A soft-bound anthology with a wrap-around cover, *Soho Square* was an occasional publication from the early days of Bloomsbury, promoting its authors and providing a civilized mix of illustration and photography. Jeff Fisher is often at his best when drawing slightly absurd, "children's book-like" covers filled with incongruous incident.

► **Will Self, *Cock and Bull*, London, Bloomsbury, 1992. Cover design by Jeff Fisher.**
An early work by Will Self (b. 1961), consisting of two linked novellas about sex change. The stories are intended to show Self's anger at the way "we fit into our sex roles as surely as if we had cut them off the back of a cereal packet and pasted them on to ourselves." The result was criticized for its "blatant sexism". Fisher's jacket is a literal interpretation of the title, bolder in style than some of his other work, but distanced from the subject through a hint of absurdity.

▲ **Peter Redgrove, *The One Who Set Out to Study Fear*, London, Bloomsbury, 1989. Cover design by Jeff Fisher.**
The fairy-tale quality of this dark version of magic realism is well conveyed in the multiple images of the jacket, which is deliberately limited in its colours, like all Fisher's work, to recapture the visual discipline of the pre-war period and its printing techniques.

► **Louis de Bernières, *The Troublesome Offspring of Cardinal Guzman*, London, Vintage, 1998. Cover design by Jeff Fisher.**
A novel, first published in 1994 and set in fashionable South America, offers scope for Fisher's style of individual images within a whole. The novel explores "Issues of freedom, power and ideology" through the tale of an imaginary hero, "a decent man, unpredictable, savage and comically grotesque."

▼ **Louis de Bernières, *Captain Corelli's Mandolin*, London, Vintage, 1998. Cover design by Jeff Fisher.**
One day soon, students will write dissertations explaining the magnetic attraction of this cover design which, in an age of computer graphics, indicates the power of hand, eye, and paintbrush.

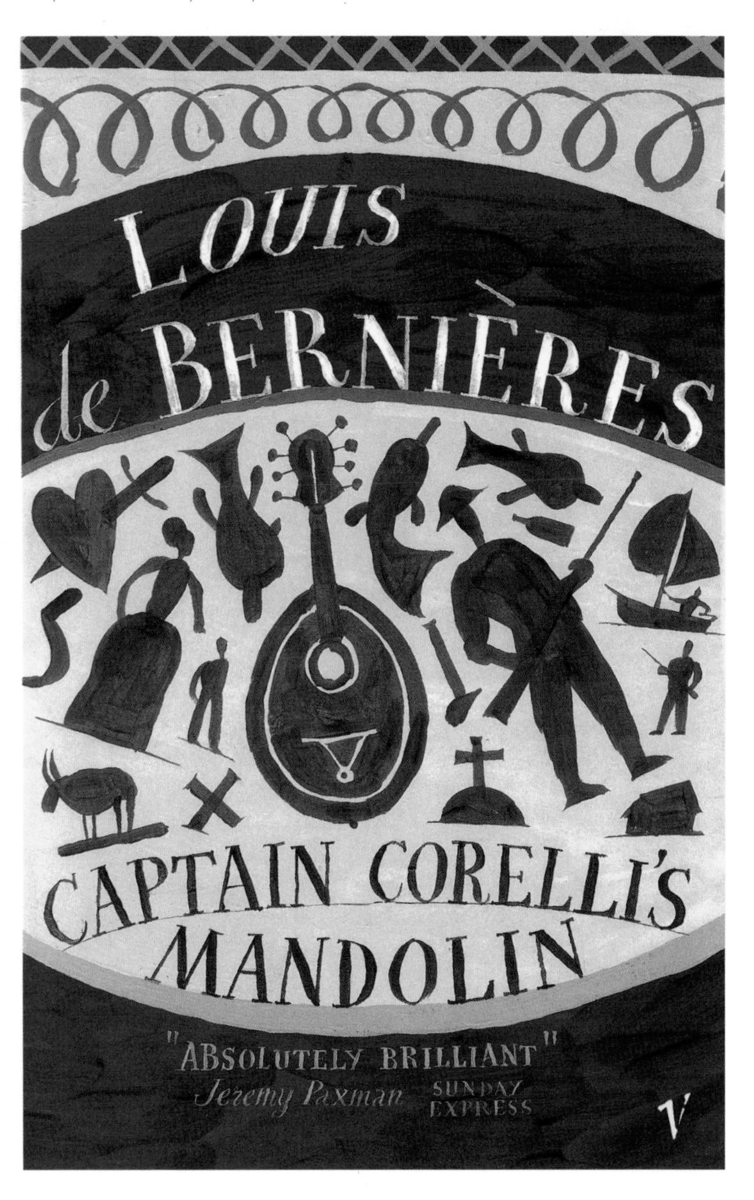

Indigo

Indigo was launched in 1994 by Liz Knight and George Sharp, formerly art director at Cassell, as the main paperback list of Victor Gollancz Ltd. The lead title was Nick Hornby's best-selling novel *Fever Pitch*, a Gollancz hardback. Gollancz was taken over by the large London-based conglomerate Orion, and Indigo was relaunched in August 2000, but only lasted until January 2001. The covers were all the work of art director and designer Gary Day-Ellison, who had left Picador in 1988. He found conditions at Indigo more difficult, however, than at Picador, as there was more committee interference and a range of viewpoints had to be accommodated on the covers, leading to less coherence. The Indigo logo does not generally appear on the books' front covers, but for its use elsewhere, Day-Ellison decided to avoid the obvious colour connotation, decreeing that the word itself should appear in any colour except Indigo, on a series of different backgrounds. This is a typical example of his pleasure in sending secret visual messages through apparently standard design elements. Another example was his rearrangeable set of covers for Douglas Adams's *Hitchhiker's Guide to the Galaxy* (published by Pan) which also include on their spines a colour-coded version of the number 42, the number declared in the book to be the answer to the secret of the universe.

▲ Nick Hornby, *High Fidelity*, London, Indigo, 1995. Cover design and art direction by Gary Day-Ellison.
A simple but ingenious use of lettering and near-abstract imagery describes the setting of Hornby's second novel in a record shop in North London Rob, aged 35, works and tries to understand what motivates the female half of the human species which does not share his obsession with music.

► Tim Earnshaw, *Helium*, London, Indigo, 1996. Cover design and art direction by Gary Day-Ellison, illustration by Chris Moore.
A story set in a lightly fictionalized version of Los Angeles starts with a character whose fly-away hair causes him problems. The cover illustration captures the tragicomic qualities of the novel with its ingenious play on the title word and its surreal isolated cloud.

▲ **Richard Glyn Jones, editor, *Naked Graffiti*, London, Indigo, 1996. Cover design and art direction by Gary Day-Ellison, photo by Robert Clifford.**
A distinguished assembly of favourite authors writing on a theme which grows increasingly important as a means of understanding society. The cover presents its information clearly, with an image which, although "red-hot", indicates that this is the land of the respectable and intellectual erotic.

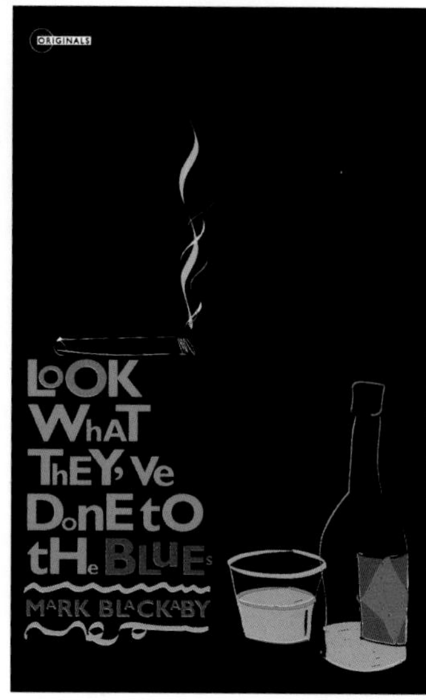

► **Mark Blackaby, *Look What They've Done to the Blues*, London, Indigo, 1996. Cover design and art direction by Gary Day-Ellison.**
The second novel by the winner of the 1995 Betty Trask Prize for fiction, this is the story of Gideon Charles Lucas, a modern-day Alfie. Educated and charming, he's been in prison and now spends his life avoiding commitment and dabbling in antiques. The cover was designed using a deliberately unsophisticated software package.

◄ **Richard Glyn Jones, editor, *Love is Strange*, London, Indigo, 1996. Design and art direction by Gary Day-Ellison.**
One of the in-house editors found this picture, and Day-Ellison adapted it to suit the design, giving full rein to his love of strong colour.

▼ **Joe R. Lansdale, *Mucho Mojo*, London, Indigo, 1995. Cover design and art direction by Gary Day-Ellison.**
A murdered child is discovered under the floorboards of a house inherited from the uncle of Leonard, the gay Vietnam veteran who forms one half of an investigative team with Hap Collins, in "an acute commentary on matters of race, friendship, and love in small town America". The cover is an another cut-price computer job with naive charm.

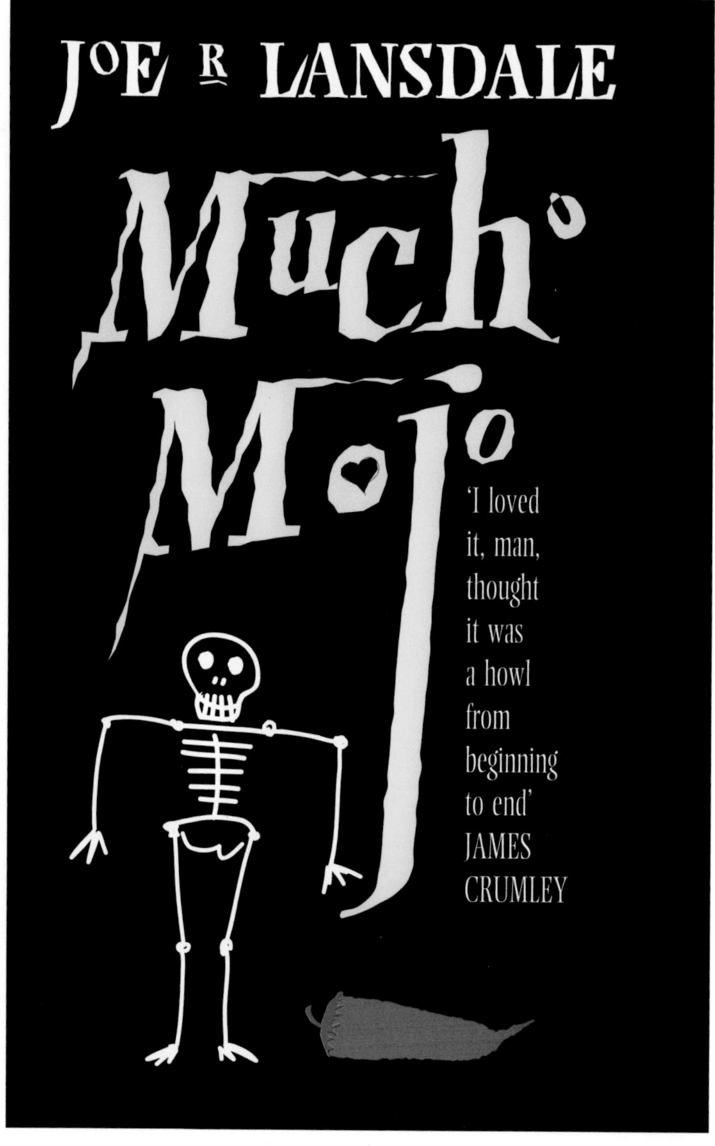

Rebel Inc

Granta and Rebel Inc indicate a trend toward launching imprints from literary magazines. Rebel Inc sounds American, but is actually based in Edinburgh, for, as far as the world of writing goes, America is a state of mind. The magazine's founding editor, Kevin Williamson, does indeed represent Scottish authors such as Laura Hird and Toni Davidson, along with European and American names, including the cult author Richard Brautigan, one of the leading lights of the "beat" generation, who committed suicide on a remote mountain in 1984 and is now a cult figure once more. Part of the list is defined as "classic outsider texts", and includes non-fiction, such as Howard Sounes's biography of Charles Bukowski (see pp.122–3). Rebel Inc is a division of Canongate Books (see pp.120–1) and its black and white photographic covers are similar in style to the Pocket Canon series, both coming from Angus Hyland at Pentagram. For the Rebel Inc Classic list, the circular title "label", positioned beside one of three edges of the front cover, is a simple device but one never actually employed consistently before in the history of publishing. As a geometric figure, it is much kinder to the visual form of photographs than a rectangular label and allows for a double-take, being both "alternative" and "classic" in the disciplined typographic layout.

◄ James Meek, *The Museum of Doubt*, Edinburgh, Rebel Inc, 2000. Cover © Arno Rafael Minkkinen, self-portrait, Asikkala, Finland, (8.8.88) 1988. Courtesy Barry Friedman Ltd, New York; NCE Paris. Cover design by James Hutcheson.
Meek introduces a series of characters through which he explores the bizarre and the perverse. The cover is alluring but strangely peaceful by contrast.

▲ Toni Davidson, *Scar Culture*, Edinburgh, Rebel Inc, 1999. Cover design by Angus Hyland/Pentagram, photos by Peter Ross © 1997.
A disturbing but compelling novel about child abuse, written in a dislocated filmic style. The cover, which scarcely hints at the contents but suggests cool with a hint of menace, is an unusual example of the integration of lettering and image.

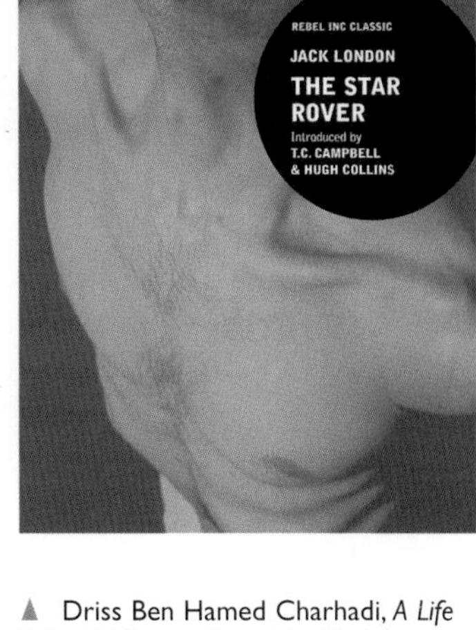

▲ Driss Ben Hamed Charhadi, *A Life Full of Holes*, tranlsated by Paul Bowles, Edinburgh, Rebel Inc, 1999. Cover design Angus Hyland/Pentagram, photo Peter Ross © 1999.
Survival, in the face of oppression. The narrator is always in dire poverty, working by turns as a shepherd, a baker's helper, and a petty trafficker in "kif".

▲ Jack London, *The Star Rover*, Edinburgh, Rebel Inc, 1999. Cover design by Angus Hyland/Pentagram, photos Peter Ross © 1999.
The last book of a turn-of-the-century writer, completed in 1915. London describes prison life in all its horror, contrasting the humanity of the inmates with the malign authority of the prison.

▲ Robert Sabbag, *Snowblind*, Edinburgh, Rebel Inc, 1998. Cover design by Angus Hyland/Pentagram, photos by Peter Ross.
A cult classic about the cocaine trade between Bogota and New York which does not flinch from glamorizing it. Sabbag's book was described by Hunter S. Thompson as "A flat-out ballbuster. It moves like a threshing machine with a fuel tank full of ether." The cover presents an appropriately disturbing image.

► Richard Brautigan, *A Confederate General from Big Sur*, Edinburgh, Rebel Inc, 1999. Cover design by Angus Hyland/Pentagram, photo Peter Ross.
Brautigan's first novel, first published in 1964. Brautigan was described by Stephen Schneck as "a special (very special) correspondent from a terribly literate sort of Field & Stream magazine."

◄ Jim Dodge, *Stone Junction*, Edinburgh, Rebel Inc, 1997. Cover design by Angus Hyland/Pentagram, photos Peter Ross © 1997.
Subtitled "An Alchemical Potboiler" and described as "a rollicking, frequently surprising adventure-cum-fairy tale", this is the best-known work of an author who lists his religion in a reference book as "reborn again Taoist dirt pagan".

◄ John Fante, *Ask the Dust*, Edinburgh, Rebel Inc, 1998. Cover design by Angus Hyland/Pentagram. Photos by Peter Ross © 1998.
The image of the period typewriter indicates the content, as one of a series of novels about Arturo Bandini, a fictional poet in the Los Angeles of the 1930s, by an author (1911–83) who was himself a screenwriter as well as a novelist.

Grove/Atlantic

The Grove Atlantic imprint was formed from an amalgamation between the Grove Press, founded in New York in 1917, and the book publishing arm of the important magazine, *The Atlantic Monthly*. It is a general publisher, mainly of fiction titles, which also formed a transatlantic link with the London firm of Weidenfeld and Nicolson, now part of the Orion Group.

The works illustrated here show the wide range of design possibilities, when an art director (Krystyna Skalski for all the examples illustrated), works with a range of artists producing imagery appropriate to very diverse book titles. These jackets are notable for a creative attitude to lettering, integrated with the illustration in style or in crossing over with the pictorial subject matter, giving a strong sense of the book's identity.

It is interesting to question whether American book jackets still have a distinctively different style, even in a time of increasing globalization. One would expect them to be more assertive and direct in content, but although some of these examples qualify under such criteria, they also include some subtle and even decorative qualities, in the jacket for Milan Kundera's *Immortality*, or even the deceptively sweet-looking design for Kathy Acker's *In Memoriam to Identity*. These designs show that there is little danger of the identity of individual books or of creatively minded publishing houses yet becoming an object of mourning.

▲ J. B. Miller, *My Life in Action Painting*, New York, Grove Atlantic, c1990. Art Director Krystyna Skalski, jacket design by Marc Lohen.
A title for a novel which invites a visual response receives a controlled piece of casual-seeeming design.

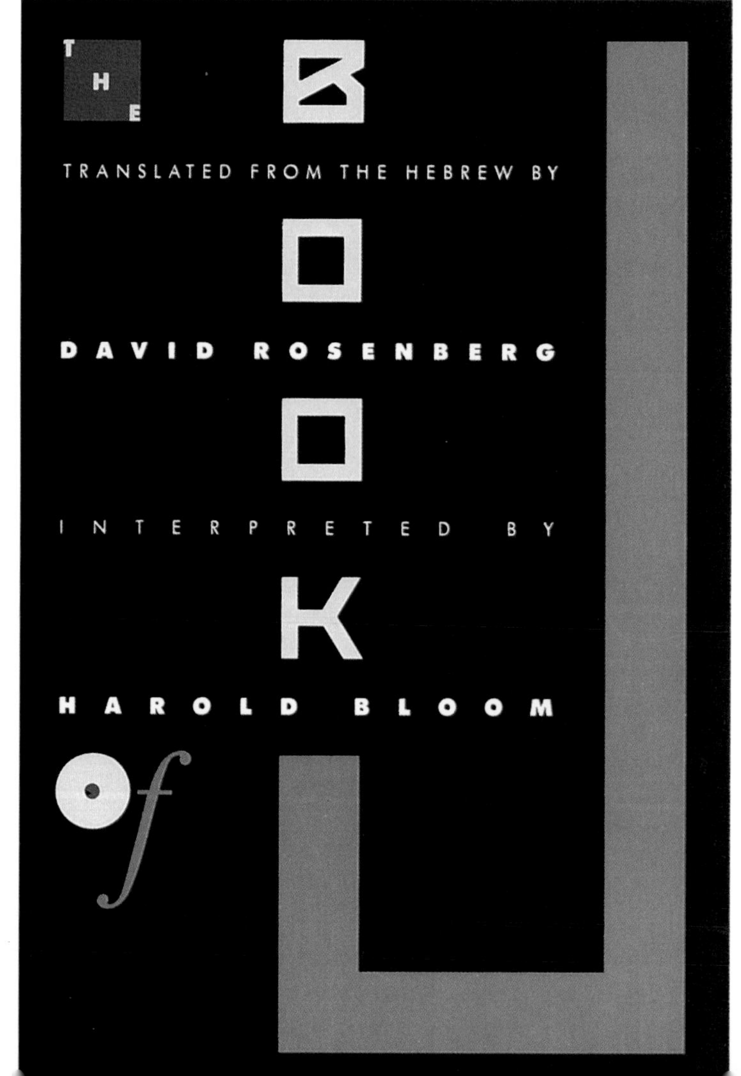

► *The Book of J.*, translated by David Rosenberg, interpreted by Harold Bloom, Grove Atlantic, New York. Art Director Krystyna Skalski, jacket design by Carin Goldberg.
This reworking of the first books of the Old Testament, described as 'an extreme form of literary revisionism', proposes that the early parts of the Bible were written by a secular and often quite bawdy author, unlike the later parts which introduce more extreme concepts of guilt and law. The jacket plays with letter forms and colours.

▲ Jamake Highwater, *Kill Hole*, New York, Grove Atlantic. Art Director Krystyna Skalski, jacket design by Bascove.
First published in 1988, this is the fourth book in a quartet which draws the reader into the author's origins in American Indian culture, crossing the boundary line between child and adult literature. James A. Norsworthy writes 'to say that Highwater did for American Indian culture what Homer did for the people of ancient Greece may seem astonishing, but it is true.'

► Milan Kundera, *Immortality*, New York, Grove Atlantic, 1991. Art Director Krystyna Skalski, designer/illustrator Fred Marcellino.
Written following Kundera's move to the West, this was his first novel to be set in his adopted France. The theme springs from the gesture of a woman towards her swimming instructor, and the suggestions this gives to a writer who observes it.

▼ Kathy Acker, *In Memoriam to Identity*, New York, Grove Atlantic, 1998. Art Director Krystyna Skalski, jacket design by Jo Boney, photograph by Michael Delsol.
A novel describing three cases of obsessive love by one of the punk movement's leading writers, who died in 1997.

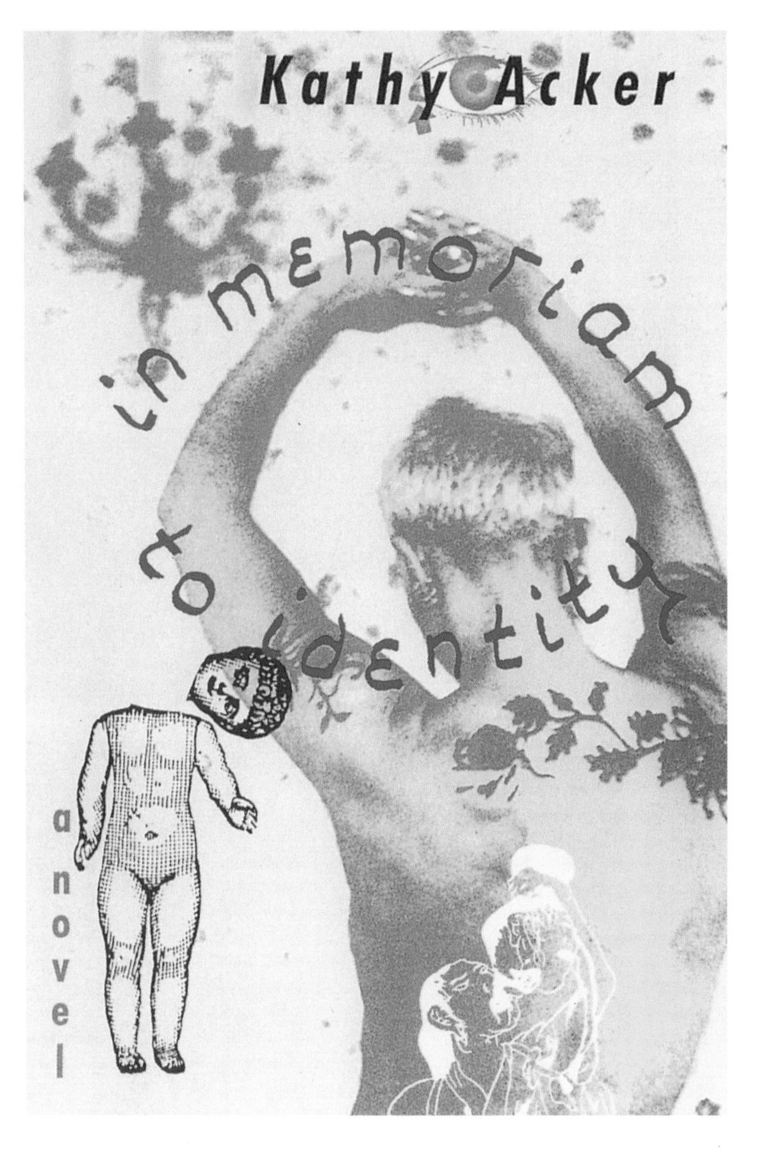

Directory of Designers

Adams, Tom (b. Providence, Rhode Island.) Studied in London and made his name as a designer with cover for *The Collector* by John Fowles (Jonathan Cape, 1962). Designer of many covers for Agatha Christie.
Symons, Julian, *Tom Adams's Agatha Christie Cover Story* (Limpsfield, 1981).

Aldridge, Alan (b. 1943) Worked as freelance designer from 1960 to 1963 before becoming art director for modern fiction for Penguin Books. Associated with The Beatles. Specialist in air-brush, later turned to children's books.
Aldridge, Alan, *The Penguin Book of Comics* (Harmondsworth, Penguin Books, 1967).

Bawden, Edward (1903–87) Studied at the Royal College of Art, London. Became known at an early age as a muralist, poster designer, illustrator and designer of book jackets. Continued to work throughout a long career. Known for his sardonic humour and use of linocut techniques.
Bliss, Douglas Percy, *Edward Bawden* (Godalming, Pendomer Press, 1979).

Chermayeff and Geismar Design practice founded in New York, 1956, by Ivan Chermayeff and Tom Geismar. Specialized in posters, book jackets, corporate identity, and public art.
Chermayef, Ivan, *TM, Trademarks Designed by Chermayeff & Geismar* (Princeton Architectural Press, New York, 1979).

Cook, Brian (Brian Batsford) Cook joined the family firm of B. T. Batsford and designed his first jacket in 1932. He continued to design the majority of jackets for art, architecture, and travel books. Known for the use of flat colours, initially with the Jean Bertè process in lurid transparent inks.
Cook, Brian *The Britain of Brian Cook* (London, Batsford, 1987).

Freedman, Barnett (1901–56) Born in the East End of London. Attended the Royal College of Art, London, as a contemporary of Edward Bawden and Eric Ravilious. Achieved fame with illustrated edition of *Siegfried Sassoon Memoirs of an Infantry officer* (Faber and Faber, 1931) and designed many jackets, usually drawn direct for lithographic printing.
Mayne, Jonathan, *Barnett Freedman, Art and Technics* (London, 1948).

Harvey, Michael (b. 1931) Lettering specialist, worked with Reynolds Stone. Designed book jackets for a living (up to 60 a year), including a long series for London publisher, The Bodley Head. Cut large-scale lettering in Sainsbury Wing of the National Gallery, London.
Powers, Alan, 'Sources of Inspiration: Michael Harvey', *Crafts* No.138, Jan–Feb 1996.

Kauffer, Edward McKnight (1890–1954) Born in Montana, studied art in Paris. Came to London in 1914, remaining there until 1939, when he went to New York. Distinguished as a poster designer and book illustrator, and designer of many jackets in London and New York.
Haworth-Booth, Mark, *E. McKnight Kauffer: a designer and his public*, (London, Gordon Fraser, 1979).

Klimowski, Andrzej (b. 1949) Born in London of Polish parents. Returned to Poland during the 1980s and specialized in poster design.
eye, London, Vol.14, no.4.
Klimowski, Andrzej, *The Depository, A Dream Book* (London, Faber and Faber, 1994).

Lustig, Alvin (1915–55) Born in Denver, Colorado. Became itinerant magician for school classes, studied with Frank Lloyd Wright for three months before becoming freelance printer and typographer in 1936. Hired by James Laughlin of New Directions in 1941 and produced notable series of mainly paperback covers for New Classics series before early death from diabetes.
Book Jackets by Alvin Lustig for New Directions Books, Gotham City Book Mart, (New York, 1947). *Collected Writings of Alvin Lustig*, 1955.
Heller, Steven, 'Born Modern', *eye*, 10, 1993, pp. 26–37.

Mackie, George (b.1920) Studied at Edinburgh College of Art. During a distinguished career in art education in Scotland, designed a notable series of book jackets for Edinburgh University Press using type, hand-lettering, and drawing. Books, mostly scholarly, and some ephemera, designed by George Mackie can be found in the National Library of Scotland, Edinburgh, 1991.

Morison, Stanley (1889–1967) Worked in printing trade in London and worked with Francis Meynell at The Pelican Press to raise general standards of typography and presswork. Worked with Victor Gollancz on creation of famous yellow jackets, designer of Times New Roman typeface, 1930, for *The Times*.
Moran, James, *Stanley Morison, his typographic achievement*, (London, Lund Humphries, 1971).

Pentagram Ltd. Interdisciplinary design practice founded in London, 1972, by Theo Crosby, Alan Fletcher, Colin Forbes, Kenneth Grange, and Mervyn Kurlansky, joined by John McConnell in 1974. Notable for Faber and Faber redesign.
Gibbs, David, ed, *Pentagram: The Compendium. The Pentagram Partners* (London, Phaidon, 1996).

Push Pin Studios Design practice founded in New York, 1954, by Milton Glaser, Seymour Chwast and Edward Sorel. Eclectic influences in line with pop art.
Mayer, Peter, ed. *Milton Glaser, Graphic Design* (New York and London, The Overlook Press, 1973).

Rand, Paul (1914–96) Born in Brownsville, Brooklyn. Studied at Pratt Institute, New York. Worked in advertising and magazine design, influenced by European modernism. Series of book covers for *'The Documents of Modern Art'* series published by Wittenborn, New York.
Heller, Steven *Paul Rand* (London, Phaidon, 1999).

Ravilious, Eric (1903–44) Studied at Royal College of Art, London. Close friend of Edward Bawden. Water-colour painter, illustrator, designer of ceramic transfer decoration, and muralist, with a distinctive hard-edged but lyrical style.
Binyon, Helen, *Eric Ravilious, Memoirs of an Artist* (Guildford and London, Lutterworth Press, 1983).

Schmoller, Hans (1916–85) Born in Berlin. Apprenticed as compositor, and came to England to work for Monotype Corporation. Head of Typography at Penguin Books, 1949, and subsequently Director until retirement in 1976. Responsible for typography and many cover designs during that period.
Hans Schmoller, Typographer, His Life and Work, Monotype Recorder, (Redhill) New Series, No.6, April 1987.

Tisdall, Hans (1910–97) Born in Germany (original name Hans Aufseeser). Came to work as an artist in London in 1931, and specialized in textile design and murals. Skilled in brush lettering (learnt in signwriting classes in German art school), and designed long series of jackets for Jonathan Cape.
Powers, Alan, Obituary, *Independent* Friday 7 Feb, p.14.

Tschichold, Jan (1902–74) Born Leipzig. Converted to modernism on a visit to the Bauhaus in 1923. Published handbook *Die Neue Typographie*, 1928, stressing an asymmetrical design with sans serif type. Held by Nazis in 1933, moved to Basel, influenced by 'New Traditionalist' typographers in England. Worked for Penguin Books, 1947–50, creating typographic rules and standards.
Tschichold, Jan, *The New Typography* (Los Angeles, London, University of California Press, Berkeley, 1995).
McLean, Ruari, *Jan Tschichold, Typographer* (London, David R. Godine, 1975).

Wolpe, Berthold (1905–88) Born in Offenbach, Germany. Pupil of Rudolph Koch. Left Germany in 1935 and came to England to work on Albertus typeface for Monotype Corporation. Worked for four years for Fanfare Press, before moving to Faber and Faber, 1941–75, where he designed many book jackets.
Berthold Wolpe, A Retrospective Survey (London, V&A Museum, 1980).

Whistler, Rex (1905–44) Studied at Slade School. Made his reputation as a mural painter, stage designer, and illustrator, in styles derived from 18th-century decoration. Designed many book jackets. Killed in action in the Normandy invasion.
Whistler, Laurence, *The Laughter and the Urn*, a Life of Rex Whistler (London, Weidenfeld and Nicolson, 1985).

List of Publishers

Jonathan Cape Ltd. Founded 1921 by Jonathan Cape and G. Wren Howard, with Edward Garnett (father of David Garnett) as literary adviser. Cape was one of the first British publishers to visit the USA in search of authors, signing up Ernest Hemingway, Sinclair Lewis and Eugene O'Neill. The imprint is now part of Random House.
Howard, Michael, S., *Jonathan Cape, publisher* (London, Jonathan Cape, 1971).

Chatto & Windus Founded in 1855 as a bookseller and publisher, by John Camden Hotten, in premises on the site of the present Ritz Hotel, London. Hotten made profits from publishing American authors (including Mark Twain) who were unable to claim royalties in Britain. Hotten was succeeded on his death in 1873 by Andrew Chatto and his `sleeping' partner, W. E. Windus, and the firm became a pure publisher. The quality of presswork and book design became notable from before the pre-1914 period, and authors in the 1920s included Lytton Strachey, David Garnett and Aldous Huxley. Famous editors Ian Parsons and Norah Smallwood continued a lively tradition into the 1980s, including many good jacket designs by E. McKnight Kauffer, Enid Marx and others. Now part of Random House.
Warner, Oliver, *Chatto & Windus. A Brief History of the Firm's Origin, History and Development* (London, Chatto & Windus, 1973).

Collins Founded in Glasgow in 1819 by William Collins, to print and publish religious books. In the middle years of the twentieth century, Collins expanded under William Collins (1900–76, the fifth in the family line of succession) to become a general and educational publisher based in London, while retaining its own printing works in Glasgow, known as Collins' Cleartype Press, using 'Fontana typeface, derived from Renaissance examples. Collins Crime Club was invented by F T. Smith, an employee of the firm, and Agatha Christie was its leading author. The `New Naturalists' series of books on the natural world, 1945–95, was notable for its jackets designed by the husband and wife team of Clifford and Rosemary Ellis in four colour lithography, initially printed at the Baynard Press. The firm now runs as Harper Collins, after amalgamation with the American publisher Harper and Row.
Collins, W. A. R., *The House of Collins* (London, William Collins, 1952).
Marren, Peter, *The New Naturalists* (London, Harper Collins, 1995).

Faber and Faber Ltd. Founded in London by Geoffrey Faber, 1924, as Faber and Gwyer. T. S. Eliot was a director from 1926, and selected the poetry list for which the firm was well known. Jackets desigers during the 1930s, under direction of Richard de la Mare, included Barnett Freedman, Edward Bawden, Ben Nicholson and Rex Whistler. With the arrival of Berthold Wolpe in 1941, a more uniform style was created, based on lettering, much of it owing to Wolpe's colleague and successor, Shirley Tucker. The house style was redesigned by John McConnell of Pentagram in 1981.
Faber Books 1925–75, *Impressions of a Publishing House* & Faber Music, notes of a decade (London, National Book League, 1975).

Heinemann Firm established by William Heinemann in 1890, noted for its attention to visual presentation of works by new authors. The artist William Nicholson made an early success with his illustrated books, such as *An Alphabet*, 1898, and created the windmill device used on all Heinemann books. The jacket for *A Dop Doctor* by Richard Dehan (pseudonym of Miss Clothilde Graves), 1910, drawn by the author, was considered to be the first 'all round' pictorial jacket with a picture running from the front to spine and back.
St John, John *William Heinemann, A Century of Publishing 1890–1990* (London, Heinemann, 1990).

Hogarth Press Founded in 1917 by Leonard and Virginia Woolf, who bought their own hand press and type and worked from home (Hogarth House, Richmond), printing small editions of avant-garde writers, including the first edition of *The Waste Land*, by T. S. Eliot. They often used coloured and patterned papers with printed labels as wrappers, but also designs by artists associated with the Bloomsbury Group, such as Vanessa Bell, Dora Carrington and Duncan Grant. The press published all Virginia Woolf's books, and had to employ professional printers, although the Woolfs owned and ran the business until 1946 when Leonard Woolf sold it to Chatto & Windus, where it remained a separate imprint.
Kennedy, Richard, *A Boy at the Hogarth Press* (Harmondsworth, Penguin Books, 1973).
Woolmer, J. Howard, *A Checklist of the Hogarth Press* (Revere, Pennsylvania, St Paul's Bibliographies, 1986).

Alfred A. Knopf As a student at Columbia University, New York, Alfred Knopf (b.1892) became interested in the works of the British author, John Galsworthy, and later met him on a visit to England. After working for Doubleday & Co., Knopf established his own imprint in 1912, specializing in Russian literature, including the esoteric works of P D. Ouspensky, which proved very profitable. The Borzoi (Russian wolfhound) was chosen as an emblem for the firm, but when Knopf and his wife owned one, they found it 'handsome but stupid'. The cover designs of Paul Rand for Alfred Knopf in the 1940s and 50s brought additional distinction.
Alfred A. Knopf (Cathy Henderson, ed) *Those Damned Reminiscences* (University of Texas at Austin, Harry Ransom Humanities Research Centre, 1995).

General Bibliography

Penguin Books Ltd. Founded by Allen Lane 1935, became the largest and most prestigious paperback publisher in Britain, with American offshoot (Penguin Books, Inc.). Employed a series of influential design directors before diversifying in the 1960s.
Williams, W. E., *The Penguin Story* (Penguin Books, Harmondsworth, 1965); *Fifty Penguin Years* (Penguin Books, London, 1985). Edwards, Russell and David J. Hall, "So Much Admired": *Die Insel-B¸cherie and the King Penguin Series* (Salvia Books, Edinburgh, 1988).

Pocket Books Inc. America's leading paperback house, founded in 1939 by Robert DeGraff. Developed series design and corporate identity, including `Gertrude', a kangaroo with a book in her pouch. Employed McKnight Kaufer and Leo Manso among other distinguished cover designers.
Tebbel, John, *Paperback Books: A Pocket History* (Pocket Books, New York, 1964).

Victor Gollancz Ltd. Founded 1928. Specialized in politics and crime, with authors including Daphne du Maurier, Elizabeth Bowen and Dorothy L. Sayers. Gollancz founded Left Book Club in 1936, as rallying point for the left and Popular Front. Famous for the yellow jackets, early examples of which were designed by Stanley Morison and printed at Fanfare Press.
Hodges, Sheila, *Gollancz, The Story of a Publishing House 1928–1978* (Gollancz, London, 1978).

Broos, Kees, and Hefting, Paul, *Dutch Graphic Design* (London, Phaidon, 1993).
Brown, Gregory, *`Book-Jacket Design' Penrose Annual*, 1937, pp. 30–32.
Curl, Peter, *Designing a Book Jacket* (London and New York, Studio, 1956).
Curwen, Harold, *Processes of Graphic Reproduction in Printing* (London, Faber and Faber, 1934).
Day, Frederick T., *`Book-Jackets and their Treatment' Book Design and Production*, Vol.II, No.2, 1959, pp. 20–23.
Flower, Desmond, *The Paperback, its Past, Present and Future* (London, Arborfield, 1959).
Heller, Steven, and Seymour Chwast, *Jackets Required* (San Francisco, 1995).
Heller, Steven and Fink, Anne, *Covers and Jackets! What the Best Dressed Books & Magazines are Wearing* (New York, Libary of Applied Design, 1993).
Lamb, Lynton, *Drawing for Illustration* (London, Oxford University Press, 1962).
Lewis, John, and John Brinkley, *Graphic Design* (London, Routledge, 1954).
Lewis, John, *A Handbook of Type and Illustration* (London, Faber and Faber, 1956).
Lewis, John, *The Twentieth Century Book* (London, Studio Vista, 1967).
McAnally, Sir Henry, *`Book Wrappers' Book Collectors' Quarterly*, VI, 1932, pp. 10–17.
Meggs, Philip, *A History of Graphic Design*, 1983 (New York, John Wiley & Sons, 1998)
O'Brien, Geoffrey, *Hardboiled America, Lurid paperbacks and the Masters of Noir* (New York, Da Capo Press, 1997).
Porter, Catherine, *Collecting Books* (London, Miller's, 1995).
Rosner, Charles, *The Art of the Book Jacket* (London, Victoria & Albert Museum, 1949).
Rosner, Charles, *The Growth of the Book Jacket* (Victoria & Albert Museum, 1954).
Sandilands, G. S. *`Book Jackets' Commercial Art*, New Series II, 1927, pp. 107–9.
Schmoller, Hans, *'The Paperback Revolution'* Brigs, Asa, ed., *Essays on the History of Publishing in Celebration of the 250th Anniversary of the House of Longman* (London, Longman, 1974).
Schreuders, Piet, *The Book of Paperbacks, A Visual History of the Paperback Book* (London, Virgin Books Ltd., 1981).
Simon, Oliver, *Introduction to Typography* (London, Faber and Faber, 1945).
Watson, David, *`On Jacket Design', Book Design and Production*, Vol.V, No.4, 1962.

Index

Author's Acknowledgments

My first thanks must go to John Jervis, who as an editor at Mitchell Beazley worked on this book with me from the beginning and played an important role in finding and selecting the jackets included. Other suggestions came from Mark Fletcher, and several afternoons were spent as the guests of London book dealers rummaging in their shelves. Peter Joliffe of Ulysses Books deserves a special mention, and I would also like to thank Simon Finch Rare Books, Maggs Bros, and Ken Lopez.

In the USA, Steven Heller, the only recent author on this subject, gave us helpful connections. Elaine Lustig-Cohen and Ivan Chermayeff provided illustrations of works seldom seen in England. Nicola Bayley, Ian and Emma Beck, Peter Sampson, Simon Rendall, Paul Stolper and John Byrne who gave advice and lent precious items from their collections for photography. Ron Costley provided information about jackets at Faber and Faber, and Gary Day-Ellison and Raymond Hawkey gave detailed information about their own design work. Piet Schreuders kindly made available transparencies from items in his own collection, featured in his invaluable work, *The Paperback Book*.

I would like to thank Jo Walton for excellent picture research, Penny Warren for patient editing and Hannah Barnes-Murphy for seeing the project to completion. My wife Susanna, in addition to the indispensable support that she provides in everyday life, also acted at times as research assistant.

I apologise to those who find their favourite artists or jackets omitted, but these throwaway items can be hard to find when you need them.

AP

Picture Acknowledgments

Mitchell Beazley would like to thank those publishers credited alongside each illustrated book cover who have kindly given permission to publish copyright images. In some cases ownership has changed since original publication and we would also like to acknowledge and thank those additional individuals and publishers credited below who have supplied material or granted permission.

Key **t** top, **c** centre, **b** bottom, **l** left, **r** right

6 t:V&K Design b.v. Netherlands; **8 t**: Constable & Robinson; **8 c**: Elaine Lustig Cohen; **8 b**: Calder Publications Ltd; **9 t**: Random House Group; **10**: Gary Day-Ellison; **14 r**: Constable & Robinson; **15 tr** & **br**: Random House Group; **17 l** & **tr**: Simon Rendall for the estate of E McKnight Kauffer; **19br** © 1961 The Estate of Vanessa Bell, courtesy of Henrietta Garnett; **21 l, tr**, & **br**: © Estate of Eric Ravilious 2001. All Rights Reserved, DACS; **24 l**: Random House Group; **25 tl**: © 1927 Harcourt Inc, renewed 1974 by Sonia Orwell, © 1961 The Estate of Vanessa Bell, courtesy of Henrietta Garnett; **26 l** & **r**: © Estate of Rex Whistler 2001. All Rights Reserved, DACS; **27 tl**: © Kingdom of Spain, Universal heir of Salvador Dalí/DACS 2001; **27tr** & **br**: Random House Group; **28 l**: Harper Collins Publishers Ltd; **33 tl**: Piet Schreuders; **33 bl**: Random House Group; **34 r**: Simon Rendall for the estate of E McKnight Kauffer; **35 b**: © Estate Brian Cook, Batsford; **35 tr**: Random House Group; **37 r**: Random House Group and the Estate of Noel Coward; **42 tr**: Harper Collins Publishers Ltd; **42 br**: Random House Group; **43 tr**: Harper Collins Publishers Ltd; **43 br** & **l**: Random House Group; **44–45**: Simon Rendall for the estate of E. McKnight Kauffer; **44 r**: Random House Group; **45 bl**: Random House Inc, New York; **46 tr**: Harper Collins Publishers Ltd; **48 t** & **b**, **49 tr** & **tl**: Random House Group; **52–53**: Elaine Lustig Cohen; **54–55**: Piet Schreuders; **56 b**: Simon Rendall for the estate of E McKnight Kauffer; **57 bl** & **tl**: Elaine Lustig Cohen; **59 tr** & **br**, **66–67**: Piet Schreuders; **68 r**, **69 bl**: Random House Group; **72 l**: Simon & Schuster; **72 br**: Calder Publications Ltd; **73 l**: Constable & Robinson; **75 l**: © 1946 Harcourt Inc, renewed 1954 by Leonard Woolf; **82 t**, **83 tr, br**, & **l**: Random House Group; **84–85**: Chermayeff & Geismar Inc, New York; **86–87**: Marion S Rand and Alfred A Knopf Inc, New York; **95 br** & **tr**, **100 l**, **101 br** & **tl**: Random House Group; **102 br, tl**: Random House Inc, New York; **104 t** & **b**: Harper Collins Publishers Ltd; **108–109**: Pentagram; **110–111**: Gary Day-Ellison; **112–113**:The Harvill Press; **114–115**: Bloomsbury; **117 bl**: Random House Group; **122–123**: Black Sparrow Press; **124–125**: Andrzej Klimowski; **126–127**: Granta; **130–131**: Indigo/The Orion Publishing Group Ltd; **132–133**: Canongate Books Ltd; **135 tr** & **bl**: Random House Group.